*f*P

ALSO BY LAURA CALDWELL

Burning the Map
A Clean Slate
The Year of Living Famously
The Night I Got Lucky
Look Closely
The Rome Affair
The Good Liar
Red Hot Lies
Red Blooded Murder
Red, White & Dead

Long Way Home

A Young Man Lost in the System and
the Two Women Who Found Him

LAURA CALDWELL

Free Press

New York London Toronto Sydney

Free Press
A Division of Simon & Schuster, Inc.
1230 Avenue of the Americas
New York, NY 10020

First Free Press hardcover edition September 2010

FREE PRESS and colophon are trademarks of Simon & Schuster, Inc.

For information about special discounts for bulk purchases, please contact
Simon & Schuster Special Sales at 1-866-506-1949 or
business@simonandschuster.com

The Simon & Schuster Speakers Bureau can bring authors to your
live event. For more information or to book an event contact the
Simon & Schuster Speakers Bureau at 1-866-248-3049 or
visit our website at www.simonspeakers.com.

Manufactured in the United States of America

1   3   5   7   9   10   8   6   4   2

Library of Congress Cataloging-in-Publication Data

Caldwell, Laura.
Long way home : a young man lost in the system and
the two women who found him / Laura Caldwell.
p.   cm.
1. Murder—Illinois—Chicago—Case Studies.   2. Judicial error—
Illinois—Chicago—Case Studies.   I. Title.
HV6534.C4C35 2010
3643152'3092—dc22   2010005544

ISBN 978-1-4391-0023-3
ISBN 978-1-4391-2302-7 (ebook)

Long Way Home

Prologue

Behind Courtroom 600, behind the majestic ceilings, the mahogany woodwork, and the judge's high pedestal desk, there is a cage. Also called a "bullpen," the cage is about twelve feet wide by twenty feet long. Its cement floor has been painted so many times it's now a jaundiced ivory color. In the far corner is an exposed urinal. Along the left wall, a bench is bolted to the floor. And sitting on that bench is Jovan Mosley.

When he sees me he looks startled. He stands. He tugs the bottom of his gray suit jacket and adjusts his tie. He walks to the bars of the cage and grasps them. He has light black skin, gentle brown eyes and long lashes. He looks like a handsome young lawyer. He does not look like a kid awaiting a verdict for first-degree murder.

It's against the rules to touch prisoners in the bullpen, but I'm past caring. I put my hands on his. They are big and soft because Jovan's home for almost six years—SuperMax, as the inmates call it—is a holding cell for those awaiting trial where there is nothing to do but wait and try to stay alive.

SuperMax is one of the toughest county jails in the state, possibly the country. And yet, if Jovan gets a guilty verdict, he faces a future in a state penitentiary. I look into his eyes, and I know that if the jury finds him guilty, if he has to go to that state pen, we will lose him. Jovan, or at least the Jovan I have come to know, will vanish if the legal system he believes in so strongly does not come through for him.

"That question?" he asks. "What did it mean?"

The question he is referring to is one we received from the jury—*Can we convict him of something less than first-degree murder?* The judge told them they had all the information they needed, and they should keep deliberating.

"Cathy says . . ." My voice drifts as I search for the rest of my answer. This has been my mantra for months now.

Cathy is Catharine O'Daniel, Jovan's lead attorney, and the person who somehow pulled me into this case. Cathy also happens to be one of the best criminal lawyers in the city. And since I'm a civil litigator—a former civil litigator, really—with no criminal law experience, I defer to Cathy on all things important. It turns out that during a murder trial, what's important is each and every thing.

"Cathy says we just have to wait and see."

"What do *you* think about that question?" he asks.

"Well . . . it looks like they're thinking of . . ." How can I say this? Jovan's gaze doesn't waver from mine. He is asking for the truth. Or at least the truth as I see it. "It looks like they're thinking of convicting you of something."

His body sways for a second. His hands cling to the bars, and I squeeze them tight. Shooting a glance down the hallway, I wonder if a deputy will come if I call for help.

But then Jovan stands upright again, and I glance the other way, thinking that down that hallway in a stuffy room are twelve people—the only people who can help Jovan now.

I turn my eyes back to Jovan, then to the white paper plate on the bench behind him. On the plate is a bologna sandwich—two pieces of brittle wheat bread on either side of stale, pinkish bologna.

"You should eat something," I say. I know Jovan has eaten little in the ten days since his trial started.

He looks at the plate too and grimaces. We both know he won't touch it. He has eaten a bologna sandwich, the only lunch offered by SuperMax, every single day for the last five years and nine months. Meanwhile, his suit hangs loose on him, his shirt collar is too big, as if he is slowly disappearing. When that jury comes back, we'll find out if he's about to disappear for good.

I feel a surge of grief.

"Seriously, eat something." I squeeze his hands again. "Cathy and I will get lunch too, and we'll be back."

He nods. He takes his hands away. I hesitate.

When I turn to go a moment later, Jovan Mosley is sitting on the bench, his arms on his knees, staring straight ahead at nothing.

In the courtroom, Cathy is finishing a discussion with one of the state's attorneys. Her blond hair is perfectly styled, and she's wearing a red suit—the perfect closing argument outfit. But when she turns to me, I see the strain on her face. Her hazel eyes are exhausted.

"How is he?" she says.

I give her a helpless shrug. I can't seem to find words.

"I swear," she says, "if he gets tagged I'm giving up my goddamned ticket." She means her law license.

"Any more questions from the jury?" I ask.

Cathy shakes her head, looks on the verge of tears. "Jesus. I can't just sit here."

"I can't either."

She picks up her bag and slings it over her shoulder. "Let's get some lunch."

At a dumpy Mexican place a block away from the courthouse, Cathy and I order food, which sits congealing on the table, and margaritas. I'm not sure how it works in other legal systems, but in Chicago, in Cook County, which happens to be the nation's largest and busiest court system, it's standard protocol for attorneys to cocktail during jury deliberations. The drinks had never been more welcome.

An hour or so later, after we've blown off steam and continued to ignore the food, the cell phone, sitting in the center of the table, rings. We both look at it for a moment. She answers and listens, then snaps the phone shut. "There's been yelling from the jury room. They've got another question."

Cathy and I race back to the courthouse, chewing breath mints, trying not to think of what might happen.

In the courtroom, Judge Michael Brown, a tall, stoic black man, reads the question: *Can we see the police records?*

The judge informs the jury again that they have all the information they need and tells them to keep deliberating.

Cathy and I huddle together.

"What does *that* question mean?" I ask.

Cathy bites her lip. "I don't get it."

A deputy enters the courtroom and hands the judge another note from the jury.

The judge puts on his glasses, reads the note. He takes off the glasses and lays them on his desk. He looks at the state's attorneys, then at Cathy, then at me. "We have a verdict."

Cathy and I turn to each other, eyes big. "I think I'm going to be sick," she says.

"Should I get Jovan?"

She nods.

This time, a deputy escorts me back to the cage.

Again, Jovan seems shocked to see me.

"They're back," I tell him.

His expression turns to terror. Sweat beads on his upper lip.

The deputy opens the cage, keys jangling.

Back in the courtroom, it's deadly silent. The three male state's attorneys stand at their counsel table, hands clasped behind their backs.

The deputy walks us to our table, and Cathy and I arrange Jovan so he stands between us. I can feel him trembling.

"Breathe," I tell him. "Breathe."

He shakes his head and swallows. It seems a real possibility he might pass out.

"Breathe," I say again.

"Bring the jury in," calls the judge from the bench.

Jovan takes an openmouthed intake of air, like someone just coming to the surface after being underwater.

The jury files silently into the jury box. We study their faces, as if we can divine, by only a twitch or a blink, which way they are going to go.

One of the jurors, Alfonzo Lewis, acknowledges Jovan with a glance and a barely perceptible jut of his head, a movement entirely unreadable. He takes his place by his jury seat and looks down. Cathy and I look at each other: *What was that?*

Jovan's trembling increases.

We keep studying the jurors.

"Uh-oh," I hear Cathy say under her breath.

And then I see what she sees. One of the jurors, Andrea Schultz, a suburban brunette with short, styled hair and glasses, is holding the verdict forms. Which means Andrea Schultz is the foreperson.

Andrea had been attentive and pleasant during the trial. But while many of the jurors had cried throughout closing arguments, Andrea had been near sobbing, something that threw the attorneys on both sides of the case. Was she weeping for Howard Thomas, the victim, and the horrible loss his family had suffered? Was she crying for Jovan and his innocence? After Cathy's closing argument to a packed courtroom, Cathy had written me a note on my yellow pad: *Did the crier cry for us?* I wrote her back, *Yes, but not as much. She makes me nervous. . . . If crier is foreperson, we're in trouble.*

"Has the jury reached a verdict?" the judge asks.

"Yes," Andrea Schultz answers in a loud, clear voice.

"Please give me the verdict," the judge says.

Hand to hand, the verdict forms are passed down the row of jurors. Jovan's trembling increases until he is shaking violently, his torso bobbing back and forth.

I put my arm around his back and take hold of one of his arms. Cathy does the same from the other side. "It'll be all right," she whispers to him.

She looks across Jovan to me. And I know we are both wondering whether she is telling the truth. Or whether this is the end for Jovan Mosley.

Part I

1

"See you when I see you."

On August 5, 1999, Howard Thomas, Jr.—or "Bug," as his friends and family called him—stepped outside the Union League Club into a dark summer night. Chicago's normally bustling Loop was quiet at eleven p.m.

"Goodnight," called the doorman.

"See you when I see you," Bug called back, like he often did.

Bug (a name often given to men who are "juniors" in their family, short for "June Bug"), with his quick quips, had been at this job—parking cars for the private club's wealthy clientele—for years, and he was friends with both staff and members.

That night, Bug and his girlfriend, Donna Harris,[1] planned on spending what was left of the evening together, in their basement room, in Chicago's Park Manor neighborhood. He was in a particularly good mood because that morning he'd seen his youngest daughter and his granddaughter, who'd returned from California, for the first time in two years.

In his fifty-one years, Bug had seen and done much. You could say he'd been a troublemaker in his youth. He'd been shot twice and stabbed and had been in a number of fights. But years ago, Bug had decided to "get with God." He quit drinking, started reading the Bible, and watched evangelists on TV. He even sent them money when he had some extra, because sometimes he felt like they were talking directly to him.

Still in his uniform, Bug tucked his night's earnings into the Bible he always carried and began to walk. It was a nice evening, cool for August, and the city was calm. According to the *Chicago Sun-Times*, that day hadn't been too exciting. "Cows On Parade: Tour No. 3," an art exhibit, had gone

3

up on the Chicago streets, featuring painted, life-sized cows; Bill Clinton had taken issue with some of Hillary's comments on adultery; and the "Timing Might Not Be Perfect for McGwire," according to the headline, as he tried for his five hundredth game homer.

Bug headed toward the El train. Sometimes he drove to work, but he preferred to walk to and from the train when he could. He took the Red Line to the Park Manor neighborhood on Chicago's South Side, then caught the 69th Street bus to 75th Street.

When he arrived at his stop, Bug went into a Harold's Chicken on 75th Street near King Drive and purchased a late dinner for Donna and himself, using the money he'd put in the Bible. By the time he turned toward home it was after midnight, but Thomas knew his way around. He had been living in the Park Manor neighborhood for years.

The boundaries of the neighborhood are from 79th Street to 67th Street and from Cottage Grove Avenue west to the Dan Ryan Expressway. A local realty company says on its Web site that Park Manor is "cradled between two of the city's major highways and the Red Line branch of the El train,"[2] but *cradled* might give the impression of a sleepy neighborhood, safe and idyllic. While one section of Park Manor was a stable working-class black neighborhood with small bungalows lining the street, the other section, particularly along 69th and Calumet, was entirely different. There, the shabby apartments, crumbling houses, and liquor stores hosted brutal gang violence, and the neighborhood was striped with territories marked by the Black Disciples (BDs), the Gangster Disciples (GDs), and others.

Luckily, Bug was living on the good side of Park Manor, and he planned on leaving the area altogether. The owner of the small brick bungalow where he stayed rented rooms to fourteen other residents, and it had grown too cramped. The energy among the residents was not as good as it used to be. So Howard had worked hard and bought himself a place at 83rd and Blackstone. He would move on Monday.

Bug walked north on Calumet Avenue toward his place in the 7200 block. Although it was late, lights burned inside the houses, and some people stood outside socializing. When he was a few houses from home, Howard saw what was a common scene in his neighborhood—a group of kids, mostly guys, standing by someone's porch.

Some of the guys were in the street by the time he reached them, but since they weren't doing anything in particular, he simply strolled by. But just as he passed them, something struck the back of his legs, then someone kicked him. He tripped and stumbled.

He recovered his footing fast and dropped his bags. Spinning around to face the punk, he said, "What the fuck is you doing?"

Another kid hit him on the back of the head. The kids grabbed him, caught his arms. He fought back, trying doing the same to them. He and the kids snatched at each other's clothes and faces, spinning around, tussling or wrestling more than actually fighting, going around in circles.

Other kids rushed up and stood around them. He was hit, then once more from another side, then another blow. He saw something swinging, felt a different kind of blow to the side of his face.

"Stop!" he shouted. "Stop!" He held an arm up to shield his face.

Someone kicked him again, and he lost his footing, crumpling to the ground. Another kick to his side. He covered his face with his arms and tried to tighten himself into a ball. More kicks to his legs . . . his shoulders . . . his head . . . more than one foot . . . more than one person.

Still more kicks, more punches.

In his peripheral vision, he might have seen a different slice of life—people on the street, watching.

2

"He could have squeezed a murder confession out of Mother Teresa."

Chicago police officers arrived at Calumet Avenue near 72nd Street approximately thirteen minutes after a report of a fight. In their report, the police wrote that the victim was in "critical condition," and really, it didn't look like he was going to make it. He'd been beaten badly— blood and dentures were on the street along with a Bible and pieces of chicken that spilled from a torn plastic bag. An ambulance arrived and carried away the victim.

Because of the neighborhood, the cops were more cautious than usual as they looked for witnesses and suspects. Police officers only made about $33,000 a year when they started out, not enough to relish duty in Park Manor, where you could get spat on, called names, or popped at any time.

The police interviewed Joseph Saunders, who said he'd been in his house when he heard a disturbance. He went to the front window of his basement room and saw three to five men in their mid-twenties beating a victim with a baseball bat. He heard one of the men say, "I told you about messing with my sister," or words to that effect.

The cops also interviewed Ronald and Derek Barnes, two men who had seen some boys walk by and later heard a commotion about two hundred feet away. They saw the silhouette of a fight. They heard some blows that were as loud as gunshots, but they hadn't seen any faces and wouldn't be able to recognize anyone.

At 1:57 a.m., Detective Bradley arrived and, after surveying the ugly scene, called the evidence techs. He interviewed the first few witnesses

6

again, as well as others, like Jori Garth, a girl of fourteen, who'd been sitting on her family's porch next to the street where the beating occurred. But no one could identify the perpetrators specifically. *Didn't hear or see anything,* Detective Bradley wrote in his report more than once. He'd written those phrases before. Such a response wasn't uncommon in that neighborhood, where everyone wanted to keep their head down and no one wanted to be involved.[3]

"I don't know if that's him or not." Donna Harris stood staring at the corpse at Cook County Hospital.

They'd told her that the body was Bug, that he'd been beaten, but it didn't look anything like him. Bug was lean, but this man's face and chest were hugely swollen, and sure, Bug had a nose that was thick in the middle and crooked to one side, but this guy's nose was puffed up and split.

Donna had been with Bug for two years. She thought she knew all the different parts of his body, all the random spots and markings that a person might have. She glanced over the corpse again, but still nothing registered. Maybe the police were wrong. Maybe there had been a mistake.

But then she noticed the hands. She blinked and jutted her head forward, peering at them. They were swollen too and covered with little scrapes.

"He must have defended himself," the attendant said, pointing to the scrapes.

Donna glanced at the attendant. "That sounds like Bug." Saying his name out loud brought a lump to her throat. She'd fallen asleep the night before, waiting for him to come home. Yet it wasn't Bug who had woken her up that morning but one of the other residents of the house saying detectives wanted to talk to her. She hadn't been too worried at first because she knew Bug had been in more than one fight in his life.

But then she'd walked down the street and seen the bloodstains. Even as she heard from the cops what had happened, she figured Bug was just injured, lying in a hospital bed talking in his fast, funny way, making the nurses crazy.

Donna looked back at the corpse now, looked even more closely at the hands this time. Around the fresh scrapes she saw a few little nicks, a few scars. For as long as she had known him, Bug had had those same old nicks on his hands, those scars. Swallowing hard, she raised her gaze and studied the man's hairline. She recognized that too.

"That's him," she said.

On August 25, a few weeks after the beating, Detective Bradley wrote a Field Investigation Progress Report. It wasn't an easy case, but from the witnesses who were willing to talk and who'd seen the fight, the detectives had narrowed things down, and three men were wanted for the beating death of Howard Thomas. All the suspects were young black males in their late teens to early twenties. The first guy had a slim build and dark complexion. The second guy was approximately six feet with a large build and a medium-dark complexion, who had been wearing a red-and-white-striped shirt that night. The last guy had braided hair.[4]

But then for six months, the case languished. Sometimes a murder remains unsolved just because of the sheer number of cases the Chicago Police Department (CPD) has to handle.

"At that time, there were three or four murders a day in that area," says Larry Nitsche, a CPD officer who was a homicide detective for thirteen years and on the force a total of thirty-three years before becoming director of investigations for the city's Corporation Counsel Office. "And there were often only six detectives on duty. *And* the day-shift detectives were often testifying in court. As a detective, you're constantly bombarded with things to do. You'd love to take a case and never stop working it, but it doesn't work like that.

"Homicide is like golf," Nitsche explains. "The case you're working on is like the first hole. The next case is the second hole—you start focusing on that one and just hope you can replay the other one sometime later." And with certain cases, Nitsche says, there are few leads and no one is saying anything to help track down your suspects. Nitsche wasn't talking about the Howard Thomas case, but he might as well have been. By early February 2000, five or so months after Thomas died, the case had stalled.

But then something happened. One frigid February day, the residents of Park Manor awoke to find white sheets of paper taped to lampposts in the neighborhood. The posters' corners came loose and flapped in the bitter winter wind, up and down busy 75th Street.

The tantalizing words CASH REWARD $7,000 were emblazoned in bold atop a photo of Howard Thomas looking uncharacteristically mournful, his gentle gaze and slim face drastically different from the grotesquely swollen figure Donna Harris had identified months before.

The reward, the poster said, would be given *for information leading to the arrest and conviction of the person(s) responsible for the death of Howard Thomas Jr.* The poster listed the date, time, and address of the murder and asked people to contact Detective Bradley, promising, *All calls are confidential.*

Howard Thomas's family had posted the signs. "Bug," as they called him, had survived so much, and he'd been about to move to a new home, but a bunch of thugs had taken his life. The family was missing Bug, angry that he had been killed so cavalierly, and frustrated at the lack of progress on the investigation.

Once those signs were posted in cash-strapped Park Manor, people suddenly remembered the fight, and they started talking.

Coincidentally, around the same time, someone else was killed with a baseball bat in the neighborhood. The Thomas case was officially resurrected.

On February 16, 2000, the day he was assigned to the Howard Thomas case, Detective Charlie Williams had been with the Chicago Police Department for nearly eighteen years and was working as a violent crimes detective in the police region called Area 2.[5] Also assigned to the case were Detectives Clarence Hill (a thirteen-year veteran of the force), Edward Howard (also a thirteen-year veteran), and Derail Easter (who had nearly fifteen years on the force).

Area 2, at 727 East 111th Street, had a reputation in Chicago—a very distinct reputation—for allowing its detectives to be freewheeling, creative, and often violent in interrogations. Frank Laverty, a CPD detective who became a whistle-blower for Chicago police brutality, said that at "Area 2 you could do anything, nobody would say anything. . . . If somebody would make a brutality complaint it wouldn't go anyplace."[6]

Most notably, Area 2 had been home to Detective Jon Burge, a name synonymous in the city with torture in interrogations. His tactics allegedly included administering electric shocks to the testicles and anus, suffocating suspects with typewriter bags, and shoving pistols in suspects' mouths. Tom McNamee, a columnist for the *Chicago Sun-Times*, wrote of Burge, "[He] could have squeezed a murder confession out of Mother Teresa."[7]

Detectives who worked with Burge at Area 2 often said that, on the whole, Burge had been a devoted police officer. Jon Burge had no wife or family, and the CPD was his world. Over the years, he had legitimately cracked unbelievably tough cases. Nonetheless, in the late 1980s, Burge was investigated by the Office of Professional Standards (OPS), which determined that Burge had engaged in systematic torture for thirteen years.[8]

A civil suit against Burge for police brutality in 1989 resulted in a hung jury. Four years later, Burge was fired from the police force and two other detectives were suspended for fifteen months without pay and demoted to patrolmen (though those demotions were later revoked due to a Fraternal Order of Police contractual technicality). John Conroy, a journalist who covered Burge for decades, wrote in the *Chicago Reader* in January 1996, "Burge's fall from grace has been well publicized and is known at some level by millions of people in the Chicago area and around the country. That torture was administered by certain Area 2 policemen is not a wild claim made by some lunatic and radical fringe; it is a fact known to well-established, well-meaning, and well-off members of the community."[9] In October 2008, the U.S. Attorney's Office seemed to recognize this when it charged Burge with lying about his torture tactics in the earlier civil suit. (At the time of the writing of this book, the federal trial had not yet begun.)

By the time of the Howard case, personnel changes had been made at Area 2, but all of the detectives assigned to the Howard Thomas case were aware of Burge's notoriety for torture, as well as Area 2's reputation for police brutality.

But there are nonphysical ways to get suspects to talk. In fact, many interrogators take pride in the fact that they don't resort to physical torture and use psychological torture, which most don't consider torture at all.[10] Yet the effects of psychological torture, which includes humiliation, degradation, threats, hunger, isolation, and sleep deprivation, can be just as devastating as, if not more devastating than, physical torture. Such methods may seem innocuous at first glance, but over a prolonged period of time these psychological techniques become coercive. "The discussion of torture," it has been said, "cannot merely be narrowed down to acts causing pain and suffering in an abstract sense."[11]

When they heard about the most recent baseball bat homicide, Detective Charlie Williams went with Detective Hill to the Sixth District, where they spoke to a sergeant about Leroy McKelker, the suspect in that case. Then they interviewed McKelker and his alibi witnesses, and it became clear that McKelker was not one of the guys they were looking for in the Howard Thomas case, and in fact the cases were unrelated.

But their interest in Howard Thomas had been reignited. They decided to start from the beginning and reinterview the witnesses who'd been listed on the original police report taken at the scene.[12]

First they spoke to Donna Harris, Bug's girlfriend, who still couldn't believe he was gone. Though she had been ready to move into Bug's new house with him, the house had gone to Bug's family when he died. Not only had she lost her companion, she'd lost her own dream of leaving Park Manor.

Next, the detectives paid a visit to the Union League Club, where Bug had worked as a parking attendant. They spoke to the doormen and other staff, all of whom remembered Howard fondly. The president of the club described him as a wonderful man who did his job cheerfully and with a great deal of care for the members. Everyone said they would miss Howard's smiling presence.

The detectives went next to the 7300 block of South Calumet and spoke to Ronald and Derek Barnes, the two brothers who had been down the street from the beating. The Barnes brothers said the same thing they had six months before—unable to identify anyone.[13]

When they turned to Jori Garth, the fourteen-year-old girl who'd been on a porch right where the fight had occurred, the detectives got their first break. Garth's father was a detective with the CPD, and, as a professional courtesy, the detectives informed Officer Garth they wanted to speak to his daughter. Shortly after, Officer Walter Garth, looking none too pleased, brought Jori to the police station along with her boyfriend, seventeen-year-old Anton Williams.

Jori Garth looked at the detectives and told them that she had a confession to make.

3

"They tried to do the good cop/bad cop thing. Like I don't watch TV. Like I don't know what's going on."

When Jori Garth was originally interviewed, she had told the detectives she had witnessed the Howard Thomas beating but couldn't identify any perpetrators. That was a lie.

Jori had not only seen the fight, she could identify some of the guys involved. The first was the boy who beat the victim with a souvenir bat. He was a tall guy who she thought was called Big Muhammad. She also identified Marvin Treadwell, the first boy to hit the man. Lastly, Jori stated that Gregory Reed, a rapper known as Fettuccini Corleone ("Fetta" for short), had also been there that night. He had run toward the fight as if to get involved but had been struck with the bat and backed away.

Although Jori's new statement was helpful, Jori's boyfriend, Anton Williams, would be their star witness.

Anton told the detectives that he had seen the fight from start to finish. When the police showed up after the murder, Anton had been inside the Garth house but didn't go outside to talk to the police.[14] He didn't want to get involved, he said, because he was afraid that if he did, the guys he saw would turn on him.[15] Officer Garth convinced him that speaking out was the right thing to do.

Anton told the detectives that on that night in August, sometime after midnight, he was on the Garths' porch talking to Jori. A group of teenagers, all black guys, came up to them. Some of the guys Anton knew. In fact, he'd seen some of them earlier in the evening at a bowling alley, including Marvin Treadwell, Fetta, and Big Muhammad, whose first name was Frad (pronounced *Fa-rad*).[16]

The group stood around the porch, Anton said, and they all talked. Someone said something about his uncle being robbed. A guy walked down the street, an older black guy. The group of boys, including Frad Muhammad, Treadwell, and Fetta, turned and "rushed" the man.[17] Marvin and Frad, along with another guy whom Anton had heard called "Red," attacked, punching and kicking the man.[18] A bat came out, and Anton saw Frad holding it, then using it to beat the man.[19] The man fell to the ground and tried to cover himself while the two other guys continued to strike and kick him. Marvin leaned on a nearby car and jumped on the guy with both feet. When the fight was over, all the guys walked away.

Had anyone tried to stop the fight? Had he? No, Anton said. That wasn't the kind of thing you did in that neighborhood. You kept to your own business and left others to theirs.

Now the case was moving. The detectives kept going—contacting the witnesses all over again. They received varying reports of how many teenagers had been involved in the attack but determined that it was between three and five persons.

After they'd reinterviewed every previous witness, Detective Williams went to work generating photos from the CPD database of the boys who had been identified—Frad Muhammad, Marvin Treadwell, Fetta, and the guy known as Red.

On February 17, 2000, the detectives hit the streets, searching for more leads on the Howard Thomas case. All those detectives were African-American, and as detectives, they didn't wear police uniforms. Chicago is particularly dangerous for "plainclothes" cops, especially cops of color.[20] In *Defending the Damned,* a book that explains the Herculean job facing public defenders in Cook County, one longtime public defender stated, "My hat goes off to the black cops. I mean they are always in danger." He mentioned that most drug busts happen in African-American neighborhoods. "Can you imagine being a black cop in this city? During a drug bust when they bust in a house, if they see a white face come through the door, they know it's the cops."[21]

Despite the hazards of performing street work in plain clothes, Detective Howard was able to find someone named Sherez Boykins. He told Ms. Boykins they were trying to locate a boy called Fetta, who was apparently a rapper.

"He lives at the end of the street," Ms. Boykins said. But no matter how many doors they knocked on, the detectives couldn't find Fetta.

They decided to search instead for Frad Muhammad. Detectives Williams and Easter drove to the 7100 block of South St. Lawrence, where Frad was supposed to live. And sure enough, they found him. He was nineteen years old and tall—about six-foot-four, 260 pounds—with an Afro. Frad sometimes wore Malcolm X–style glasses—black on the top and wire-rimmed on the bottom—and had a tattoo of initials on his upper arm.

Frad, they would eventually learn, was a member of the Gangster Disciples, one of the nation's largest gangs. When he was younger, his mother noticed something a little different about Frad, something slightly vacant in his eyes and a way of responding that always seemed a beat late. Eventually Frad's mother was told that he had a learning disability, which was helpful in a way, since it entitled the family to a certain amount of state money meant to treat the disability. The checks rarely went toward Frad's education, however, and he eventually dropped out of school. Yet Frad had done well enough for himself. He'd gotten a job at the corner store and, later, a position at an ice-cream company. He was the guy in the neighborhood who helped grandmothers around their houses and mowed lawns as a favor. He had three children, two of whom he'd had with Marvin Treadwell's sister.

"Frad Muhammad?" Detective Williams said to the man at the place on St. Lawrence.

"Yeah."

"Do they call you Big Muhammad?"

"Yes," Detective Williams recalled hearing.

"You're under arrest."

The detectives took Frad to Area 2 and put him in an interrogation room.

"We're investigating the beating death of Howard Thomas," they told Frad.

"I don't know anything about it."

On February 18, the kid known as Fettuccini Corleone was at his mother's house when two detectives came to the door. He thought they were Jehovah's Witnesses at first because they wore hats and long coats.[22] But Jehovah's Witnesses didn't search your house like these guys did, Fetta said.[23] Even though they didn't have a search warrant, they flipped over his bed and rummaged through his drawers.

Detectives Williams and Easter brought Fetta to Area 2 and placed him in an interrogation room. Fetta was of medium height and build, with hair cut close to the scalp and slightly bulging eyes. He was a member of the Black Disciples gang. The police began interviewing Fetta, and Detective Williams wrote *tipsy* at the top of the report.

"They tried to do the good cop/bad cop thing," Fetta said. "Like I don't watch TV. Like I don't know what's going on."

In the meantime, Frad Muhammad was still in custody. Detective Hill questioned him, and Frad admitted he had been present at the beating.[24] That night, he said, he'd been with Fetta, Lawrence Wideman (whom they called Red), Marvin Treadwell, and someone named Jovan Mosley. This was the first time in the investigation that the name Jovan Mosley had been raised.

Frad told the detectives that the altercation started because Red saw a man and told him he was tired of the guy "sticking up his family." Red and Thomas began to fight. The guy had a knife and Frad got the knife from him and threw it on the street. Red had a bat, which he'd gotten from someone's yard, and used it on the guy.

Frad Muhammad was placed in a number of lineups.[25] At the time, the procedure for lineups involved using the subject as well as four or five "fillers"—persons similar in size, shape, and color to the subject. The fillers were usually other people being questioned by the police at the time.

At the first lineup, which Jori Garth saw, she stated that Frad looked similar to the person who was using the bat during the fight but that he was not the person.[26]

The detectives went back to Fetta and continued to question him. They reminded him that a man named Howard Thomas had died. They explained what Jori and Anton had told them—that he was present at the time of the fight.

"And I'm like, okay," Fetta said. He told them that on the night of the fight, "I was drunk as hell."[27] Specifically, he said he informed Detective Hill that he was so intoxicated at the time of the incident he didn't even know how it started. The information he possessed about the fight he'd only learned from others who were there.[28]

The detectives then told Fetta their version of what had happened that night.[29] They told him that Marvin started the attack and that Frad accidentally hit Fetta with the bat.[30] They also told him that Jovan Mosley helped in the fight.[31] Fetta hadn't seen Jovan strike Howard Thomas, and he told them that.[32] He had, however, heard that Jovan might have been involved in the fight from the guys talking about it later.

The detectives showed Fetta a department photo, and he identified the guy in it as Red.[33] Then they took Fetta from Area 2 to 432 East 71st Street, to look for Red. When they couldn't find him, they went back to the station, Fetta in tow.[34]

Frad Muhammad was interrogated throughout the night of February 18 and into the early morning hours of February 19. At one point, during questioning by Detectives Easter and Howard, Frad changed his story. He told them that he had, in fact, struck the man (whose name the detectives told him was Howard Thomas). He had also punched him and kicked him.

An assistant state's attorney (ASA) was called to Area 2 to talk to Frad. This particular ASA was on the Felony Review Unit, a unit that provided either the first attorneys on the scene of a crime or those called to police stations when cops considered pressing charges. The ASA spoke with Frad and learned that he had dropped out of high school during his sophomore year.[35] She brought up the fight, and Frad told her the victim had pulled a knife and Frad had then "football-tackled" him and punched him in the face, shoulder, and rib cage. He also kicked him about five times.[36] Red then used a bat, which he had found in a yard, to hit Howard Thomas.

The detectives went back to Fetta.

"I told them," Fetta said, "I can't really give you all what happened because I was drunk. I can inform you from what I've been told, what people have told me. And they said, okay, we're going to bring you some pen and a paper and you could put your statement down. I said, okay."[37]

Despite the fact that Fetta told the detectives on three or four occasions that he'd been drunk on the night of the fight and that he could only give them a version of the events he'd heard from other people,[38] the police gave Fetta forms known as General Progress Reports (GPRs). GPRs are meant for cops' handwritten notes, not civilians' confessions.

"I was giving them a statement," Fetta said, "so they would leave me the hell alone.[39] I was writing down basically what I had heard throughout my peers," he said. "Like Marvin and them. They [Marvin and Red] had told me what happened that night because I had asked them. I mean, we talked about stuff like that because we was guys."[40]

In Fetta's statement, he referred to a boy named "Jason" (but later said that he meant "Jovan"),[41] as well as Jori, whom he referred to as "Jury," and "Farad," which was how he spelled Frad Muhammad's first name. The statement (in which the spelling, grammar, and punctuation are taken verbatim) read in part:

I see Marvin again he asked where I was going I said the bowling alley he said I'll be up there. He catches up to me while I'm walking and we run into Red, Farad and Jason. They ask what we were up to, we said we just heading to the damn bowling alley. So they strolled with us, we get inside see what's up but Anton and them were about to leave, they were almost finished bowling. So Red, Farad and Marvin go outside me and Jason follow about five minutes after. At this time, Jury and Anton, Larry, LT and Greg were getting up to leave the bowling alley.

Me and Jason meet back up with Farad, Marvin and Red on Prairie 75th. I asked who had some money to put on some liquor Farad said he had about two dollars, but I mean his two and my five can't get all five of us drunk. So that plan was over, I heard Marvin mention a cigarette, and Jason said hell yeah he needed a cigarette too. I slowed down some cause Farad was walking kind of slow I asked what was wrong he said nothing Fetta I'm all good.

We catch up with the rest of the pack and I hear Red say something about he'll fuck a nigger up and Marvin and Jason start laughing and Farad said who and Red said nobody in particular I just would. That brought forth the idea of Jason telling Marvin they should whoop a nigger ass for some money. So everybody was saying what they would do and how they would do it including my stupid ass just talking shit being one of the fellows but nobody was too much serious we were just talking shit. So we make it in front of Jury's house and Jason was still talking about it to Red but it didn't seem like Red was paying no attention.

Then Anton asked me to say a rap verse or two for him so I told him hold on let me think of what I'm gone say. In the meantime I guess Marvin has spotted his victim he walked past him and turned around and jump kick the man in the back. So the guy stumbles forward then Marvin punches him to throw his balance off then Jason gets in and gives him two or three quick punches. During this time I turned to Anton and say "these motherfuckers crazy as hell" he laughs and says "hell yeah they too crazy." I then turn around and see Red with a baseball bat hit the man in the back, then the side then the leg. Jury says, damn he bogus as hell while Farad was screaming fuck that just get the money.

Now nobody else tried to get close to stop him from swinging the bat but my dumb ass and then I get hit on the side. I grabbed my side instantly in pain and drop my head Anton and Farad asked me am I ok I just shake my head yes. I stood by Jury's porch 45 seconds to a minute I kept hearing the bat and the man, but I felt like I wanted to cry from my side being in pain.

I looked up and seen Marvin, Red, Farad and Jason running off and I told Anton we a catch up with each other later and rap for him then he just said alright Fetta holler at me tomorrow. I shook my head and I said bye Jury and told him Im going to put some ice on my side. I jogged and caught up with them on damn near 72nd and Vernon. I asked what they get somebody said a pack of Kools and six dollars. I laughed and said that ain't shit y'all crazy ass hell.

At the end of the statement, Fetta wrote:

Personal Note—Red told me a couple of days after it happened that Farad hit the man with the bat also but I didn't recall seeing that or it was just after I got hit and had my head down in pain and I just didn't bother trying to see it.

Continuing, Fetta wrote:

(Anton—witness). (Jury—witness). (Greg (Fetta)—Injured witness). Farad, witness (who shouted get the money and who was accused of having a bat also

or having that bat Red had). (Marvin—Participant—He delivered the first and second blow) (Jason—Participant—He delivered the third, fourth and fifth blow.) Red—Participant—He had the bat and if anything him being a homey to me I'm sad to say is responsible for the victims death. He says Farad helped and hit him with the bat but I can only go off of what I seen.

I'm willing to testify this statement in court in front of a judge.

My feelings—I'm sorry I had to witness a man's life get took even though I didn't find out until yesterday 2-18-2000. And I realize if someone does the crime they should do the time even if it means telling the truth on your homeys and yourself. If it had been me I wouldn't expect them to feel sorry and hold back information so I'm not feeling sorry and holding back information. Red my prayers are with you but you were wrong and you know you were wrong. Farad if you did help swing the bat in the end you will get yours. Marvin and Jason you really didn't do anything but passed a couple licks maybe God will forgive you.

After writing a total of six pages, Fettuccini Corleone ended his statement saying:

Anton and Jury I'm sorry you had to witness this just as well as myself but look at the bright side I got hit y'all didn't. (Laughs).
This is the real story in the words of (Gregory Stephen Reed).

4

"They was looking for him then. I guess they had found everybody else but him."

With Fetta and Frad still in custody, the detectives drove back to the neighborhood in search of Lawrence "Red" Wideman. They got lucky this time and found him at an apartment. Red was seventeen years old, heavyset, about six feet tall. He wore his hair on the long side, combed straight back from his face, and he spoke with a very slight lisp.

The detectives told Red he was under arrest and took him to Area 2. Initially, Red said he had nothing to do with that fight, but later that day he changed his story and said that he was present for the fight, as were Frad, Marvin, and Fetta. Marvin was the "aggressor," he said.[42] Frad hit the man with the bat. Red initially said Fetta hadn't hit Thomas, but then stated that Fetta did punch the man twice. Red insisted that he himself had not done anything to cause Thomas's death.

At 8:10 that evening, Fetta and Red were placed in a lineup, and Jori Garth was once again asked to view it. Jori told the detectives she couldn't identify any of the perpetrators, but she identified Fetta as someone she knew from the neighborhood. She had not seen Fetta involved in the fight.[43]

That same night, the detectives had Anton Williams view another lineup, this one consisting of eight guys, including Frad, Fetta, and Red. Anton identified Fetta as being present on the night of the fight. Anton then pointed to Red and Frad and stated that they had participated in the beating.

On February 20, 2000, three days after being arrested, Frad Muhammad was still in custody. But the detectives weren't getting anywhere with him. Changing tactics, they moved Frad from the interrogation room at Area 2 to 1121 South State Street. Frad Muhammad was placed in another interrogation room. There, Officer Bartik, a detective who wasn't primarily assigned to the case, told Frad about the lineup results and continued to interrogate Frad. Finally, Frad admitted he had hit Howard Thomas with a small bat. Afterward, he said, he gave the bat to Red, who hit Thomas multiple times.[44] He dropped the story of Howard Thomas wielding a knife or any mention of Thomas being involved in a prior robbery.

Frad Muhammad was returned to Area 2, and at seven-thirty that evening an ASA named Victoria Ciszek arrived to take his statement, in which he confessed to beating Howard Thomas. No mention was made of Jovan Mosley participating in the fight. Frad Muhammad was charged with first-degree murder.

Frad's statement was just what the detectives needed. That same day they convinced Lawrence "Red" Wideman that he should take a polygraph exam.

When it was over, the detectives told Red the examination had shown "deception."[45] Then they told him Frad had given a statement and implicated Red in the beating.

According to police reports, Red then stated that he wanted to tell the truth,[46] and an assistant state's attorney was called to take his statement.[47]

Red's statement is very close to Frad's. According to him, on August 6, 1999, he was with Frad, Fetta, Marvin (whom he also knew as "Leno"), and Jovan (whom he also knew as "Jovizzle.")[48] They were on Calumet when Marvin began a fight with Howard Thomas, who had come walking down the street. Marvin and Red attempted to force Thomas to the ground and Red struck him in the side. Frad then hit Thomas with a baseball bat. Frad also mistakenly struck Fetta, who quickly backed off. Marvin continued to hit Thomas with his fists, while Frad hit him with the bat. Red then got the bat from Frad and hit Thomas a couple of times as Thomas fell to the ground. Red walked away with Fetta, Frad, Marvin, and Jovan, and they drank a pop that Thomas had in his bag.

Neither Frad's nor Red's statement suggested that Jovan Mosley had been involved in the fight. Lawrence "Red" Wideman was charged with first-degree murder.

About a week later, on February 24, a stop order was submitted for Marvin Treadwell. A stop order essentially identifies a person as being wanted by the police, someone they have probable cause to arrest.[49]

On March 5, 2000, the detectives found their third man, although at eighteen years old Marvin Treadwell was barely a man. He was a short guy, about five-five, who weighed maybe 130 pounds. His hair was usually braided into cornrows and he had dark skin. If you talked to him for a while, you noticed he spoke in seventies lingo, referring to people as "those cats," and used phrases like, "Man, this is bull-jive."

Nine officers descended on East 71st Street, where they heard Marvin had been seen.[50] They arrested him and took him to Area 2.

After interviewing him numerous times, Detective Howard informed his fellow detectives on the case that Marvin could identify another participant in the beating, someone he called "my guy."[51] "My guy" was described as having a bump on his nose.

Jori Garth and Anton Williams were once again asked to come to the station and view a new lineup. Both Jori and Anton definitively identified Marvin as one of the men who had beaten Howard Thomas to death.[52]

After learning the lineup results, Marvin Treadwell agreed to confess. He was questioned by an assistant state's attorney with Detective Edward Howard present. This time the statement was recorded by video, providing an exact question-and-answer format for the confession.

"Marvin," the ASA said, "before we spoke I explained to you that I am an assistant state's attorney, a lawyer, and a prosecutor, and not your lawyer. Is that correct?"

"Yes," Marvin answered.

"And before we spoke, I advised you of your constitutional rights. Is that correct?"

"Yes."

"Okay, Marvin. I talked to you earlier and you told me about the murder of Howard Thomas. At that time you told me you, Frad Muhammad, Lawrence Wideman, Gregory Reed, and a friend of Frad's beat a man to death, is that correct?"

"Yes."

The state's attorney stopped at that point and read Marvin his constitutional rights. With each, Marvin was asked if he understood, to which he replied, "Yes," each time.

The assistant state's attorney took some background information, then started asking Marvin questions about that night. According to Marvin, he'd been walking around with Red, Fetta, Frad, and Frad's friend, whose name Marvin didn't know.

"You don't know his name?" the ASA asked.

"No."

"Do you know his street name?"

"No."

"How do you address him when you see him?"

"As my guy."

"As your guy?"

"Yeah."

Marvin continued, stating that after a while Fetta started talking about "whooping somebody."

"What did Fetta say?" the ASA asked.

"He say, 'I'll punch a nigger out and take his money.'"

Frad had said the same thing too, but in a different way, as had Red. "When he asked me, would I fight—help him fight," Marvin stated, "I say, 'Yeah, whatever.'"

They went into a bowling alley, where they saw Anton Williams and his girlfriend. Then they went to 73rd and Calumet, where they ran into them again. "They were sitting on Anton's female's porch."

The group was talking with Anton and his girlfriend when a man came walking down the street. Marvin said to the group, "There go one right there," meaning "a person we could probably beat up." Frad then said, "Go get the nigger."

Marvin walked past the man, then turned around and kicked him in the back. The man stumbled and swore at Marvin. At that point, Red came up on his blind side and hit him with his fist.

"Where did Red hit him?" the ASA asked.

"In his face."

"And after Red hit him, what happened next?"

"Everybody—Greg, Frad's friend, and Frad—rushed toward him."

"And what did they do?"

"They got to beating him up."

"Okay," the ASA said, "and when you say beating him up, what were they doing?"

"Punching him."

"And what were you doing?"

"I was holding him," Marvin said.

"And you said that, that they were—Frad and Frad's friend and Fetta and Red—they were all hitting him."

"Yes."

"What were they hitting them with?"

"Their fists."

The next thing Marvin saw, he said, was Frad pulling a bat from the side of his pants. Frad hit the man in the face with it.

"Okay," the ASA said. "Now, you're holding him, right?"

"Yes."

"As you're holding him, how many times did Frad hit him?"

"Three."

After Frad hit the man with the bat three times, Marvin said that he and all the guys ran away. When they got to the corner he saw that Red had money, which he hadn't had before.

Marvin said, "[Red] put it in my face, like, 'Look what I got from him.'" The ASA continued to question Marvin on this point. Eventually, Marvin changed his story—saying that Red actually said something specifically about the money.

"What type of money was it?" the state's attorney asked.

"Dollar bills."

"Okay, and again, what did Red say to you? How do you know he got it from the man?"

"Caused he showed me the money."

"And what did he say?"

"'Look what I got from him.'"

"Did anyone take anything else?" the ASA asked.

"Fetta took a pop," Marvin said.

"Okay, when you said he took a pop, where did he get the pop from?"

"The victim." The pop was a two-liter, Marvin said, which the man had had in the bag he was carrying.

"What did you guys do with the pop?"

"They drunk it."

"Okay. Who drank it?"

"Frad and Fetta and Red."

After that, Marvin said, he went home.

Marvin Treadwell was charged with first-degree murder and armed robbery, the armed robbery charge stemming from the fact that a weapon, the bat, was used during the beating, and the participants had allegedly robbed the victim of his property (the money and the pop). In Illinois, a "felony murder" such as this, the combination of first-degree murder and armed robbery, carries the possibility of the death penalty.

The person Marvin Treadwell called "my guy" was never identified by Marvin, but he did tell the detectives that "my guy" resided at 503 East 71st Street.

The detectives picked up Fetta, and once again they placed him in an interrogation room, where he was kept for nearly a day.[53] They showed Fetta a number of photos. According to Fetta, the police said the photos might be a man named "Jason" from his neighborhood.[54]

"I was like, 'That's not him,'" Fetta said.[55] "But they was looking for him then. I guess they had found everybody else but him."[56]

Eventually, Fetta's mother brought a lawyer to Area 2 and was able to get her son released.[57]

Using the CPD database, the detectives obtained a computer-generated photo of Jovan Mosley, age nineteen.[58] According to the database, Mosley had no convictions, a rarity in his neighborhood, and had been arrested only once, for a mob action charge (essentially loitering) that was never prosecuted.

At that point in the investigation, the statements police had received from participants or witnesses can be summarized as follows: (1) Anton Williams stated Marvin, Frad, and Red had been in the fight, and Anton picked them out of a lineup; (2) Jori Garth said that Big Muhammad (Frad) and Marvin had been in the fight. Fetta had been present; (3) Frad admitted he had punched Howard Thomas. He then hit him with a bat, as did Red; (4) Fetta said Marvin drop-kicked the guy, Jason (Jovan) got two or three quick punches, and Red hit the man with the bat; (5) Red said Marvin started the fight. Red hit the guy and Frad struck him with a baseball bat. Red then got the bat from Frad and hit the man. They all walked away (including Jovan) and took a sip of pop; and finally (6) Marvin said he started the fight by kicking the guy. Red then hit the man. Then everybody—Fetta, Frad's friend (Jovan), and Frad—rushed toward him and "got to beating him up." Frad hit the man with a bat, then they all ran away. Frad, Fetta, and Red had the man's pop and drank it.

Though no stop orders or arrest warrants had been issue for Jovan Mosley, as they had been for Frad, Red, and Marvin, the detectives took to the streets, speaking to people in his neighborhood. And this was how the detectives learned that Jovan Mosley had previously resided at the address Marvin had given for "my guy"—503 East 71st Street. The detectives also learned that Jovan had since moved to the vicinity of 83rd and Kingston, and they headed in that direction.[59]

5

"It was just life. And I was just living it."

On an overcast Sunday in March 2000, nineteen-year-old Jovan Mosley left the house and stopped to say hello to some girls he knew.

"The house" was the place in the 8300 block of Kingston Avenue where Jovan and his father were staying with Jovan's grandparents, uncle, aunt, her two sons, and other family members who crashed there sporadically. It was a tight squeeze—his aunt and cousins stayed on the first floor, Jovan and his dad on the second. His uncle stayed in the attic, with a lock on his door.

Jovan and his father were not living together because they were close. When asked about his father, Jovan said, "He was there. There isn't much to say about him."

While Jovan was growing up, his family lived in a few different places depending on their financial situation. Until he was twelve, the Mosleys lived in the 500 block of East 71st Street. Then they moved to the 4400 block of South Lawler in Le Claire Courts—a housing project. The complex was inhabited by five or six different gangs and was extremely violent. They left, and moved to 90th and St. Lawrence. Next, Jovan lived with his mother in Park Manor in an orange brick building with nine apartments and a tavern. It was in that apartment where he'd spent his latter high school years, but money issues once again had forced them to leave. So in March 2000, a year and a half after graduating from Dunbar Vocational Career Academy, Jovan was living with his dad's side of the family. His parents were still technically married, but they lived together only when they could afford a place large enough for all of them.

On that Sunday, Jovan was telling one of the girls that he'd just had a job interview. He'd been busy lately, trying to figure out what to do with his life.

Jovan had enjoyed school at Gillespie Elementary in the 9300 block of South State Street. But in seventh grade, when his family moved, he transferred to Hearst on South Lamon and found they were teaching things he had learned years ago. He was bored. He stopped doing his assignments and got bad grades for the first time. Whenever he was challenged he would "step it up" and get A's. But then he'd find the classes tedious again and his grades would dip. This pattern would follow him into high school.

However, in high school he'd gotten a job as a clerk in a law office. Jovan had always wanted to be a lawyer, and he liked the job. He filed documents at the Daley Center, provided copy services, and made bank runs and deliveries. When he had a little extra time, what he liked best was reading the documents that he filed and copied—complaints initiating lawsuits, motions demanding depositions of experts, interrogatories disclosing evidence. They thrilled him, though they seemed nonsensical at first. By the time he'd graduated from high school and had to leave the job (since it was part of a work-study program), he'd made sense of those documents. Someday, he intended to write those kinds of documents himself.

Jovan had done well enough to be accepted into Ohio State—the school he'd set his sights on (in large part because of their football program). He would be one of the few kids from his family or even his side of the neighborhood to attend college. But nobody had been able to help him through the labyrinth of financial aid applications, and he balked. So, instead of going to college, Jovan worked a factory job at Federal-Mogul in Skokie. But it took him hours to get there on the bus. And so he'd quit.

In March 2000, Jovan, like many people in his neighborhood, was unemployed, with no real certainty of what he would do in the future.

"It was just life," Jovan would later say. "And I was just living it."

Jovan recalls that while he spoke to the girls that Sunday afternoon he saw, out of the corner of his eye, his grandmother leaving the house. He knew she was likely going to the store, and when he finished his conversation, he started off to meet her. Just then a car pulled up and three or four plainclothes police officers jumped out.[60]

"C'mere," one said.

Jovan walked up to them.

The officer snatched the soda can Jovan was carrying and poured the liquid on the street. The others grabbed him and spun him around. They yanked his hands behind his back and cuffed him. As this was happening, a number of other squad cars pulled up to watch and offer assistance if necessary. It wasn't. Jovan didn't fight or resist arrest. The officers shoved him into the back of a squad car. One of the officers got in the back with him.

"Can you tell me what this is pertaining to?" Jovan asked the officer, anxiety making him formal.

"We'll let you know when you get there," the cop said. Then he laughed.

A voice in Jovan's head hollered, *What is going on?* But he wasn't truly scared yet. He knew he hadn't done anything wrong or broken any laws. And, like most other young guys in the neighborhood, he'd had some exposure to the police before. Cops frequently came through the neighborhood looking for witnesses or information on different cases. They would stop Jovan and his friends on the street and tell them to come to the car. They'd say, "Put your hands on the hood." Then they would ask them if they knew people who had guns, whether they had any information about where a drug deal was going down. If the cops were in a bad mood, they'd handcuff them and shove them into the back of a police car, questioning them there instead. If you couldn't come up with any information, they sometimes threatened to take you to territory in the neighborhood that was ruled by the GDs (Gangster Disciples) and tell them that you were a Blackstone, which would guarantee you'd get your ass handed to you, if not killed. Jovan's real concern, as he sat in the back of the squad car, was how he was going to get home from the police station. He'd heard that after you were questioned by the cops you had to find your own way back.

One of the officers spoke to the cops outside, while the two officers inside the car remained silent. Jovan asked questions, but no one spoke to him. He was never read his *Miranda* rights.

When the final officer got in and started the car, Jovan turned his head. As the car pulled away, he watched the house disappear. It was the last time he would see it for almost six years.

6

"We know what happened that night."

Jovan was taken to Area 2. Never having been formally interrogated by the police before, he didn't know the station was infamous for police brutality, particularly the cruel tactics of Detective Jon Burge.

But Burge wasn't the only detective with honed interrogation skills.

At Area 2, two of the detectives brought Jovan into an eight-by-eight-foot interrogation room. (The CPD prefers such rooms to be called "interview rooms.") One of the detectives had a mustache and a slightly crossed eye tinged with pink. The other was skinnier, had lighter skin, and wore glasses. Jovan thought absently that he looked like a children's book character. The detectives told Jovan to sit on a bench with no back. One of his wrists was freed from the handcuffs, the other attached to a ring a foot or two higher than the bench and hanging on the wall behind him. The room was made of cinder blocks. There were no windows. In the center of the room was a desk and two chairs. A mirror was embedded in a wall on one side of the room.

"Why am I here?" Jovan asked the detectives again.

The detectives turned and left without a word. The door banged shut behind them.

Although there was no clock in the room, it seemed to Jovan that at least an hour went by. He shifted around on the bench, but it was hard to find a comfortable position because of the handcuff bolting his wrist to the wall. His arm began to ache.

Finally, the detective with the glasses entered the room. Jovan later learned their names—Detective Edward "Charles" Howard and Detective Derail Easter.

"Why am I here?" Jovan asked him again.

The detective stared intently at him. "We investigate violent crimes. Is there anything you want to tell us?"

"No," Jovan said.

The detective left again. It seemed like a few more hours went by, each one an eternity. He began to feel queasy. The feeling grew until he couldn't take full breaths into his lungs. His eyes swept the room, but there was nothing to focus on, and the queasiness evolved into something like panic.

Eventually both detectives returned. The one with the glasses was the first to speak. "Is there anything you want to tell us about what happened in the early morning hours of August sixth, 1999?"

August 6 . . . August 6 . . . Jovan searched his mind, but he didn't know what they were talking about. "No," he said. "I don't remember what happened on that day."

"*Anything* you want to tell us?" the detectives asked again and again.

"No," he said each time. He had nothing to tell them. He didn't know why he was there.

The detectives locked the door behind them.

Jovan began to squint. The bright lights were starting to mess with him. He fought mounting panic, telling himself he had nothing to worry about, because for the most part he had done the right things with his life, made the right choices, just like his brother had told him.

His brother, Christopher Michael, whom they called Michael, had warned him to be careful who he hung out with and never to join a gang. It was Michael's membership in the Gangster Disciples that had landed him in jail for arson murder. Michael had staunchly denied setting the fire, particularly because there was no reason for him to do so—the building was controlled by his own gang. It was well known in the neighborhood that the fire had been started by two teenagers, but a woman from a rival gang told the police she believed Michael had instructed the teenagers to start the fire. No one seemed to care that during the fire Michael had kicked in doors to help people get out and had caught babies thrown from upper floors. Michael had been convicted anyway, sentenced to an Illinois penitentiary.

"Once you get in a gang," Michael had said, "you can't get out."

And he wasn't just saying that to scare Jovan. The different gangs had rules about when, or if, you could leave. Certain gangs said you could opt out if you'd reached the age of thirty-five (as if this was unlikely) or if you'd found religion. Others maintained that the only way to quit was to be shot in the head. And survive.

Jovan's other brother was gone, dead of an illness related to HIV. Jovan had been the youngest of the three boys, and he'd watched his brothers' lives carefully, the way he was always watching everyone. So he'd listened to Michael's warnings and avoided the gang life. It hadn't been easy, but he befriended everyone, no matter who they were affiliated with. Unlike most of his neighborhood's residents, Jovan had no criminal convictions. Though he'd been arrested once for loitering outside a convenience store, the case was never prosecuted, and so he had essentially no experience with the criminal justice system. Jovan drank alcohol when it was offered, smoked an occasional cigarette, and sometimes something a little stronger, but his quick smile and kind demeanor made him the sort of boy that nearly everyone liked, gang members and grandmothers alike. So far, he'd led a relatively charmed life, a neutral island in a complicated neighbor-hood sea.

In the interrogation room, Jovan was beginning to lose his grasp of reality as time steadily grew more elusive. Nothing moved in the room, nothing shifted, the bright lights never changed. Jovan had to use to the bathroom but he didn't want to admit that to the cops. His back hurt from lack of support. The one arm cuffed to the wall went numb for a time, then began to ache more and more. He was given no food or water.

Finally, one detective came into the room. "Do you know these guys?" the detective asked. He rattled off names like "Big Mack" and "Leno."

"No," Jovan said. He'd never heard them.

The cop looked pissed off. "Yes, you do."

"No, I don't."

The detective insisted Jovan knew the guys they were talking about. He used other names, like "Marvaline."

The detective left, then returned with his partner to question Jovan about the same names, then left again. Jovan lost track of how many times they visited him, questioned him about the names, then left. He was exhausted, his eyes gritty and red from the unchanging light.

At one point, the detective with the pinkish eye left and the skinnier one with the glasses stayed.

Jovan looked at him, ready for another question, but the man did nothing. He simply sat down at the desk across from Jovan and stared at him, quiet.

"Can you loosen this?" Jovan said, shaking the hand against the wall. It felt as if the blood flow to his hand and wrist had been cut off.

The detective ignored him.

Five silent minutes later, the door opened, and the pink-eyed detective came back.

He was a stocky guy, and he grunted as he sat next to the other detective. "Let's talk again about whether you know these guys." He laid out three photos on the desk.

"Yes." Jovan nodded at each one, saying, "Red, Fetta, Frad."

The detective pointed at the photos of Frad and Fetta. "Did you ever hear them referred to as 'Bear' and 'Fettuccini Corleone'?"

"No." Jovan told them he had heard Gregory Reed referred to only by "Fetta," and had never known the full name behind it.

"These guys are in trouble."

Now it started to make sense. Jovan began to think about something that had happened weeks ago when he'd gone to visit Frad. Frad wasn't there, and on Jovan's way home, he ran into Fetta. Fetta told him Frad and Red had been arrested. The whole thing was about that fight last summer.

"For real?" Jovan had said to Fetta. It was not the first time someone in the neighborhood had been arrested. Far from it. But for Jovan, that particular night was long behind him. He had walked away before the end of the fight. He had never talked to Frad or to any of the other guys about it.

Jovan had seen plenty of brawls. Sometimes "guys would jump you even though they *knew* you were gonna see them later," Jovan said. He'd been mugged numerous times himself.

The truth was, he'd seen plenty of people shot too: twice in Park Manor Park while he was playing basketball; once at a restaurant while he was getting carry-out.

Once, Michael's friend Sniper drove by the house and shot at them.

About four houses down, he stopped, got out of the car, and started laughing. "Dude," Michael yelled. "What's wrong with you?"

Yet another time, Jovan heard shooting in the neighborhood—*bow, bow, bow, bow, bow.* He ran home and saw Michael running toward the house. He thought Michael must have been near a shooting but had been one of the first to get away. But then Michael crumpled to the ground. It turned out Michael had been shot by a member of the Vice Lords who was known around the neighborhood as Ronnie Poo, and who had mistaken Michael for a Blackstone gang member. Michael had been hit in the buttocks and was in the hospital for a while. Years later, a cousin was sent to Stateville prison in Joliet for two murders. One of the victims was rumored to be Ronnie Poo. It was the way of the neighborhood.

The frequency of the violence inured residents to it. Jovan often thought of the scene in the movie *Boyz N the Hood,* in which the kids check out a dead body. They look at it, kick the body, and then walk away. That about summed up the prevailing neighborhood attitude, which was that people got beat up, people got shot all the time. Sometimes the cops came out right after an incident. Sometimes they investigated a few days later. Sometimes it took weeks for someone to tell the authorities about a body lying in an alley. Sometimes the cops simply didn't seem to be investigating the case at all. Most people didn't call the cops for fear of retaliation from the perpetrators. The older Jovan grew, the more neutral he became. He understood that the violence was mainly in the service of revenge, and there was no way to stop the cycle but to opt out of it entirely.

A week after Fetta had told him about Frad's arrest, someone else told Jovan that the guy in that fight had died. Jovan felt a cold sadness when he heard that, but he pushed it away, not wanting to think about it. That was how he dealt with things.

"Is there anything you want to tell us?" the detectives asked again.

What was the right thing to do here? He had been there for the start of the fight. More than the start. But as far as he knew, no good had ever come to anyone who dealt with the cops. In his world, a snitch was the worst kind of person.

"No," he said.

One detective sighed heavily; the other puffed up his chest and looked like he was about to shout. But then they both stood and left.

Jovan shifted around on the bench, trying again to find a slightly more comfortable position for what he assumed would be another hour or two-hour wait.

But only minutes later the door banged open, startling Jovan.

"We're investigating the murder of Howard Thomas. We want to put away the guy with the bat," the pink-eye told him. "But we know you threw a few punches. Just tell us you threw a few punches, and tell us about the guy with the bat, and you can go home."

"I didn't hit that man," Jovan said.

More sighing and frustrated stares from the detective. He stomped out of the room.

Time dragged on. At last, the one with the glasses came in and loosened the cuff around Jovan's hand.

"Look," the detective said in a soft tone. "We know what happened that night."

And he began to tell Jovan a story. Jovan was walking around last August, he said. He was with a bunch of guys. They had planned a robbery, then they jumped a guy and killed him for his money.

"That's not true," Jovan said. "That's not what happened."

He thought back to that night. Then he dialed his mind back further, and further again, to the very beginning.

7

"You're playing games with me!"

It had seemed like any other lazy summer evening.

Jovan put on his baggy jeans and a loose cotton shirt, yellow plaid with black stripes. Then he tried to match his shoes to his shirt.

He walked to the front hall closet, where he kept some clothes in the one-bedroom apartment he shared with his mother. All his shoes were athletic trainers except for the pair of loafers he used to wear to work at the law firm. Jovan chose a pair of black Nikes with yellow-gold stripes. He sat down on the couch that he used as a bed and began to put on the shoes, wondering what to do with this muggy night. He had made loose plans to visit a girl who lived a few blocks over. You couldn't really call her a girlfriend, because Jovan was seeing two other girls on that same block.

The front door buzzed. Jovan went down a flight of steps to open it.

Waiting outside was his friend Frad Muhammad. Frad was a year younger than Jovan, and they'd met when Frad worked at the corner store, where he was a jack-of-all-trades—unloading stock, filling the shelves, ringing up customers, all of whom seemed to like him very much.

"You going out tonight?" Frad asked.

"Not sure."

"Let's go kick it," Frad said. In other words, *Let's hang out.*

"I don't know," Jovan said, one hand still on the door.

"Let's go."

Deciding not to visit the girl he'd been seeing, Jovan agreed.

Leaving Frad downstairs, Jovan went back to the apartment to get some cash. Since he and Frad were only going out in the neighborhood, where

36

there was little to buy, Jovan figured he wouldn't need much. He went into his mother's bedroom, where he kept a dresser, and took $10 and his ID from the top drawer. He debated over the four watches he owned. Jovan loved watches, absolutely loved them—cheap or expensive. But none of them went with what he was wearing, so he put them away. He pushed his money and ID into his pocket.

He left the apartment with Frad and went to Meyering Park at 71st and King Drive—the place everyone in the neighborhood called Park Manor Park. It was a large place that held basketball courts, a spray pool, and a playground. It was packed that night, mostly with shouting kids. Later, down the street, Jovan and Frad ran into some guys Frad knew well: Marvin, Red, and Fetta. Jovan had met them all a few times around the neighborhood. They were seventeen and eighteen years old, and they were in gangs, Jovan knew—either BDs (Black Disciples), like Fetta or GDs (Gangster Disciples), like Marvin. In his neighborhood certain gang members socialized with rival gangs, and Jovan used that fact to skate his way through it all, being friends or acquaintances with everyone but never joining a gang. Jovan's number one survival tactic was to let people think whatever they wanted. If somebody assumed he was a GD like his brother Michael, he let them think that. If they thought he was a BD or a Vice Lord, that was fine too.

The five of them kept walking away from the park because there was really nothing for teenagers to do there. They walked five blocks to a bowling alley. Inside, they saw Anton Williams, who'd gone to Jovan's high school. Anton, a BD, was a slight guy with a fast smile. He was with a small, curvy girl.

The group hung out at the bowling alley, talking to people, but they got bored with that too. The guys—Marvin, Red, Frad, Fetta, and Jovan—went to a liquor store. Frad, who looked at least twenty-one, went in, while the rest of them stood outside talking about nothing much.

Frad came out with eight or so beers, giving each of them one or two cans. They walked down Calumet Avenue, drinking their beers, heading north, but heading nowhere. Just walking.

Fetta and Marvin were talking, but Jovan was only half paying attention because Fetta, a constant drunk, was always going on about something.

Marvin said something like, "My pockets are light."

"Yeah," Fetta said. "We should get someone. Take their money."

Fetta and Marvin kept shooting off their mouths, joking.

Frad said, "We should reroute a nigga."

But it was just guys kicking it, talking their shit. Their tone was joking. Jovan didn't think much about it.

They strolled down a stretch of Calumet Avenue, tiny brick bungalows lining the street. When they passed one of them, they saw Anton sitting on the porch with his girlfriend.

Fetta bounded up the stairs and started talking to Anton. The rest of them stayed at the base of the stairs. Jovan said something to the girl, smiling at her. He later learned her name was Jori.

Marvin walked away then, and Jovan turned his head to see what he was doing.

A guy, an older man, was coming down the street carrying groceries. Marvin suddenly kicked him in the back.

The man stumbled, then threw his bags down and turned to Marvin, first shouting, then swinging at him. Red raced up to the two men and hit the older guy in the back of the head. Marvin and Red started wrestling with the guy, trying to get him to the ground.

Jovan, Frad, and Fetta moved toward the street to see what was happening. The guy was on the ground now, and Red and Marvin were hitting him. Then all of a sudden Frad pulled out the souvenir bat he carried for fights and started swinging it.

Fetta yelped, saying something about getting hit with the bat. Jovan and Fetta both moved away and went back to the porch where Anton and Jori sat. Jori was flinching. "It's just a fight," Jovan said to her, wanting to assure her, to somehow impress her.

"Why are they doing that?" she asked, looking over Jovan's shoulder.

He started moving around, being silly, trying to get her to look at him instead of the fight. But she was still watching, and it occurred to Jovan, *Someone is going to get in trouble here.*

He took off, walking fast down Calumet. It was after midnight, and with trees obscuring some of the streetlights, it was dark.

Fetta caught up with him. A minute later, Marvin jogged past them. Jovan remembered Marvin saying earlier that he was broke, but now he was counting singles.

"What did you get?" Fetta said.

Marvin slowed down. "Nothing but a few bucks."

Frad and Red caught up to them then. Red was saying, "I beat his head in."

"That was *bogus*," Frad said.

Jovan had had enough of the group. When they reached the end of the next block, he turned toward his mom's apartment, said good-bye, and walked away. He had managed to stay out of the whole thing. Just as he had all his life.

But the detectives didn't want to hear what he had to say about that night. They kept leaving and coming back, telling Jovan they knew he had thrown punches in that fight. He kept denying it, and every time he did, they would storm out.

He tried to pay attention to the time, but without movement or natural light, he couldn't.

The skinny guy with the glasses came back in. "You know, this guy died, and somebody is going to have to take this murder."

"I didn't do anything."

The detective left.

The detective with the damaged eye returned. But this time he had a different detective with him.

He gazed at Jovan. "You need to tell us something you did during the fight."

"What can I tell you?" Jovan said. "I didn't do anything."

"You're playing games with me!"

"I'm *not* playing games with you."

The detectives turned and left.

Jovan's eyes scanned the room, again looking for some place to land, for something to stop the fear. But it kept growing.

———

The officer with the glasses was the next to come in. The detective sat at the desk. "*Somebody* is going down for this."

The door opened and the detective with the pink eye came in, strode toward Jovan, and leaned over him.

"I didn't hit that guy," Jovan said. Then he said it again, and again. He began enunciating his words. If he said it enough, maybe it would mean something. Maybe they would hear him.

"I'm gonna slap you," the detective said, mere inches from Jovan's face, spittle flying from his mouth. "Don't play with me."

"I'm *not* playing with you." He wanted out of there so bad. He knew he couldn't budge his wrist cuffed to the wall, but he pulled at the cuff just the same. It felt like glass cutting into his skin.

The detectives started to leave.

"I didn't do anything!" Jovan yelled at their backs.

Then Jovan thought of something. "I want a lie detector test."

One of the detectives stopped, turned, gave Jovan a curious look. "*What?*" he said, as if he couldn't believe what he'd just heard.

"Give me a lie detector test."

"That's bullshit! Why do you want a lie detector test when you *know* you hit him?"

"I didn't hit him!"

This seemed to enrage the detective. In a fast second, he was in front of Jovan again, leaning close to his face. "Now, you listen, you son of a bitch!" Jovan felt spittle spray from the detective's mouth again and land on his cheeks and nose. "You know if you take that test and you fail, you're going to jail for a long time? I mean a *long* time."

"Fine. Let me take it." If a machine could tell them that he was telling the truth, this would all stop.

Hours and hours passed. No lie detector machine was brought in. Jovan's stomach hurt, from nerves and lack of food. The black-and-white cotton shirt he was wearing grew rank.

Suddenly the detectives returned and walked to the ring on the wall. Jovan watched as they uncuffed him. Relief soared through him. It was over.

But then one of the detectives yanked Jovan to his feet and cuffed his hands behind his back. He pulled Jovan from the room, leading him down the hallway.

"Where are we going?" Jovan asked.

No response.

"Where are we going?"

The detective yanked his arm once again, pulled him faster down the hallway.

"Please. Where are we going?"

No one answered.

8

"Even if your son was here, we wouldn't have to tell you."

Delores Mosley had always wanted to have children, and in particular, she always wanted boys. She couldn't say exactly why, only that she remembered playing house as a young child in Arkansas and jostling with the other kids to get the boy dolls, so she could arrange her "sons" just so. Delores would eventually get her wish.

Her family moved to Chicago when she was seven years old, and she spent most of her childhood and teenage years in the Robert Taylor Homes. The Taylor Homes, a cluster of high-rise towers on Chicago's South Side, built in 1962, were the world's largest public housing development. But the Taylor soon became known for abject poverty and extreme violence. The project was built to house eleven thousand people in its roughly forty-three hundred apartments, but at its peak the Taylor Homes were believed to have a massive population of twenty-seven thousand. When Delores was a teenager, she met William Mosley at the Taylor Homes. He was a short man with a smart mouth, and she had an immediate and deep crush on him. With William, whom she called "Brother," she became pregnant when she was sixteen. Their son, William, Jr., whom they called "Wimpy," was born when she was seventeen. When she became pregnant by William with another son—Christopher Michael—they got married. Delores was twenty-two.

Their third son, Jovan, was born on July 23, 1980. "I didn't take any medications for his birth, and he came out hard," Delores remembered. "He came out being a judge," she said, referring to the often somber expression Jovan still maintains. "You could put him in a little baby outfit and tickle him, and he would never do the baby thing. He would just give you this look."

She named Jovan after cologne she'd seen in a commercial on TV. He was sick a lot as a baby, allergic to everything, it seemed, but still he was "the prince of all kids."

By the year 2000, Delores Mosley had gone through a lot of heartache over her other boys. She was a woman in her mid-forties with braided, cornrowed hair. She had a kind smile, which she often covered with her hand to hide a chipped front tooth that embarrassed her, but she couldn't afford to repair it. Years before, she suffered through her husband's arrest for a shooting at the Robert Taylor Homes. He was convicted, but after he'd spent a few years in the penitentiary, the court overturned the case for lack of consistent evidence. Those years on her own had been hard. And it seemed the hard times wouldn't stop. Her son Wimpy died of complications of HIV. Then in 1996 her son Christopher Michael, who they called Michael, was arrested; he was eventually convicted of murder, arson, and attempted murder.

Because of the sorrow and anguish surrounding most of the men in her life, Delores had placed all her hope in Jovan. And he lived up to her expectations. He was a smart kid, the smartest she had ever known. He went to class every day, and carried around a backpack full of books. She was so proud of him when he got a job at a law firm. He'd always said he wanted to be a lawyer, and she knew he could do it, even though no one in her family had gone to college. Many hadn't even graduated from high school. But Jovan did, and as that high school graduation approached, she was so proud of him, she wanted to burst. They bought the cap and gown, even though they had no money for it. But on the day of the graduation, she and Jovan were both sick with the flu. They were both upset that they couldn't attend the graduation. But that was okay, Delores told herself, because there would be others.

Jovan didn't go to college as he'd planned, but she knew he would eventually, and in the meantime, he was a good kid. He came home every night—every *single* night—exactly when he said he would (unlike other kids who would stay out for hours, sometimes days, and make their mothers worry). No, Delores never had to worry about Jovan.

But then came that Sunday afternoon in March 2000.

She stopped by the house on Kingston Avenue to see her husband and his family. They told her Jovan hadn't been home for hours. They had asked around the neighborhood and learned that he had been picked up in a police car.

Delores was terrified. She could not only remember, she could feel, the other times that her boys—her husband and her sons—had been arrested. But this had never happened with Jovan.

She called the Area 2 police station.

"No, ma'am," the officer said. "He's not here."

She got out the hefty Chicago phone book and looked up other police stations south and west of the city. But each time she called, she got the same answer: *He's not here.*

What had happened to Jovan? Had he really been taken away in a police car? It didn't feel right. Maybe the neighbors had seen someone else? But then, where was he?

She called Area 2 once again. She demanded more answers this time. "I'm sure my son is there. People saw him being picked up."

"Sorry, ma'am, we have no one by that name here." The cop paused, then asked, "How old did you say he was?"

"Nineteen."

"Well, even if your son was here," the cop said, "we wouldn't have to tell you."

9

"He didn't do anything."

Jovan tried not to stumble as they pulled him down the hallway, but he felt light-headed from the movement after all the time he'd spent sitting still in the holding cell. He was going to be in a lineup, the detectives told him.

They brought him into a room with four other men. He didn't recognize any of them; most of them looked older. Jovan had never been in a lineup, but he'd heard that the cops were supposed to stand you by other people who looked somewhat like you. Jovan had broad shoulders. His nose had a bump at the top. These guys really didn't look much like him. Still, he thought this lineup was a good thing. Whoever saw the lineup would tell the cops he hadn't been involved.

"Pick your spot," one of the detectives said. Jovan thought he'd heard someone call the man Detective Clarence Hill.

"What?" He squinted in confusion.

"Pick your spot," the detective said loudly, as if Jovan should know exactly what he was talking about.

When Jovan continued to look around in bewilderment, the cop lined up the other guys against the wall, then pointed to the group. "Pick. Your. Spot."

Jovan understood now. He looked up and down the line of men. Did it matter where he stood? He couldn't see how. He took a few steps forward and got in line.

After a minute, one of the detectives issued orders. "Turn left." Then, "Turn right." Then, "Now everyone face forward."

Anton Williams watched as the cops shuffled the grim-faced men into a line. He couldn't blame them for their expressions. It was eleven thirty at night. Too late to be doing this.

Anton scanned the faces, moving up the row, then back down. He landed on a dude wearing dark baggy jeans and a black-and-white shirt.

"That guy," Anton said, pointing to the man.

"He was there?" the cop asked.

"Yeah, he was there."

"What did he do?"

"He didn't do anything," Anton said.[61]

The detectives took the guys in the lineup out of the room and into a hallway, where someone took their pictures. Then Jovan was shuffled back into the same windowless eight-by-eight-foot room. Once more, he was cuffed to the wall and left alone.

Time dragged. And dragged.

At last the first two detectives came in—the skinny one with glasses and the guy with the pinkish eye.

"You were identified in the lineup," one said. "They said you did it."

"Who said that?" Jovan said.

"Doesn't matter. They said you threw a couple of punches."

"Who?" Jovan said again, almost shouting now.

When no answer came, Jovan said, "I want a phone call. I have a right to a phone call." He wanted to call his mom.

Hour after relentless hour passed. When the door opened next, it was two different detectives, both black, one very tall. Where had the other ones gone? Jovan studied them nervously. They took a seat. "Let's talk about what happened on August sixth, 1999."

"I didn't do anything," Jovan said.

Had he tried to stop what went on that night?

No, he told the police. He tried to steer clear of fights. He'd walked away. The detectives left.

Hours later they came back, with another story of how they believed things had gone down that night. Jovan kept repeating himself—*I didn't hit that guy, I didn't hit that guy*—but they kept insisting he had.

"Two punches isn't murder," they said. "That's not killing anyone."

"But I didn't hit him." He started to feel as if he were going crazy. How was this happening?

They left. Again.

Criminal justice and police interrogation experts have determined that different types of false confessions exist.[62] A "stress-compliant" confession occurs when the stresses and pressures of custodial questioning overwhelm the suspect, who comes to believe that the only way to terminate the punishing experience of interrogation is by confessing. Interrogators ratchet up or continually change the intensity of interrogation, often being confrontational, demanding, deceptive, and hostile. This in turn brings about anxiety and distress designed to whittle away at the suspect's self-confidence. Because the interrogators don't let the suspect proclaim innocence or deny guilt, the suspect feels powerless and trapped. Even though the person privately knows he is innocent, the stress-compliant interviewee complies with the interrogator's demand that he confess because the prospect of continued interrogation is intolerable.

According to John Laskey, a former Chicago homicide detective, handcuffing a suspect to the wall in a stark room with bright lights was standard police practice for the thirty-four years he spent with the CPD.

The fact is, some form of persuasion in criminal investigations is probably, generally, required. The Chicago police had often found themselves hampered by the "no-snitching" street code, resulting in no witnesses stepping forward even on cases, like that of Howard Thomas, where many people saw the crime. "There is a strong wall being built where kids will not come forward, and it literally is killing us," said Chicago Police Superintendent Jody Weis.[63]

But Jovan Mosley knew nothing about the typology of false confessions or police practices. All he knew was that he was exhausted from hunger. From fear. His muscles screamed from being in the same position for so long. Surely it had been days now. Why had no one come to help him? He grew confused and frantic.

Every time detectives returned to the room, Jovan told them, "I didn't hit that guy. I didn't touch him."

At one point, the door suddenly banged open and a detective exploded into the room. It was a new detective. He was older than the others, and Jovan recognized him as one of the men who'd been around when he was arrested. He stood in the doorway with his arms crossed tight, as if he were holding himself back from attacking Jovan.

"Is this the guy right here?" the man asked another detective behind him.

"Yeah, that's him. He's not cooperating." They stepped into the room.

"Charge this guy!" the detective shouted.

Jovan kept quiet, but felt the situation reeling away from him—far, far away from his control.

"Charge him with battery, murder, robbery, armed robbery, attempted murder!" He kept yelling a litany of crimes, his face contorted with fury.

"Wait a minute," Jovan said loudly. "What do you mean, you're going to charge me with all that stuff?"

Jovan watched the man's mouth, felt things careening further out of control. Who was this guy?

"Hold on, hold on," Jovan said, his heart hammering. "Don't do that. Don't do that."

They left.

Another detective came in. Someone else he didn't recognize. "Do you want to go home?"

"Yes."

"Then why don't you just cooperate with us? Tell us you threw two punches. Two punches ain't murder. Tell us that, we'll let you go."

Jovan said nothing. What should he do?

With a disgusted look, the detective left, the door clanging shut behind him.

Finally, Jovan gave in and began to cry. Tears streamed down his face. He wiped them with his free hand. He yanked at the cuffed hand, but he was going nowhere.

Over and over, the detectives spoke with Jovan and then disappeared. Twenty or thirty times, they came in the room, insisting he had hit Howard Thomas, telling him if he just signed a statement he could go home.

Two punches isn't murder, they kept saying, and when he insisted he hadn't done anything, they'd say, *Stop lying to us.*

Jovan would insist he hadn't been in the fight, and they'd be gone again. They came at him from so many different angles. They left him alone, they shouted, they vanished. At times, two detectives were there, one spitting and screaming in his face, then stalking out. The other would remain, talking nice, saying Jovan could go home if he'd just tell them what they wanted to hear. So many things were coming at him at once, he felt he was going insane. When the detectives weren't there, every hour seemed like ten days. One arm remained cuffed to the wall, and his back screamed along with his bladder. He was hungry.

Once, a detective entered the room with two sheets of paper. He held them out one by one, pointing quickly to what Jovan could see was his name written on those pages. "Your name is right here, and right here, so we know you did something."

He snatched the papers away, so Jovan couldn't read anything other than his name. Then he was gone.

The detectives who'd arrested him returned at one point.

"Look, I know you're tired," one said. "I know you want to go. Just say you threw a couple of punches, and you can go home. We know this is what happened."

Again, they told him their story. By this time they had the names right. Jovan had been walking around on that night in August, they said. He was with Frad, Marvin, Fetta, and Red. They stopped at a liquor store, and Frad bought some beer. They walked northbound on Calumet and while they walked Marvin said that his pockets were hurting, and then Frad said, "Let's reroute a nigga."

"Okay," Jovan said, because so far what they had said was essentially true.

"And so pretty soon, you saw a guy, and you decided to rob him," the cop said.

"No." Jovan shook his head now. "I didn't decide to rob anyone."

"But Marvin kicked the guy."

They kept telling him the story. They never asked if what they were saying was true. They never asked Jovan for any information at all. They just kept telling him what had happened.

He sat across them, his head drooped from exhaustion. Occasionally, they'd pause to see if he was still listening. He'd murmur okay and they'd continue.

"And then Red started in there."

"Okay."

"And then they started beating him."

"Okay."

"And then you got in there."

"No, I didn't," Jovan said. "I didn't touch that man."

"C'mon, it's no big thing. You punched him twice in the left side, that's it."

Jovan shook his head again. "That's not what happened."

"Yeah, it is." They told him the rest of the story. Frad ran up with a baseball bat and started swinging really hard. "He almost hit you and Fetta with that bat." After Frad kept swinging the bat, Jovan backed off, and he and Fetta walked away. "And one of those guys—Marvin or Red—they came up to you with some money."

"Marvin was counting out some money," Jovan admitted.

"And he gave you some."

"No."

"Your buddy, Frad—he had some pop with him, right?"

"No."

"Yeah, yeah, he had some pop," the cop said.

Jovan just looked at him, not knowing what he was talking about. "He gave you the pop, and you took a sip."

"No," Jovan said.

"Yeah," the cop said. "That's what happened. That's exactly what happened. And if you just say you threw a couple of punches, you can get out of here." And once again they left.

10

"If the police think you're the one, you're in trouble."

Police detectives are under immense pressure to solve crimes, often atrocious ones. Arguably, they have one of the hardest jobs in the world. They're underpaid, undermanned, and they get little or no assistance from the street. So they decide who they think is responsible. "And then they buy into their own theory," says Rob Warden, the executive director of the Center on Wrongful Convictions at Northwestern Law School. "It's the whole tunnel vision phenomena."

Warden is an award-winning journalist turned innocence crusader who helped expose numerous wrongful convictions that often came in the wake of forced confessions. "We usually don't see any truly evil people," he says. "Even cops who do evil things, like Jon Burge, believed they had the right guy."

Francis Wolfe, a former Cook County public defender, agrees. "This is inherently an issue in criminal investigations and prosecutions—they're based in large part on the hunches of everyone involved. The system is dangerous because even good cops have intuitions they believe. They say, 'I know in my bones you did it, so I have to assemble evidence that shows you did it.'"

Tunnel vision in law enforcement was specifically noted in a later report by the Illinois Commission on Capital Punishment, convened by then Governor George Ryan. The members of the commission included judges, senators, state's attorneys, public defenders, U.S. attorneys, and Scott Turow, the author who was once a federal prosecutor on death penalty cases. The commission was created in response to a trend in Illinois of individuals being found innocent after serving time on death row.

After two years of extensive investigation, the commission made recommendations, some of which addressed police procedure and pretrial investigation. One of their unanimous recommendations was that law enforcement agencies take steps to avoid "tunnel vision," in which the belief that a suspect committed a crime obviates objective evaluation of the case.

The commission stated, "Pressure always exists for a police department to solve a crime, particularly where that crime is a homicide. Law enforcement agencies very often undertake heroic efforts to bring the guilty to justice, and their efforts in this regard should be applauded and supported. In any investigation, danger exists that rather than keeping an open and objective mind during the investigatory state, one may leap to a conclusion that the person who is a suspect is in fact the guilty party. Once that conclusion is made, investigative efforts often center on marshaling facts and assembling evidence which will convict that suspect."

Tunnel vision is not a problem associated with any one particular group of police officers or any one department, the commission said. Rather, it is a potential problem for all investigative agencies. The commission specifically pointed to agencies in other countries that have experienced the same problem. Quoting from the findings of a special investigation in Canada, they noted, "Tunnel vision is insidious. It can affect any officer, or, indeed, anyone involved in the administration of justice with sometimes tragic results. . . . Anyone, police officer, counsel or judge can become infected by this virus."

Once tunnel vision sets in, detectives can start to believe that torturing a kid and getting him to confess is for the greater good. And if the kid didn't do this, then he did something else. And if he didn't do something else, he's going to do it in the future. The detectives are meant to get the bad guys off the streets, and they'll do what they have to do to perform that job. Their tactics, when exposed, sometimes manifest as evil, but they don't see themselves that way at all.

John Conroy, the journalist who investigated the Detective Jon Burge scandal at Area 2, puts it this way: "Torture has long been employed by well-meaning, even reasonable people armed with the sincere belief that they are preserving civilization as they know it."[64] "When most people imagine torture, they imagine themselves the victim. The perpetrator appears as a monster—someone inhuman, uncivilized, a sadist, most likely male, foreign in accent, diabolical in manner. Yet there is more than ample evidence that most torturers are normal people, that most of us could be the barbarian of our dreams as easily as we could be the victim, that for many perpetrators, torture is a job and nothing more."

In Conroy's book *Unspeakable Acts, Ordinary People,* he describes how torture targeted toward a victim's mind is often as effective as bodily force. "When presented with a list of cruel tortures," Conroy says, "it is hard not to fixate on the more exotic methods, yet . . . some of the most brutal tortures are the simplest, requiring no imagination, no technology, and little effort on the part of the torturer. Depriving someone of food, for example, is remarkably economical and as effective as the most elaborate methods. Depriving a man or woman of sleep is only slightly more difficult and is equally effective."[65]

Conroy goes on to investigate how such techniques are favored because they leave no physical scars on the subject. "Depriving prisoners of sleep or food, forcing them to stand for long periods of time, confining them in positions that cause acute muscle strain, depriving them of the use of a toilet, all allow interrogators to proclaim that they never laid a finger on the men or women in their charge."[66]

The problem is, "when you are innocent, you think your innocence can protect you," says Dr. G. Daniel Lassiter, a psychology professor at Ohio University in Athens, Ohio. Lassiter is the editor of the book *Interrogations, Confessions, and Entrapment,* and he has studied the psychology of interrogations for years, from the perspective of both law enforcement and the interrogee (a suspect in questioning). But once the police go into interrogation mode, he says, they've often made the decision about who is the guilty person. "They're not looking for anything for you to say that will change their mind at that point. They're just trying to get you to say something that's going to be damning in a court of law."[67]

Scott Christianson, a longtime investigative reporter and former criminal justice official, agrees. In his book *Innocent: Inside Wrongful Conviction Cases,* he writes, "Innocent defendants can end up being penalized at a number of key decision points. In exchange for fully cooperating with the police, a person may make himself more likely to be arrested."[68]

The problem, many have said, is that the word *interrogation* can be a misnomer, since it rarely plays a significant role in the fact-finding part of a police investigation. Instead, the process usually dictates that the detectives identify the guilty person, and only then start interrogating that person.

"You don't bring a guy in unless you have him," says Larry Nitsche, the former CPD homicide detective, "unless you know they did it. Your own experience tells you how much evidence is good enough."

Dick Devine, who served as the Cook County State's Attorney for twelve years, including the time of this investigation, disagrees. "When detectives have information about a suspect, they will usually at some point bring that person in for questioning. Based on my experience, that does not mean that the decision has already been made to charge the person. It often happens that people are brought in for questioning and later released. Most detectives conduct their investigations with professionalism and common sense, constantly evaluating evidence, following that evidence where it leads them, and refusing to put blinders on to other possibilities."

Devine acknowledges however that the pressures of the job can lead some detectives to focus on a particular suspect early in the investigation. "Some officers will either make the wrong judgment or reject exculpatory statements out of hand and focus solely on building a case against the original suspect to the exclusion of other options."

But ultimately, Devine says, "the felony review assistant state's attorneys have to approve charges, so the police don't make the charging decision anyway."

And yet, if a suspect confesses, there's little chance that the ASA won't press charges.

Nitsche says that he never liked to have a suspect make an outright confession, since it usually led to a motion to suppress—a hearing in front of the judge to exclude the evidence—which in turn led a detective to have to spend his or her time in court, rather than on the street.

But Nitsche seems to be one of the few who subscribe to such a theory.

Scott Christianson says, "A confession is considered one of the strongest forms of evidence of guilt in criminal law—so much so that it can dominate everything else presented at trial. For that reason, police and prosecutors have always done everything they can to get the suspect to admit his guilt."[69]

In fact, the only purpose of an interrogation, Professor Lassiter says, is to get evidence that will stick in court and back up the detectives' decision of who is guilty. To do this, police are taught to pursue the interrogation aggressively and to ignore claims of innocence, no matter how compelling. They isolate the person in a cramped room designed to increase anxiety and insecurity. These rooms are typically devoid of windows or clocks.

"Everything is made to make the person feel nothing but despair," explains Professor Lassiter.

And yet, what are the police to do? Find out what makes each individual comfortable and take the necessary steps to put that person at ease? Cases would rarely get solved with such a scenario.

The famous U.S. Supreme Court case *Miranda v. Arizona* considered the issue of "voluntariness" in confessions and guilty pleas. It instituted new procedures to protect a suspect's rights, such as the reading of "*Miranda* rights." However, following *Miranda,* police just became more sophisticated in their interrogation techniques, says Scott Christianson.[70] "Gradually, the emphasis became more psychological than physical."[71]

And there is a particular problem for an innocent interrogee, Professor Lassiter says. Innocent interrogees believe that if they can just explain themselves, the police will understand and matters will be resolved. As a result, such interrogees often don't avail themselves of their *Miranda* rights, such as the right to remain silent or a meeting with an attorney.

Meanwhile, courts have held that police are allowed to play on the ignorance, fear, and anxiety of an interrogee.[72] In addition, the police have no duty to disclose facts known to them from other sources.[73] It's only when affirmative acts of the police amount to fraud, deceit, and trickery that the results of an interrogation will be invalidated.[74] One of the seminal cases on the issue is the U.S. Supreme Court case of *Frazier v. Cupp,* in which the court held that even though the cops had lied to a murder suspect and told him that his cousin had implicated him in the crime, this deception had not changed the voluntary nature of the confession.[75] In other words, the cops can lie all they want to a suspect, as long as nobody can prove they've resorted to fraud, deceit, and trickery.

Lying to a suspect, Professor Lassiter says, "is extremely problematic for innocent people. If they're lying and telling you something that makes you think they're going to nail you, you get confused. You're in there for hours and hours, and you become more susceptible to their tactics. They play on your confusion. They might tell a suspect that it's not unusual for people to blank out events."

And so the detectives often lead interrogees to believe that there is nothing they can do to extricate themselves. They use "maximization techniques," telling the suspects they have irrefutable evidence against them. Or they use "minimization techniques," implying leniency if the person confesses. The detectives say, "This is looking really bad for you. We know you're the kind of person who didn't want to do it, and you feel bad about it."

According to former CPD Detective John Laskey, "The detectives knew, or should have known, that there was no credible evidence to implicate Jovan Mosley in the murder of Howard Thomas, yet they held him in custody for over twenty-nine hours."[76] They did that, Laskey says, even after an eyewitness to the murder identified Jovan as being on the scene but not participating in the murder.

The detectives also had the confessions of Frad, Red, and Marvin, so technically they could have stopped there. But for most detectives, their work is not just about clearing the case. "In general, it's about people answering for what they did," says CPD Detective Andy Perostianis.

So if the detectives believed Jovan had something to do with the fight, then stopping the investigation before they'd proven that would be lazy. "How would that look in court?" one detective asked. "If a defense attorney can reasonably show lazy police work, it can jeopardize the whole investigation."

11

"He's giving it up!"

In the late afternoon, more than a day after his arrest, Jovan Mosley couldn't know that Detective Maverick Porter was about to come on duty on the Third Watch—the 3:00-to-11:30 p.m. shift.[77] Nor could he know that Detective Porter was known around Area 2 and the halls of the courthouse as a "closer"—a guy who could go into an interrogation room and get a defendant to say just about anything.[78]

All Jovan knew was that he was weak from hunger, bleary and confused from lack of sleep, and that his stomach ached from not having used the bathroom for so long.

Just then, a large barrel-chested man burst into the room. This was Detective Maverick Porter.

"We know you did it," Porter shouted at Jovan. "You're a liar! You're a liar!"

Jovan shook his head fast.

"You're going to take responsibility for what happened out there on the street! Somebody's dead, and you've got to take responsibility for that!" He paused.

Jovan said nothing.

"I'm sick of you playing dumb!" Porter yelled. "You're not getting out of here until you tell us you punched Howard Thomas. Punches don't kill someone. Punches aren't murder. Tell us you hit him, and we'll let you go home. We're not looking for you. We're looking for the guy with the bat." On and on he shouted.

Jovan said nothing, but he wanted to. He wanted to say anything to make the detective stop shouting, anything to get out of this place. Finally

57

Porter stopped and then said in an insistent voice, "Just say you threw *two* punches. Two punches isn't murder. Say you threw two punches, and you can go home."

Exhausted and famished, Jovan bowed his head. Then he raised it. He bowed it once more, then raised it again. He kept doing that, nodding slowly, finally agreeing.

Detective Maverick Porter stormed, triumphant, from the Mosley interrogation room. "He's giving it up!" he yelled. "He's giving it up!"

Detective Hill looked up from his desk.

"Let's go," Porter said to Hill, gesturing at the interrogation room. In order for a suspect to properly make an oral admission to a crime, Porter would need a third person in the room to hear it.[79]

They entered the room together this time, and Jovan Mosley was still there alone, crying.

"So let's talk about it again," one of the detectives said.

Jovan felt his world careening away from him. This was all so wrong. And he was so tired. So hungry. Slumping, he peered at the two detectives, but they almost blurred into one.

Then the big dude, the one who'd come in yelling, cleared his throat. That was all it took to make Jovan sit up straight.

One of them had a sheet of paper. Jovan couldn't see what was on it, but the officer began reading from it. "So this is what happened," he said. "You were walking around that night." He paused and looked up at Jovan.

"Okay," Jovan said.

"On August sixth, 1999, you were out with your friends."

"Okay."

"Your friends were Frad, Marvin, Red, and Fetta."

It wasn't really true. He was good friends with Frad, but not the others. They were just guys from the neighborhood. Still, he'd told them that before and they hadn't listened. Besides, what did it matter? "Okay," he said, like, *If that's what you want me to say.*

"Marvin said that his pockets were hurting and Frad then said, 'Let's reroute a nigga.'"

Jovan felt as if he might drop from exhaustion, from hunger. "Okay."

They kept reading him their version of what happened that night. Jovan went into a hole in his mind as he repeated, "Okay. Okay. Okay."

"And you knew the robbery was going down, so you got in there and punched the man twice on the left side," they said.

It wasn't right. It wasn't true.

"We know you're tired," the first detective said again. "And we don't want you. We want the guy with the bat. Tell us you threw two punches, and then we'll let you out of here. You can go home."

Jovan gulped, sucked in lungfuls of stale air. He nodded.

They kept talking: *Frad swung the baseball bat and then you backed off; you walked with Fetta two houses away and talked to Anton Williams; Red took the bat and beat the dude's head about three times; Frad and Marvin had the dude surrounded while Red used the bat; you and Fetta walked northbound on Calumet, where Marvin ran up counting money; Frad and Red caught up to the group; Marvin didn't split up the money—seven dollars—but you would have taken some if he did; Red had a bottle of pop that he opened; you, Red, Frad, Marvin, and Fetta all drank from the bottle of pop.*

Jovan thought about the house. It was right there near the fight, not two houses away. And Jovan didn't know what had happened with the entire fight because for much of it his back had been turned and then he'd walked away. Afterward, he'd seen Marvin with money, but there had been no bottle of pop.

His eyes swung from one detective to the other, searching for help. But somewhere in the hole in his mind, he began to feel a little bit of relief that this nightmare was ending. And so all he said was, "Okay."

To Assistant State's Attorney Allen Murphy, Jovan Mosley must have looked like so many other black teenagers he'd seen in Area 2—sitting with slumped shoulders and a sullen expression, a guy whose eyes were slightly glaring, but mostly defeated.

The criminal justice system had many parts to it, and ASA Murphy must have known, rightly so, that he was only one cog in a large and complex wheel. And his job as that cog at that moment was to work in the Felony Review Unit, to show up in the middle of the night and to determine whether there was enough evidence to press charges.

"People think that there's a cozy relationship between the Felony Review assistants and the police," says John Rock, a former Cook County assistant state's attorney who was once assigned to the Felony Review Unit. "Once the case is on trial at 26th and Cal [the criminal courthouse], that may hold some truth, but during the investigation? Not so much." The job of a Felony Review assistant, Rock explains, is to look at all the evidence collected so far, talk to the witnesses and the suspect—if they're talking— and determine if felony charges are warranted. So that ASA is essentially looking at the case as if he or she had to try it. "As a Felony Review assistant, you have to make a very important decision, and I can't tell you how many times I decided not to approve charges," Rock says. "Once, I was followed to my car by a detective yelling at me about my decision."

Judge Thomas Lyons recalls the same thing about being an ASA on Felony Review. He rejected many charges, he says. Often, he would tell the cops, "We don't have the horses." Lyons explains that knowing a guy did it and proving it are entirely different things. "You can feel in your mind a degree of moral certainty, but proving it in court is something else." The ASA Felony Review team acts as a series of checks and balances for the police investigation, he explains. The ASA's job, he says, "is to test the evidence, poke holes in it, and make sure that the case is supported by credible, admissible evidence." At trial, the defense lawyers become a system of checks and balances for the state's attorneys. The judge or jury puts checks and balances on the testimony and argument. It's all part of the system. Lyons adds, "It's not a perfect system. We're human. And so mistakes are possible even when everybody is trying to do the right thing."

But the fact is that the initial part of the system prides itself on arrests and convictions, and particularly on the "clearing" of crimes. And the detectives pride themselves on solving crimes and getting everyone involved off the street.

And for Allen Murphy, the crime in question probably appeared solved. He showed up, talked to Detective Hill, and was told they had a suspect in custody who wanted to confess. He was likely told that the suspect had been identified in a lineup as being at the scene, and some of the other guys involved, including Fetta and Marvin, had said the suspect had thrown a few punches. And now the suspect wanted to say the same thing.

Murphy introduced himself to the teenager in the interview room and told him that he was a prosecutor, which meant he wasn't Jovan's lawyer.[80] The kid then told him in a flat voice exactly how it had all gone down, all in chronological order—how he'd been walking around with some guys named Marvin, Red, Fetta, and Frad, how one of them had said, *Let's reroute a nigga,* how his buddies jumped some guy a few blocks later, and how he, the teenager, had gotten in a couple of licks, throwing two punches to the left side of the body. The teenager ended the tale, telling ASA Murphy how he and the other guys walked away and how they had a bottle of the man's pop, how they all took a sip of that pop.

It must have sounded perfectly simple to ASA Murphy as he wrote down the details of the story in his Catholic boy's even penmanship. And yeah, the kid didn't have too much to do with the fight, but the rules in Illinois stated that if you were part of a crime, you were responsible for the whole of it, no matter how small your part. According to what Murphy knew, the kid had just confessed to a murder. And that sip-of-pop bit? Well, that pop had been the property of the victim, and it had been stolen from him while he was murdered. With a bat. That meant he could charge him with first-degree murder and armed robbery. Which meant the crime was automatically death-penalty-eligible.

When Murphy was done writing all the details, he took the sheets of paper on which he'd been writing and flipped them to the last page, turning them to the teenager. "Sign here," he said.

Innocent people really do confess, according to the Innocence Project, an organization devoted to exposing wrongful convictions. Although forced confessions may be hard for some to grasp, the Innocence Project has found that false confessions are involved in 25 percent of all cases in which DNA evidence shows the defendant could *never* have done the crime.[81]

"Confessions are so powerful to jurors," says Professor Lassiter of Ohio University, "because they think to themselves, why did the person say it if it's not true? And so the concept of false confessions is hard for people to accept. Most think they would be strong enough to resist 'mere' psychological tactics, but if they haven't been in that situation, it's likely they will underestimate the pressure and tension that actually exists." Some subjects later say they confessed to avoid physical harm.[82] Still others were told they would be convicted with or without a confession, and that their sentence would be more lenient if they confessed.[83] Some were told a confession was the only way to avoid the death penalty.[84]

Ultimately, a dangerous mixture of causes—duress, coercion, intoxication, diminished capacity, mental impairment, ignorance of the law, fear of violence, actual infliction of harm, threat of a harsh sentence, and a misunderstanding of the situation—leads to an innocent person signing his or her life away.[85] But the Innocence Project says there is one thing common to most innocent people who falsely confess—they believe they can "go home" once they admit guilt. "Regardless of the age, capacity or state of the confessor, what they often have in common is a decision—at some point during the interrogation process—that confessing will be more beneficial to them than continuing to maintain their innocence."[86]

The police then turn up the heat by telling suspects that the legal system is about to come crashing down on them. They tell them, often in the form of outright lies, that the evidence is piling up.

Suspects, particularly innocent ones, grow demoralized as the situation becomes less tolerable. No one will listen to them, no one seems to understand. They don't get to see other people. A lack of sleep and food can make them vulnerable to the relentless demands of the police. The longer an interrogation lasts, the more likely it is that an innocent person will break.

In the end, despair drives suspects to do whatever they can to escape. "Instead of thinking, 'Geez, I don't want to say something that will look bad for me six months down the line,'" Professor Lassiter says, "they think, 'I can't bear this any longer. If I just admit to this little bit, I'll get out of here, and I'll be able to defend myself.'" Law enforcement personnel understand this very well, and so they keep going.

"You don't even have to pressure them very hard at that point," Lassiter says. "It's an absolute psychological wearing down."

And once the police get what they want, "they end up putting so much weight on an admission or confession that they coerced," says Professor

Lassiter. "The fact that little other evidence exists to corroborate the admission or confession just doesn't matter."

According to John Laskey, the former CPD homicide detective who was with the department for three decades, Jovan Mosley's interrogation had the classic warning signs of a false confession—Jovan's eventual statement "did not fit the investigative facts. It did not fit the eyewitness testimony. It was made after more than twenty-four hours of being in custody . . . with threats and deprivation of comfort items." Jovan was deprived of sleep, he notes, did not have experience with the police, and during the interrogation he was left alone and not permitted to make a phone call.

A teenager from Jovan's neighborhood with a criminal record would most likely have known the detectives were lying about his being able to go home. That teenager would never have signed a confession. But Jovan wasn't an average teenager from the neighborhood. Yes, he'd dabbled in just about everything that teenagers (from Connecticut to the South Side of Chicago) dabble in, and yes, he'd been walking around with those guys the night of the beating. But he was the good kid in the neighborhood; he was the one who had managed, against the odds, to stay out of a gang and to stay out of jail. In a sense, he was now a victim of his own innocence. He'd always risen above the lot he'd been dealt, and he saw no reason why he couldn't continue doing that. And in this interrogation situation? Well, he hadn't done the thing they were talking about. So if he could just get out of there, he could take care of it.

Jovan signed the handwritten statement that the lawyer gave him.

The lawyer told him to initial at the bottom of each page. He hadn't read the thing, but he scribbled his initials, eager to be done with this and to go home.

12

"You're not going home anytime soon."

Jovan was led to lockup.

The police officer who took him there was nice enough. "The guys who had the bat," he said. "They're going to get a lot of time."

Jovan said nothing.

"We're just going to finish processing you," the cop continued.

Joy surged through Jovan. He'd gotten through this. It had been a nightmare, but as soon as he was out, he could figure how to set it straight. And if he couldn't exactly straighten it out? Well, like the police said, it wasn't as if two punches were murder.

He was put in a cell, where he waited for a few hours with a bunch of other guys. Finally someone arrived, handcuffed all the men, and put them in the back of a paddy wagon.

As they drove, Jovan asked the guy next to him, "Where are we going?"

"To the county."

"The county?" He knew what that meant: jail. But he didn't want to believe it.

There were no windows in the paddy wagon. When it finally stopped, the prisoners were led inside a building and deposited on benches in a hallway. People bustled back and forth. No one paid them much attention, and for a while Jovan lost himself watching the hallway traffic—doctors, lawyers, cops, guards, and administrators—all in a rush, all doing their jobs.

Exhaustion replaced fear and began to overtake him. He'd almost nodded off when he heard, "Hold up!"

Six guards appeared, and they stopped the hallway traffic, waiting until the hall was clear but for the prisoners on the benches.

"Get up!" one of the guards yelled. "Strip!"

The guys on the benches jumped up and started unbuttoning shirts, shrugging them off, unzipping and stepping out of pants, pulling off socks and underwear, putting them in a pile in front of them.

"Strip!" a guard barked at Jovan.

Self-conscious, blinking fast, Jovan followed, taking off his shoes, his shirt, his jeans, and finally his underwear.

"Turn!" the guard shouted. "Hands on the wall. Legs apart."

The other men spun around and placed their hands high on the white brick wall, spreading their legs wide. Jovan followed suit.

"Hurry up!" a guard yelled at another inmate down the hall. A minute later, the same guard, seeming to be talking to another officer, said loudly, "Didn't you just hear me tell him to hurry up?"

"I did," the other officer said.

Smack! The blow itself was so loud, so stinging; it reverberated in Jovan's ears. The human cry of pain that followed was even louder.

Jovan was flooded with anxiety. He glanced down the hall and saw a prisoner on the ground, a guard standing over him. When the guard raised his fist again, the guy scrambled to his feet, shed his clothes, and spun around to face the wall.

The guards made their way from prisoner to prisoner, sifting through the piles of clothes, looking, Jovan figured, for weapons.

When they were done, he felt grateful, but then a guard yelled, "Bend over!"

The guy to Jovan's right shuffled his feet back, then bent over at the waist, his naked butt now thrust into the hallway and on display. He looked at Jovan and nodded, like, *Do it.*

Scared, Jovan followed. The guards strolled the hallway, leaning over to visually inspect genitalia, asses.

"Squat!" was the next order.

The other prisoners, who all seemed to know the routine, bent their knees and sank a foot or so toward the ground.

"Cough!" a guard yelled.

The hallway was filled with the sound of fake coughs and throat-clearing. Again, the guards moved up and down the hall, peering at bodies to see if a foreign object had dropped from someone's ass.

Finally, "Put your clothes back on!"

But Jovan's relief was short-lived. Once clothed, the prisoners were led from the hallway to a square room about twenty or thirty feet wide and packed with what seemed like hundreds of men. The prisoners were in a line that snaked back and forth across the room, stopping at a set of double doors, where the men were allowed to enter one by one. The room was hot, the air overripe. It seemed every time someone went through the double doors, potentially shrinking the crowd, a new group of inmates crowded in from the other end.

Some of the men in the room were dope-sick, coming down hard from their drug of choice. One guy swayed back and forth, then suddenly threw up, his vomit splashing on the floor, on people's shoes. The other prisoners shouted insults at the man, who sank to the floor. No one came to clean up the mess. The room stank, and the tension shot skyward. The smell grew so overpowering that Jovan began to feel sick, layering nausea atop his exhaustion, anxiety, and fear.

A few moments later, the tension reached a breaking point. Jovan heard a murmur across the room. He looked up to see what appeared to be sparks flying from an old man's shoulders.

"Dude, what the fuck?" someone yelled at the man.

"Yeah, what the fuck?"

"It's lice!" someone yelled.

Three or four guys pounced on the old man, beating him with their fists. Jovan looked around, expecting a guard to intervene, but no one arrived to stop the thrashing. When they were done, the old man lay crumpled on the ground. He managed to inch his way on all fours to the wall, where he huddled until his turn came to go through the doors.

Jovan's nerves felt sliced. Apprehension jangled inside him.

He heard some guys talking a few feet in front of him. "You got a square?" one asked.

"Yeah. It's two," the other said.

"Two bucks for a square?" the guy said incredulously.

The man gave an unconcerned shrug. "I got a short for a buck."

The first prisoner grumbled, but he pulled a single dollar bill out of his pocket and gave it to the man. In return he was handed a cigarette that was smoked two-thirds of the way down. Jovan watched as the man lit his abused cigarette. He closed his eyes, inhaling deeply. Although Jovan had only smoked socially, he envied the calm that spread across the smoker's face.

Jovan turned to the man next to him. "Do you have any cigarettes?"

"One for a femp," the man answered quickly.

"Five dollars?"

He nodded and looked away like, *Take it or leave it.*

Jovan dug from his pocket a five-dollar bill and gave it to the man.

He took that cigarette, enjoyed the look of it and anticipated the pleasure of it as never before, then he smoked the cigarette down to its very, very last ash, trying not to panic, trying to tell himself that everything was all right.

His respite was short-lived. More fights broke out, and the rank smell of men and vomit worsened. An hour later, the tortuous line had barely moved, and Jovan bought a half-smoked cigarette for three dollars. When another hour was gone, he bought a "short."

He was almost done with the short, exhaling long and slow, when suddenly he heard, "Joe?"

Jovan looked across the room. "Pretty Ricky?"

The man nodded, a big smile on his face. Pretty Ricky was a guy Jovan knew from the neighborhood. He was a black guy with light skin and eyes that were somewhere between green and gray.

Jovan looked down at Pretty Ricky's foot and saw blood pooling beneath it. "What's going on, man?"

Pretty Ricky lifted up his leg. A metal pin was lodged into the sole of his foot, surrounded by blackened skin and oozing blood.

"They chased me from my house," Ricky said, sounding kind of proud, kind of amused. He didn't say why the cops had been chasing him, but he didn't seem surprised or angered by it either. "They chased me all the way to the El tracks. Man, I jumped the turnstile and landed on this." He gestured at his foot.

"Does it hurt?"

"Yeah," Ricky said cheerfully.

Seeing a familiar face made Jovan feel a bit better, but it was tough to talk with so many people between them. Meanwhile, the line crawled toward the doors. Jovan didn't know what was behind those doors, but he could hardly wait to escape into them.

When he finally reached the front of the line and stepped through the doors, there wasn't much to see. At one table sat a doctor in a white lab coat. At another sat a clerk. The doctor had medical supplies in front of him, the clerk paperwork. The doctor gestured at Jovan to come toward him.

He was about to sit at the table when the doctor stood from his collection of medical supplies. "Please take your clothes off."

Jovan exhaled hard, but it was easier this time without so many people around.

When Jovan was nude, nothing to protect him, the physician lifted what look like a long Q-tip. Before Jovan could ask what was happening, he raised Jovan's penis, aimed the Q-tip at the head, and then shoved it far inside.

Screams barreled into Jovan's throat, but he held them back.

Just as fast as the doc had inserted the Q-tip, he pulled it out. Jovan would later hear guys call him the "Dick Doctor." He never did learn exactly why the Q-tip test was necessary, but he assumed they were looking for sexually transmitted diseases.

"You're done," the doctor said. "You're ready to go."

From there, the clerk led him through a series of questions about his medical history, but Jovan was so startled by the Q-tip he could barely pay attention.

When he left the room, a guard told him he could have his phone call, which must mean his processing was over. He could get out of there.

Jovan called his mother. He told her he'd been at the police station for the last few days, but that now that he had signed something and was processed he would be leaving soon.

Delores was with Jovan's dad, William, who quickly came on the line. "You signed something?"

"Yeah." Jovan explained what had happened.

"They're not going to let you go."

The thread of joy Jovan had been holding on to snapped.

"Not a chance," his dad said.

When he was off the phone, Jovan was approached by a guard. "Hands," the guard said.

When Jovan did nothing but give him a confused look, the guard barked at him, "Hold out your hands. Make a fist."

On the back of each fist, the guard wrote the number 11 with a thick black marker.

Jovan stared at his tattooed hands. Shortly another guy was led into the hallway.

"Where you going?" the guy asked Jovan.

"Home."

The guy noticed the numbers on Jovan's hands. He leaned forward and looked at them, then looked back at Jovan, giving a sad shake of his head. "That's Division Eleven. You're going to SuperMax."

"What?"

"Man, you're not going home anytime soon."

Part II

Part II

13

"Cathy is a straight shooter. If something comes out of her mouth, it's the truth."

Outside the Cook County Jail, life in the U.S. kept moving and was largely rosy. No planes had yet crashed into any notable buildings. As a nation, we were thriving, enjoying our economic prosperity and our status as the relative darlings of the world. And the city of Chicago, Jovan's city, grew without him. It was bustling and booming, as was the criminal defense practice of Catharine O'Daniel.

Cathy can best be described as the soul of a grizzled male criminal lawyer in the body of a hot blonde wearing Prada. When I first met her, I was fascinated by her clients, if a little repulsed. She represented Mexican cartel families, suspected white-collar criminals, alleged murderers, smugglers, gun runners, and people who got in all sorts of odd trouble with the law. One particular client of Cathy's was pulled over in his RV. The problem was that literally every inch of the RV—the bathroom, the bedroom, the shelves, the glove box—was stuffed with pot. Another client, who was busted with what Cathy called "a boatload" of drugs, was also carrying around his Israeli assault rifles. She represented a woman who, with a network of others, was accused of draining $38 million from the Royal Bank of Scotland in one day.

Cathy's family had lived in Indianapolis most of their lives, but traveled around the world too. She received her undergrad education at Indiana University, then moved on to law school at John Marshall in Chicago. As she approached graduation and considered what area of the law she wanted to get into, Cathy kept coming back to criminal defense.

"Criminal is the guts of the law," Cathy says. "And it's exciting. And, as opposed to civil cases, you don't wait seven years to get to trial."

When asked why she hadn't entered the holier side of the criminal arena—the prosecution—Cathy explains, "I didn't go state because it's not in my makeup to send someone to jail. Everyone fucks up. A lot of people seriously belong in jail, but I don't want to be the person sending them there." Essentially, Cathy saw the good in everyone.

So Cathy decided to hang out her own shingle. She rented an office from some senior lawyers, Larry Axelrood and Richard Mottweiler, covering cases for them when they needed it and learning from them. Cathy quickly realized she loved her job. One of the most gratifying aspects was what she saw as the importance of her role in the criminal justice system. It's Cathy's belief that everyone who is arrested is entitled to lawful treatment and a fair trial. If defense lawyers like her didn't make sure there was due process, the system would slide into chaos.

"I'm a big due process person," Cathy says, "because *due process* is just a fancy way of saying *fair*." By making sure the legal system treats a defendant fairly, "you can do some serious good for someone."

Moral convictions and beliefs aside, the money that Cathy earned didn't hurt. She wouldn't touch a murder trial without $25,000 retainer, usually more. And it seemed there was rarely a lack of defendants wanting her help. By the year 2000, Cathy had been trying cases in numerous Illinois counties, as well as in Indiana, Missouri, Michigan, Texas, Ohio, North Carolina, Florida, New Mexico, and Wisconsin.

Cathy already spoke French, which she'd taken in school, and broken Polish, which she'd learned from her kids' nanny, and then from many of her clients she learned to speak Spanish as well. She'd gotten to the point where she could, as she put it, "limp along" and no longer needed an interpreter for her Spanish-speaking clients, unless she was preparing the client to testify at trial.

Cathy had become the go-to girl for many Mexicans and Mexican-Americans who'd gotten in trouble in the United States. In one case, Cathy represented a cartel family member caught for running drugs. When the client decided to plea-bargain, therefore giving up the goods on a number of other family members and colleagues, he begged Cathy to fly to Laredo, Texas, and meet with the family just across the Mexican border to give them the heads-up. Days later, Cathy was in Nuevo Laredo, explaining to her client's immediate family, and one trusted advisor, exactly how the plea bargain would happen. The next day, the advisor was beheaded, an obvious message to Cathy and her client that cooperation with the government was frowned upon.

Cathy rushed back to Illinois to give her client the horrible news about the killing. He decided to go forward with the plea bargain anyway. But Cathy hasn't returned to Mexico since. She says it's unlikely she'll ever go, given the clients she's represented and the high rate of kidnapping there. "You could not *give* me a hotel down there," she says.

Cathy met her lawyer husband, Eddie Shishem, in the Gold Coast highrise where they both lived. Their children, Caroline and Sam, are blond like their mother and have her same wide grin. She and Eddie bought a house in Burr Ridge, Illinois, a beautiful house with a pool outside. When she was at home, Cathy was the typical suburban mom, tying on an apron, cooking up a storm, decorating her house. All the while, around the hallways of Chicago's various criminal courthouses, Cathy was garnering a stellar reputation.

Jim McKay, a longtime ASA, says of Cathy, "She's well respected, well liked, and always courteous. A very good lawyer with a great reputation."

"Cathy is a straight shooter," says Brian Sexton, another career ASA. "If something comes out of her mouth, it's the truth, and you can trust her. Plus, she's smart as hell."

Some people talk of being lucky in love. In 2000, I was fortunate enough to be lucky in law as well as love.

I'd been married for a year to Jason, a man I'd been with for seven years. I felt blessed. And my law career seemed to be blessed too.

Cathy's passionate career notwithstanding, law school is the great repository for people who don't know what else to do with their lives. I was no exception. I had graduated Phi Beta Kappa from the University of Iowa, sure, but my major was general communications. What I was going to do with that, I had no idea, especially when my unofficial minor had been football and beer.

My best course seemed to be graduate school. My father had attended Loyola University Chicago School of Law, as had his brother and their father before them. When my dad told me that he'd pay my tuition to law school if I continued with my education directly after college, law seemed the only option. I had skills for no other graduate programs. I applied to Loyola and got in. I graduated with honors from Loyola, and after multitudes of interviews, I got exactly one offer of employment—from Clausen Miller, a big, prestigious litigation firm.

Back in those days, associates with an offer from a big firm had little or no say in the department they would work in, and therefore minimal input in what legal specialty they would end up practicing, likely for the rest of their lives. At Clausen, the assigning of new associates to partners operated roughly like the NFL draft. Partners in need of an associate checked out the talent, then put in a bid for the ones they liked. I had no medical background to speak of, but I ended up as a medical negligence attorney and spent years learning how to read medical records and depose neurosurgeons. And I liked it. A lot. Eventually, I moved to medical boutique firms with a few other lawyers, and I became a partner.

It was my law partners, along with Jason, who gave me my career in the publishing world.

The fact that I liked the law was fortunate because many lawyers find that they flat-out hate the practice. By the time they figure that out, though, they're trapped by their partnerships and the money they're making to support their families. Even if they considered the bold move of leaving the law, there remained that question—*What would I do with myself?*—which, of course, was the question that got so many of them into law school to begin with.

Thankfully, I had discovered something I did love—writing. I remember exactly when I discovered this passion. It wasn't at the University of Iowa, which hosts the Writers' Workshop, one of the best writing programs in the nation. No, at the University of Iowa I was so focused on that football/beer minor that I got the worst grade of my college career in creative writing. And it wasn't during law school, when I got the lowest grade in my legal education in first-semester legal writing.

But I'd always been a voracious reader, and about a year after I started practicing law I went to a local bookstore to pick up something new. I stood in that bookstore, reading the back covers of what seemed like hundreds of books, unable to find what I was searching for. I kept thinking I'd like to read a novel about a woman who takes a vacation that changes her entire life.

A year before, I had taken a fun but relatively uneventful post–bar-exam trip to Rome and Greece with some girlfriends. But as the year progressed, and as I became indoctrinated into the world of depositions and billable hours, a particular what-if scenario gnawed at me—what if my life had somehow changed during that vacation? What if that trip, during the span of a month, had altered my entire existence—everything from my family, to my friends, to my relationship, to my job?

Despite my lack of experience, I decided that day in that store that I would write a book. Instead of buying a novel, I bought a notebook.

Eventually, my scribblings in that notebook would make up about seventy typed pages, double-spaced, when the average novel is around four hundred such pages. But ignorance really is a delicious bite of bliss, and all I knew when I left that store was that I was bursting with an optimism and motivation that only comes from a new project that's got you by the throat.

I signed up for a series of writing classes and workshops. Over the course of three or four years, I wrote *Burning the Map,* about a woman whose life gets rocked while on a European vacation.

So by the time the year 2000 rolled around, I had the nice law practice, the writing hobby that ignited me, and a husband I loved.

But I was living at a breakneck pace. So much so that in the spring of 2000, my husband proposed a halt—six-months off of work.

"Call it a sabbatical," he said. "You love this writing thing. Work on your new book."

By the time, I had lengthened and finished the novel about the woman whose vacation changes her life. *Burning the Map* had gone through about fifty-five thousand four hundred and eighty-two drafts and revisions and been rejected by scores of agents. At the time, the "chick lit" genre had yet to descend on the literary world. There were no book covers with martinis or high heels. And so what I kept hearing from agents was, *I like it, but I just don't know what I would do with it.*

None of this rejection deterred me from writing, because it was the act of writing—of creating something entirely from the jagged, random, and often freaky shores of my imaginative sea—that turned me on, made me more satisfied in all other parts of my life. So I'd started writing another book, a suspense novel called *The Other Rebecca* (the one novel that, to this day, I've never been able to sell), and by the time my husband made his bold suggestion of a sabbatical, I was halfway to finishing it.

Tentatively, I took the idea to my law partners the next day, fully expecting a what-in-the-hell-are-you-talking-about? reception. But instead, they patted me on the back and said I should take those six months off. They gamely offered to take over my cases for a few months, adding on to their already mountainously high workload. The gods, it seemed, were smiling on me, and so I left the "wall of fame" in my office (the one holding all the diplomas and bar certificates). I left the Tiffany-style lamp my partners had given me for my birthday. I left all my files and notes and books and pens and tchotchkes.

"I'll be back shortly," I told my partners before I sailed out the door for the last time.

14

"He's been charged with murder."

The morning after Jovan's phone call from the police station, Delores Mosley was in agony. Despite his assurances during the call, Jovan was not home.

"I told him," her husband said. "He shouldn't have signed nothing."

When the phone rang, Delores lunged at it. The man on the other end said he was a reporter at the *Chicago Sun-Times*. "Do you know Jovan Mosley?" the reporter asked.

"Yes. He's my son." She had always felt proud saying that. She still did.

"He's been charged with murder."

Delores Mosley felt her world veer away. She had been through terrible things in her life. She had gone through another son being arrested and convicted. Her husband too. But she couldn't remember feeling any more pain—more *terror*—than this.

On March 8, 2000, Jori Garth and Anton Williams testified before a grand jury. They were placed under oath and an assistant state's attorney took them through the facts of the fight they'd witnessed in August 1999.

Jori testified more than once that she saw three men beating Howard Thomas, one of whom was Marvin Treadwell. She didn't know the other men.[87]

Anton described the beating, saying he saw Frad Muhammad hitting Howard Thomas with a bat. He saw Marvin Treadwell kicking the victim and throwing the man against a car. He saw Lawrence "Red" Wideman hitting him. The fight, he said, went on for about five minutes. Anton was shown photos. Using them, he identified the three men he had seen attack Howard Thomas: Frad Mohammad, Lawrence Wideman, and Marvin Treadwell. When asked about Jovan Mosley, he said, "I didn't see him beat him."[88]

But the grand jury heard about Mosley's confession. And indicted him for murder and armed robbery, eligible for the death penalty.

15

"We're GDs from Lo-town."

Jovan found himself in a jail that was, in many ways, its own cruel country ruled largely by the inmates deep inside.

The Cook County Jail system, in its entirety, housed roughly nine thousand to eleven thousand people a day when Jovan entered it. Division 11, or SuperMax as the inmates called it, was the maximum-security division. It was was shaped like an X from above and had four pods. Each pod, housing forty-eight men, was distinguished by the color of the doors and the trim around the thresholds. A Pod, for example, had yellowish doors. B pod was green-blue, C Pod royal blue, and D Pod orange. The pods were further divided into tiers. Each tier was triangular and had an upper and lower deck that faced the day room, the place where everything happened outside the cell. In that room, meals were eaten at round tables bolted to the floor. One or two TVs were attached to the walls, the remotes generally controlled by the chief of whatever gang was most prominent on the tier. One hour, three times a week, inmates would get to go "on rec" to lift weights in the meager, dirty weight room or play basketball. The basketball court was fenced in, and, like so many things at SuperMax, shaped like a triangle.

Initially, Jovan was put on BA Deck, considered the intake deck, where most inmates stayed until it could be determined where they should be placed more permanently. As Jovan was led to his cell, he could feel the burn of the inmates' stares and hear them yell a chorus to the new guy: *On the new! On the new!* It scared the shit out of him.

When he was given his uniform—khaki pants and a khaki V-neck shirt with the initials DOC (Department of Corrections)—he looked at the shirt's tag and saw it was a size 1X.

Jovan held up the shirt and looked at it. "Is this a small?"

The guard nodded.

Jovan looked down at himself. He was about five-ten and weighed 240 pounds. "I usually wear a double XL or larger."

The guard shrugged, like that wasn't his problem.

A few feet away, another new inmate (a guy even bigger than Jovan) was ordered to put on a uniform. The inmate struggled into what looked like extra-small pants, tugging and grunting. He managed to get the pants half up, managed to pull the shirt over his neck, although it went only halfway down his chest.

Jovan looked back at his own guard. *Please,* he said with his eyes.

The guard stared at him for a second, then went through the bins where he had other uniforms stored. He tossed large pants and a large shirt at Jovan.

Jovan, who had always taken pride in the way he dressed, soon learned that inmates were required to wear that same uniform continuously for a week.

At SuperMax, you wore your uniform to the day room, to the gym, to sleep, and to eat. If you spilled something on it? If you perspired or soiled it? You still waited a week. If an inmate needed to wash his uniform, he did so at night, with the hard, white "state soap" sometimes available in the showers. Then he'd toss the uniform over the deck rails or hang it below the vent in the cell and pray it dried by morning. If a uniform tore, he might get a new one. But otherwise, no other clothing was provided by Division 11.

Each cell at SuperMax held two men. The cells were not protected with bars but with a thick steel door whose small window (one foot tall, four inches wide) looked onto the day room. Below the window was the "chuck hole," the size of a shoe box, where meals were slid in when inmates weren't allowed out of their cells. At the far end of the cell was a wall with a window, which generally looked at the outside wall of the pod next to it. The air the prisoners breathed was entirely recirculated and incredibly dry. The light, aside from the minimal amount that filtered through the window, was artificial.

The "mattresses" at SuperMax were thin sponges laid atop a concrete slab if you were on the bottom bunk, steel if on top. The sheets were rough and as thin as paper. Sometimes they were, inexplicably, cut down the middle and the inmate slept with only half a sheet. The blankets were coarse gray wool and full of holes.

The most horrible part of the cell, however, was the steel toilet, which sat uncovered at the entrance to the cell. Every time someone used it, he did so in front of his roommate (or "cellie"). The flush was powerful and incredibly loud, and the ice-cold water rose up to soak and freeze your ass. Despite the great flush, the odor of piss and shit was nearly impossible to control.

When Jovan was at SuperMax, sexual assaults happened—never to him, but the inmates all heard about them from the guards. Half the guards were male, half female. While it seemed that SuperMax was always 97 percent full of black guys, the guards were a mix of blacks, whites, and Hispanics. The morning shift was usually composed of women guards, while the 3:00-to-11:00 p.m. shift, which saw the most trouble, was overseen by male guards. The guards were trained to be stern and forceful and to assert their authority. Most did this very effectively.

Although weapons had been confiscated on the way into Division 11, inmates could fashion knives from just about anything—the metal of a utilitarian light fixture, a piece wrenched from a heating vent. Some of those knives were the length of a man's leg. And they were sharp. In fact, one member from each gang, on each deck, was given the full-time job of sharpening knives on the cement floor. Those knives were used in the frequent fights that broke out. Sometimes those fights would escalate and turn into all-out melees. Jovan would later say that when a "massacre" started, "the only thing you could see was knives and blood." If there were a handful of people in the altercation, the guards would jump in and stop it, but if the fight involved most of the deck, the officers would let the prisoners go at each other, waiting until the fight had calmed before intervening.

Even worse were the lockdowns, when prisoners were kept in their cells for hours or days at a time, following a stabbing or a particularly nasty fight. During that time, there were no showers, and food trays were slipped through the chuck holes. When Jovan was first at SuperMax, an additional mandatory three-day lockdown occurred every month, during which the guards searched the cells for weapons or contraband. The lockdowns were torturous with just two men and a toilet. The air was ripe. Irritation grew. And grew. One lockdown Jovan experienced, which followed the knifing and killing of a prisoner, lasted for two straight weeks. The tension in the cell was as thick as the odor of two men living all their hours in it.

Jovan's first meal at SuperMax was dinner. He and Pretty Ricky went to the day room, right on time, both anxious and stressing. The TV blared a rap music video, showing a girl in a tank top writhing her upper body.

Soon, a few other inmates arrived. One of the guys eyed Jovan and Pretty Ricky. "What is you?" he asked, no expression on his face.

Jovan understood the question. He'd heard it before in his neighborhood, and it meant, *What gang?*

"We're GDs from Lo-town," Pretty Ricky said, gesturing at himself and Jovan. Ricky had, Jovan realized, assumed Jovan was a Gangster Disciple because so many people in their neighborhood were and because his brother had been a GD.

The guy who'd asked the question nodded his approval and gestured at one of the round tables behind them. Jovan and Pretty Ricky sat down and others joined them. The day room filled in.

Jovan had always been a watcher, an observer of people and behaviors. The watching was how he'd survived growing up. And in the day room, Jovan watched everything, listened to everything. Someone at the table occasionally filled in the blanks for Jovan and Ricky about who was who. Their table and the ones next to them were soon filled with "One Love" gang members—guys who were GDs or BDs (Black Disciples). At another table sat the Latin Kings with the Blackstones. The Vice Lords and the Fours (the Four Corner Hustlers) sat together too.

And Jovan, who'd always tried to escape the gang life, slid into his role as a GD, thankful for it.

Two days after Jovan arrived, he was awakened at three thirty a.m. by a *pop . . . pop . . . pop-pop-pop,* then a *click, click, click*

Jovan sat up fast. He immediately grimaced and put his hand to his lower back, which was in spasm from lying on the steel bed.

He'd missed breakfast the day before. His cellie, a forty-year-old white guy whose face was bruised from fighting with his girlfriend's son, told him that the popping sounds indicated the opening of the cell doors, the only signal the inmates would get that breakfast was about to be served.

Inmates who got up and made it to the day room received breakfast. They were required to be back in their cells at four a.m. so the guards could transport anyone who had to appear in court. If you didn't get up soon enough after the door opened, you'd miss breakfast, as the guards would lock the doors again from their office. At seven-fifteen, the doors would pop open once more. If you didn't get out then, you wouldn't have another chance to step out of the cell until three thirty in the afternoon.

That second day, Jovan slid off the bunk as soon as he heard the first noise, hungry.

A guard stuck his head in the cell and looked at him. "Court today."

And immediately the back pain seemed to go away. If he went to court, someone might be able to help him. He straightened his uniform as best he could, tugging down the cotton shirt he'd spent another sleepless night in, smoothing the front of his pants.

After breakfast, he and the other inmates expected in court were taken into a room and placed a foot apart.

"Take 'em off," a male guard ordered.

Two other guards stood by, arms crossed, holding flashlights. In the next room, visible through a window, was a female guard.

With resigned expressions, the other inmates dropped their pants and pulled off their shirts.

"Let's go," a guard said to Jovan.

Jovan shed his clothes.

"Spread 'em," the guard ordered.

Dutifully, the men reached behind themselves, grabbed their ass cheeks, and pulled them apart.

Jovan, however, glanced again at the female guard, who was still in the next room, acting like she wasn't watching.

"Let's go," the guard said in a bored voice.

Jovan was later told that the guards were looking for "kites"—notes being smuggled out, usually to other gangs. On the way back from court, they searched for drugs being smuggled into SuperMax. He also learned women were prohibited from being present during the strip-search process or viewing it in any way. But no one seemed to have told that female sergeant who often appeared in the next room just as the inmates undressed.

"Let's go," the guard said again, not so bored this time but rather irritated, bordering on angry.

Jovan did what he was told.

"Cough," the guard said.

Meager throat-clearing from the other inmates.

"Cough," the guard said, raising his voice. "Three times."

The other men obediently complied. And eventually Jovan did the same.

It was black as night as the busful of inmates, handcuffed side to side, drove down a ramp to the underbelly of the great courthouse at the intersection of 26th and California Streets and known as 26th and Cal. There, the men were sectioned into different bullpens based on when and where their hearings would be. But there were too many prisoners and not enough bullpens. In Jovan's bullpen, a bench ran along each side of the room and down its middle. But the benches were quickly occupied. The rest of the inmates, including Jovan, crammed into the bullpen, standing shoulder to shoulder.

"There would be hundreds of them down there,'" says Francis Wolfe, a former assistant public defender for Cook County. "They couldn't eat; they couldn't take a piss; there's no water. Most of them couldn't even sit down." He grimaces, remembering the sight. "There's not a jail in Turkey that's worse than that." As for the racial composition of the bullpen, he adds, "they're almost all black."

Wolfe says he's surprised by the black population's acceptance of the way they're treated when arrested. "They think, 'That's just how it is,' but sometimes I'm surprised there isn't a revolution about this."

For Jovan, the torture of standing in the bullpen for hours and hours was worth enduring because he was headed to court. But just when his name was called, he was transported to another bullpen. More hours went by. At last, he and a number of other inmates were led from their bullpen to an elevator. *Now* something would happen, something would change. But their destination was yet another bullpen behind the courtroom that packed them in shoulder to shoulder once more.

Another wait. A long wait. There was a urinal in the corner of this cage, but no one wanted to use the thing unless he absolutely had to. Some of the men smelled terrible, and you couldn't get away from them. Some were mentally ill, talking crazy to anyone, even though no one was listening, others were drug-sick and shaking.

Then Jovan saw Red, Marvin, and Frad. They looked mystified when they saw him.

"What you doing here?" Red asked.

"You tell me."

Red shook his head.

More waiting. Finally, Jovan's name was called along with Red's, Marvin's, and Frad's. He was led from the bullpen. "Don't say nothing when you're in there," the guard warned them. *"Nothing."*

In the courtroom, Red and Marvin had private attorneys. (Marvin's mother apparently knew a lawyer, who represented him, and Red's family had come up with some money.) Frad had a public defender. No one noticed Jovan didn't have counsel. The judge and the other attorneys seemed to assume he was represented by one of the three attorneys or their associates, who all strode forward to the bench, spoke in legal shorthand to the judge, and asked for the case to be continued. Continuances, or extensions for court dates, in legal or civil cases, can be requested at any time, for nearly any reason. Sometimes a continuance is needed because one of the attorneys doesn't show, sometimes one of the attorneys has just received the case and needs time to get up to speed. It may be that the judge is about to start a trial that he or she is covering for another judge, or that a defense attorney is picking a jury in another courtroom.

In the civil courtrooms in Cook County, a case management system was implemented to set deadlines in a case and keep it moving. The judges were relatively strict in forcing parties to comply. But the criminal courts in Cook County, at the time Jovan was arrested, had no such system. That, combined with the fact that the state's attorneys, PDs, and judge are all in the same courtroom with each other day after day, means that continuances, for whatever reason, are often granted. Once a continuance is granted, a defendant who can't afford to post bond, like Jovan, is returned to the county jail without input or redress.

The words Jovan heard and understood were, "By agreement." Then the judge said, "Next case."

The guards began rounding up the four defendants. "But . . ." Jovan started to say. He wanted to say, *But what about me?* The guard silenced him with a sharp look.

Before he knew it, Jovan was in the bullpen, hoping for the best. Maybe that continuance was only for Frad and those other guys. Maybe he would be called again in order to be assigned an attorney.

But a few hours later, Jovan was on the bus back to SuperMax. Next time, he told himself. Next time it would be different.

Delores Mosley was tortured by her son's arrest.

A few days after that terrible phone call from the reporter, the following article appeared in the *Chicago Sun-Times*.

A 19-year-old was being held Wednesday on $1.5 million bond in connection with the beating death of a South Side man.

Jovan Mosley of the 8300 block of South Kingston Avenue was charged with murder and armed robbery. Three other men also face murder charges in the incident.

Authorities said Howard Thomas, 51, was beaten with a baseball bat, apparently in a robbery attempt Aug. 6 in the 7300 block of South Calumet Avenue.

Mosley's mother, Delores, said Wednesday she believes her son was not involved in the fight.

Delores went to Jovan's court date, which seemed to her a flurry of attorneys and defendants, of words tossed about that she couldn't comprehend, and then Jovan was gone. She promised herself she would be there anytime he appeared in court, and that she would visit him every week. She would not let her son down.

16

"Does anyone even know I'm here?"

"There's a saying that you're innocent until proven guilty, but that's bullshit. That's a myth." Francis Wolfe, former PD, has an interesting view of the public defender's office, because he didn't start there out of law school in his twenties like so many others. Instead, Wolfe began working with the PD's office at age sixty-five.

Following the Korean War, Wolfe was employed at the Chicago stockyard, which led to nearly three decades as a trader at the Chicago Board of Trade and the Mercantile Exchange. Wolfe quit in 1987, while taking liberal arts classes at the University of Chicago, where he was constantly told that he should attend law school. At age sixty-three, Wolfe became a first-year student at the Loyola University Chicago School of Law. At a cocktail party he met a public defender who invited Wolfe to watch a trial. Soon, Wolfe found himself on one of the hard benches at 26th and Cal.

"I was horribly impressed with the power of the state," he says. Remembering the defendants, he says, "Those poor bastards don't have a chance."

Wolfe began volunteering for the public defender's office and soon had a license that allowed him to engage in a limited practice of law as a law student. Hypothetically, such limited practice should be "under the supervision of a licensed attorney," but the reality was that the public defender's office was continually stretched to its limits. Wolfe was given a few cases, wished luck, and sent off to a courtroom. As Kevin Davis pointed out in *Defending the Damned,* his book about the Cook County Public Defender's Office, "Finding and inspiring lawyers to represent the poor has been a challenge as old as the legal system itself."[89]

A few years later, when Wolfe graduated from law school, he took a job with the PD's office and began working, with no training, at the traffic court. "Assistant state's attorneys get a little more training," Wolfe says, "but not much. The judges in traffic are all beginners too. They don't know squat."

Wolfe had just as little training when he moved to Belmont and Western, a misdemeanor courtroom, then to 13th and Michigan, which hears the bulk of Cook County's domestic batteries, and eventually to a felony courtroom in the famed halls of 26th and Cal.

Scott Christianson, an investigative reporter and former criminal justice official, backs up the reality of presumption of guilt in his book, *Innocent: Inside Wrongful Conviction Cases*. Such a presumption is particularly true, he says, after arrest. "Once the police have made their arrest, based on "probable cause" that a person committed a crime, prosecutors tend to presume that the accused is most likely guilty of something. So do most juries."

But more than the presumption of guilt, more than the lack of training for PDs, Wolfe was struck by the overall bleakness of the criminal justice system.

"It's such a cultural thing," Wolfe says. "Really, how many white defendants do you see at 26th and Cal?" He shakes his head. "The whole system is so bad, I try not to think about it."

When pressed, Wolfe talks about how degrading the arrest process is. Among other things, he mentions the way police often throw an arrestee to the ground or against a car. But Wolfe, an admirer of the hard work of Chicago cops, is quick to add, "It's probably all necessary."

Jovan's family couldn't afford the $1.5 million bond (which would have required them to put down $150,000 in cash) or a private criminal defense lawyer. Such attorneys usually asked for a minimum $25,000 retainer—often much more—for murder cases. So Jovan spent the next few months on the BA Deck of the B Pod, waiting for the next court appearance, when he could be assigned a public defender.

In the meantime, there was little to do. Mostly, Jovan sat around for months, watching music videos and playing cards. Jovan's first cellie left after a few days and was replaced with a Vice Lord, a short skinny guy with a scary nervous energy. Jovan tried to keep quiet and stay out of the guy's way.

After two weeks at SuperMax, Pretty Ricky was retrieved from county by the New Orleans Police Department. He was wanted in nearly fifteen states, Jovan learned. Jovan's next roommate was a stocky homeless guy named Ronnie, who left the cell a mess.

Although Jovan ate his meals with the One Love group, there wasn't much gang activity on the BA Deck. Gang members were supposed to watch out for each other, but really it was each man for himself. Jovan often asked a GD for one of the smuggled-in cigarettes many inmates had. He wanted something to take the edge off his desperate anxiety. Most refused.

Finally, one guy said, "I'll give you the tobacco. You'll have to find rolling papers."

"How should I do that?"

The inmate said something about "doodle brown."

"What?" Jovan asked.

The guy explained that he was referring to the brown paper used to wrap rolls of toilet paper. "Use that," he said, and he showed Jovan how to do it.

Jovan smoked his cigarette. There were no ashtrays. He ashed on the floor like everyone else.

Finally the next court date arrived. Again, Jovan was strip-searched. Again, he went through the chain of bullpens at 26th and Cal. This time, he appeared in front of a different judge—Judge Ralph Reyna—but still they were instructed by the guard not to say a word. The result, a continuance, was the same.

Jovan was moved from the intake deck to the DJ Deck on D Pod, the place where he really got a feel for jail. When he stepped in the door, his cellie, who was sitting on the lower bunk, introduced himself as "Kenfolks."

"What is you?" Jovan asked. He'd learned to use the lingo by now.

"Used to be a GD. But I dropped my flag. I'm doing this right here." He nodded at the Bible on the bunk next to him. "I can't read but I'm trying."

"For real? You can't read?"

Kenfolks's eyes flashed. "I'm not stupid." He shrugged. "But a lot of things I can't pronounce."

A guy came in the cell. "That's Cat Eyes," Kenfolks said, pointing at him.

"What up?" Cat Eyes said. He had big round eyes that curled up at the ends in a feline way.

The next guy to stop by was LP. He was fat, about six-three, and he was blind in one eye, which he kept closed. LP was a GD, Jovan realized, and so were Cat Eyes and the others. Soon another GD stopped by, then another. They introduced themselves and told Jovan who the other GDs were on the deck.

LP would later become the chief of the GDs, not just on DJ Deck or D Pod, but chief of the whole jail. Eventually two guys, his security, would accompany him everywhere he went.

The gangs at SuperMax were incredibly organized. In addition to the chief, there were other positions, such as chief of security. Each gang filed paperwork, smuggling kites to other pods to report how many members were in their pod, how much "literature" (the rules of the gang) they knew, where weapons had been hidden.

Meanwhile, Jovan learned how to live day to day at SuperMax. Breakfast consisted of oatmeal or grits. Lunch, every single day, was two sandwiches—feeble bread with two pieces of thick, pink bologna in between. The spots in the bologna varied—sometimes green, sometimes red, sometimes brown. Most days, the dinner was "slop," so called because no one ever knew what was in it, although it appeared to be meat mixed with rice or macaroni, maybe some old vegetables. Sometimes the slop was an orangey color, sometimes brown or gray. Technically, a "salad" sat on the tray with dinner, but it was made of inedible, plasticky lettuce.

During each meal, inmates were allowed only a short time to eat before the heavy plastic trays were collected again. So at mealtimes the day room was filled with bleary-eyed men shoveling in cementlike oatmeal, wolfing stale bologna sandwiches, or spooning in slop. The place smelled like nursing home food, only staler and more pungent.

Jovan noticed something interesting right away about how the meals were handed out. The trays were brought to the day room on carts, forty-eight trays to each deck. But you couldn't just grab your tray or even line up for it. Instead, a representative from each gang would retrieve the trays for their group and place them on their designated tables. If you weren't in a gang, sometimes there was a tray left for you, sometimes not.

As on B Pod, there was little to do. Jovan and Kenfolks began reading the Bible together every day. Jovan taught Kenfolks how to phonate. He would point to a word and Kenfolks would sound it out. The Bible that Kenfolks owned was a King James Bible with a lot of "thee's" and "thou's."

One guy on D Pod was called Pops, because he was older than most. Pops was a guy you wanted to know, because he made hooch more potent than any alcohol you could get on the outside.

Generally speaking, hooch is made with corn, sugar, water, and yeast. The interaction between the yeast and sugars converts the combination to ethanol, the basic form of alcohol in alcoholic drinks. This sounds rather scientific, but at SuperMax the production of hooch was a process of trial and error, using anything and everything inmates could find that might contain the necessary ingredients. The occasional apple or orange was hoarded from the meal trays. Items purchased from the commissary cart such as honey, packets of sugar, and Jolly Ranchers were also saved for hooch production. Sometimes the guards brought packets of yeast from home; other times the inmates made their own yeast by putting bread in a container with water in the bottom and letting it sit.

The commissary cart came around once a week and offered food like tuna ($2.50 a can), honey ($3.50 for a little plastic bear full of it), mayonnaise ($3 for a small plastic jar), juice, bread, barbecue sauce ($2.50), tortilla chips ($1 for a tiny bag) and candy ($1 a bar). Each inmate—if he could convince a family member to send a money order to the jail in his name—got to put a certain amount a week toward commissary food.

The commissary also offered products like deodorant, lotion, hair products, shaving cream, combs, and hair picks, none of which the prison provided. They sold soap, toothpaste, and razors that were better than those the county provided. (The "state toothpaste" was so thick and gummy you could hang pictures on the wall with it.) Jovan's mom sent him a money order whenever she could, and one of the first things he bought was a pair of rubber sandals. The commissary sold both those and flip-flops.

The commissary carts were owned by Bob Barker, a name that was emblazoned across many of the products.

"That's the *Price Is Right* guy," other inmates told Jovan. Although untrue, the myth was widely accepted at SuperMax, by both guards and inmates.

Either way, you couldn't simply step up to the cart and buy what you wanted or what struck your fancy at the time. Once a week, on Wednesdays, inmates received commissary slips, which they filled out, noting exactly what they wanted and the quantity of the items. A few days later they received their items. If you forgot to note something you needed? Too bad, wait for next week.

Once Pops had collected the ingredients for the hooch—either from the commissary or the meal trays—and put them in a plastic bottle, he burned a stack of old milk cartons in his cell and held the bottle over the flame. He would bring the mixture to a boil and cook it as long as possible, because the longer it brewed, the stronger it was. Eventually, he took it off to let it ferment.

"Then a cup of it would get you hammered," Jovan said.

Food, especially from the commissary carts, was like money. You could trade food for hooch or smuggled-in weed. But often Jovan's mom couldn't send money and so he had no access to commissary food. And yet Pops gave him hooch and others gave him weed. People didn't know anything about him but they seemed to like him because he was young and quiet.

Still, Jovan was bored all the time. There was nothing to do. In the day room, LP controlled the TV, flipping from Jerry Springer to music videos and back. Every once in a while a guard would bring in a movie. Jovan noticed that no one ever watched court shows.

But that was what Jovan longed for—court. Even though reasons were always given—usually the schedule of one of the attorneys—the result of his court dates was always a continuance.

Because Red's attorney often had an associate with him, at least four attorneys appeared at each court date. The judge dealt with the cases of Jovan, Frad, Red, and Marvin together, and he seemed not to notice that none of the attorneys represented Jovan. The defendants continued to be told sternly not to speak during court, and in fact there was no opportunity. The status calls were fast-moving and tightly orchestrated.

A case was called and the attorneys would step up to the bench. Someone—the prosecutors, or one of the defense lawyers or PDs—would request a continuance, and it would be granted. The whole appearance would take minutes, usually less, and then the inmates were sent back to the bullpen for hours of waiting. Frad, Marvin, Red, and Jovan rarely talked about the case until after such status hearings, when they would share any information they'd heard from their attorneys. Then they were returned to their separate decks at SuperMax.

Jovan told the guards at the jail he didn't have a lawyer, but no one seemed too concerned. His mother always looked helpless during those court dates, and she told him at their visit every week that she had no money to hire a lawyer, but she was trying. Jovan began to wonder, *Does anyone even know I'm here?*

Jovan spent most of his time keeping his head down, and in an effort to prevent anyone from giving him trouble, he worked out—sometimes with weights when the weight room was operable, sometimes with plastic bags filled with water. He took twenty pounds off his five-foot ten-inch frame until he was 220 pounds of muscle. And although Jovan's face could break into a huge smile when he was happy, he also had a stern, intimidating way of looking at people when his face was in repose. The fact was, he didn't smile often at SuperMax. In order to cover his constant fear, he wore that stern face, trying to intimidate people into staying as far away from him as possible.

It was even harder to stay out of gang trouble in jail than it had been on the streets. But Jovan found that if he acted tough and knowledgeable, he could skate by without getting involved in gang activity. When new inmates came in, he sussed them out right away, finding out where they were from, what gang they were in. People started coming to him for advice—how to handle someone who was giving them grief, someone who was stealing from them.

In the meantime, he came up with his own internal rules for surviving SuperMax: (1) watch and listen until you get to know how everything operates; (2) respect others; (3) don't touch other people's stuff; (4) don't join in on just any conversation, wait until you're invited in; (5) don't borrow money; and (6) never be a snitch.

Jovan adapted and remained optimistic because he knew he wouldn't have to do it for long. He hadn't done the crime he was accused of, and the truth would come to light eventually. He believed that. He *had* to.

17

"You ready to die?"

The Bill of Rights says that everyone has a right to a fair and speedy trial. Specifically, the Sixth Amendment of the U.S. Constitution requires a speedy trial by an impartial jury. In Illinois, arrestees are entitled by statute to a speedy trial within 120 days of being taken into custody "unless delay is occasioned by the defendant." In other words, it's the state's burden to seek and ensure the speedy trial. This statute is rarely observed.

There is a good deal of confusion among criminal lawyers regarding the right to a speedy trial. Many believe that the defense has to demand it for the concept even to come into play. In fact, when later interviewed for an article in *Chicago* magazine about Jovan's case, Judge Paul Biebel, the respected presiding judge of the Criminal Division of the Circuit Court of Cook County, asserted that Jovan's public defender, whenever he eventually got one, needed to make a written demand in order to gain his right to a speedy trial. After being asked to review the statute again, Biebel told the reporter, "OK, he doesn't have to make a demand. It's been a while since I looked at this."[90]

As the *Chicago* magazine article stated, "For people like Mosley, caught up in this dysfunctional system, the right to a speedy trial can become a joke."

Approximately five months after he was arrested, Jovan still didn't have a lawyer. Court records indicate that a PD was assigned to him one month after his arrest, but no attorney had ever spoken to him. In court his case was always called with those of the other defendants, so that a number of attorneys stepped up to the bench together, giving the court the impression that he was represented. Jovan, to his detriment, kept quiet, taking his cues from the guards. But finally, at a status hearing, Jovan couldn't wait any longer, and he had a rare chance to speak to Frad's attorney. He quickly explained his situation.

The PD looked surprised and said, "No one has talked to you?"

Shortly thereafter, Jovan was assigned Public Defender Edwin Korb. (The exact date Korb was assigned to the case is unclear, given that Jovan's file from the public defender's office later disappeared and was still missing even when subpoenaed.)[91]

Around the same time Jovan was assigned a PD, another inmate told him he should request a transfer to the "Christian Deck." Although he had attended church before his arrest, Jovan didn't identify himself as religious. But he was told the Christian Deck was a little less dangerous, there was less gangbanging (fighting on behalf of a gang) going on, fewer knives. Still, things were mostly fine on DJ Deck. He had learned the ropes and didn't want to adjust to something new.

Then one day on the deck a GD named Pork Chop stirred up trouble by disobeying gang orders. Pork Chop, a big guy, had been put in a cell with "the opposition," a Vice Lord. The guards, knowing the gang members preferred to stay together, were going to move him out of the cell, but Pork Chop said no, he was fine. The truth of the matter was he wanted to stay there because the Vice Lord cellie had a big supply of hooch and weed.

When other GDs told him that he couldn't stay in the cell, Pork Chop decided he wanted to go "off count." He wanted to drop his flag and leave the gang.

Other gang members said to him, "You know we have to beat you up. You can't leave."

Somehow, all the GDs ended up in Jovan's cell to discuss the matter.

LP, whose weapon of choice was a few toothbrushes melted together inset with sharp spikes, assigned tasks to different members. They would, he decided, guard each set of stairs at the top deck in order to trap Pork Chop.

As usual, Jovan tried to stay out of it, but no one was letting him this time. He was assigned one set of stairs, while the other guys went up the back stairs to find Pork Chop in his cell.

Seeing no other alternative, Jovan reluctantly left his cell. He trotted up the stairs. Surprisingly, there was Pork Chop, sitting at the top, waiting.

Pork Chop smiled at Jovan. In his hands he twirled a knife the size of his arm—a large piece of steel that had been sharpened on the floor. It glinted in the fluorescent lights. "You ready to die?" he asked Jovan.

The answer was a distinct no. Jovan quickly retraced his steps, found the other guys, and told them what had happened. A guy named Four Tré, the inmate in charge of the GDs on that deck, went nuts. He was tall and skinny, with dark, animated eyebrows. "We're going to get this guy!" he said.

Four Tré handed Jovan a knife.

Jovan shook his head. "I don't want a knife."

"You need it."

"No, I'm all right."

LP looked at him. "He don't like carrying knives."

Four Tré directed someone to put Murray's grease—a hair pomade— into a sock, forming a hard ball that could be swung around. Then he gave it to Jovan.

Jovan took the sock. He told them he had to go to the bathroom. In the stall, he looked up and at the ceiling and whispered, "God, forgive me for what I have to do."

When he got to the day room, he saw that a mattress had been laid over the bottom of the staircase so Pork Chop couldn't run down all the way. Pork Chop was still sitting at the top.

Just then, a guy who had snuck up the back stairs behind Pork Chop began beating him with a cane. Pork Chop ran down the stairs, slid down the mattress, and began stabbing a guy who stood right next to Jovan. Jovan glanced around, realizing he was separated from most of the other GDs. There were no guards to be found. They were up in the area they called "triage," watching movies and playing cards.

Jovan swung the sock. He made contact with Pork Chop's back.

Pork Chop turned around, saw Jovan, and yelled, "I'm going to kill you!"

He came after Jovan, who turned and ran. Jovan lost one of his shoes and tripped. Before he knew it, he was on the floor and Pork Chop was standing above him with a knife. With a roar, he began to bring the knife down, but just then a guy named Ike came from behind Pork Chop and hit him with a cane. Someone else hit him with a chair. And Jovan rolled away.

Jovan ran back to his cell. They were still fighting outside. He sat down, panting, thinking, *I can't do this, I can't do this, I can't do this.*

When the fight was over, the guards put the deck on lockdown. No one had died, but many, like the guy who'd been stabbed, had been badly injured. The next day, the guards divided up the deck, sending Pork Chop one place, some of the GDs, including LP, somewhere else.

The GD who had been assistant chief of security took over security for the building, becoming the third most powerful GD in the jail. Jovan's cellie took the position he'd vacated.

Then they went looking for a GD to be a chief of the DJ Deck. Someone said to Jovan, "It should be you."

"No, I don't want it," Jovan said.

But before he knew it, he'd been assigned chief of DJ Deck.

It didn't last long. A week later, one of the GDs came to him. "You're not keeping the paperwork, so you're out. We're taking the position from you."

It was true. Jovan hadn't been keeping track of how many members were on his deck or who knew the literature or where knives were hidden.

He acted indignant, but he was beyond relieved.

The next day, Jovan requested a transfer to the Christian Deck. A week later, his request was granted.

Being on the Christian Deck made things the tiniest bit easier. But the fact was, the gangs were still there. The beatings and the stabbings continued. Suicides were not uncommon. One prisoner popped out the blade from one of the razors delivered every night and managed to cut his wrists before the guard came around ten minutes later to collect them. One guy ripped his sheets apart, tied them together in a long rope, and hung himself over the rails of the top deck. *The guy must have really wanted to die,* Jovan thought. But Jovan didn't want to die. He was going to get out of there.

Jovan's first roommate on the Christian Deck was Papa T. He had a wide part in his hair from which big waves rolled down the side of his head. Jovan heard he was the deck snitch, the one who kept the guards apprised of anything bad going down. Jovan didn't care. He had nothing to hide.

Jovan's public defender, Edwin Korb, had a quick visit with Jovan every time they appeared in court. Korb later said that he found Jovan to be "very cooperative, intelligent. . . . He was not an anxious type of person. He was sort of, you know, low-key and soft-spoken." Korb spoke to people at the law firm where Jovan had worked during high school and planned to call them as character witnesses. "Most of the time you can't put on a character witness because your clients are pretty bad, and they are going to bring up the rest of it. Jovan, I don't think, had any background at all. He was a good candidate for character witnesses."[92]

It was Korb who finally explained to Jovan what he was up against: murder, specifically death-penalty murder.

Jovan was confused. No one had told him, much less explained to him yet, the charges for which he'd been indicted. He asked Korb why was he in here being charged with murder if the only thing they said he did was hit the guy twice in the side.

Korb explained the accountability rule, explained that if a jury believed he had thrown those two punches, he was guilty of the murder of Howard Thomas.

Jovan felt cold, hit by a wave of fear. "Are you serious?" he asked.

Korb said he was.

"No way. How? How? I don't understand." In his head, he heard the echo of a detective's voice, *Just tell us you threw two punches, that's not murder.*

Korb wanted Jovan to consider a plea bargain.

Jovan shook his head. "I didn't do it. I'm not taking a plea."

According to Scott Christianson in *Innocent: Inside Wrongful Convictions Cases,* "Plea bargaining is notoriously coercive and dishonest."[93] He quotes Professor John Langbein of the University of Chicago Law School, who compared the practice to "ancient medieval torture."[94] "And like torture," Christianson says, "instead of getting at the truth, plea-bargaining may simply pressure some defendants to cop a plea to cut their losses."[95] He points out that both the judges and the prosecutors are reliant on plea bargaining. Steve Bogira, who spent a year in one courtroom at 26th and Cal and wrote about it in his book *Courtroom 302,* reported the same thing. He maintained that the situation is worse when a defendant is innocent.

"Prosecutors are apt to make pleading guilty an especially attractive scenario for the innocent. The weaker the case against a defendant, the more likely his acquittal if the case goes to trial—and therefore the better the bargain offered by the state in its attempt to get the conviction."

Some maintain that prosecutors and judges penalize those who exercise their right to a trial.

The *Chicago* magazine article that investigated Jovan's case stated, "Defendants who exercise their constitutional right to a jury trial must wait. Those defendants who do ask for a jury trial risk a particularly severe sentence."[96]

Steve Bogira mirrored this sentiment in *Courtroom 302.* "Defense lawyers who demand trial risk alienating the prosecutors, who couldn't possibly adhere to the time limits if every defendant in their courtroom demanded trial. Prosecutors sometimes consider trial demands to be inconsiderate if not a personal affront . . . and so work extra hard to convict defendants who demand trial. . . . Of course the defense lawyers themselves, the PDs especially, have their own caseload problems, and that's often the real reason they agree to continuances—though they're likely to tell their clients it's purely for tactical purposes that they're not pushing the case to trial."[97]

In *Chicago* magazine, Edwin Korb called the phenomena the "jury tax." "The judge will never say on the record, 'You went to trial, so you'll get your butt kicked'—that would be grounds for appeal—but if your client is found guilty, you can bet he won't get the minimum. The common wisdom is that it adds more than 20 years to time for murder."[98]

Korb was a part of the public defender's unit known as the Multiple Defendant Division, which represented clients in felony and first-degree murder cases where more than one person was accused. MDD was known around the courtroom as "Mud" and had the reputation for being one big mess, a futile place to practice law, where the PDs worked mostly with gangbangers and rarely with winnable cases.

It was widely known that "Mud" cases took longer than others, and there were a number of reasons for that. Many times, says Moses Collins, a PD with the MDD, private attorneys came in and out of the case based on when the families could pay them, causing a PD to have to jump in (and then out again) with each switch. The public defenders might get transferred to a different courtroom too, as could the state's attorneys or judges, and with all that going on, added to the number of defendants, the case could grind to a near halt.

In fact it became a strategy of Edwin Korb's (as it was for many public defenders) to postpone the trial in the hopes that as it got older, it would favor his client. It's the conventional wisdom in criminal trials that witnesses and memories fade with the passage of time, and that works in favor of the defense.

As Steve Bogira says in *Courtroom 302,* "The state's witnesses disappear, or get cold feet, or get arrested themselves, hurting their credibility. If the defendant is in jail, prosecutors often don't feel much urgency about getting to trial either."[99]

Delaying the trial wasn't hard to do. The court was liberal in granting continuances. "I mean, anybody that wanted a continuance, it was fine," Edwin Korb has said. "The State never seemed like they were ready to go. . . . There was not a lot of effort involved in terms of trying to delay this case. It just happened on its own as many cases do at 26th Street."

According to Dick Devine, who was the official Cook County State's Attorney from 1996 to 2004, during the time Jovan was at SuperMax, "A trial judge needs to take hold of the case. Everyone has problems, everyone has excuses—transfers of PDs, retirement of ASAs, furloughs of the cops. A good trial judge has to say, 'You're not leaving this courtroom until it's tried.' You have to be an equal opportunity grouch and stay on top of everyone—the state and the defense. If you stick to it, people will eventually learn that and follow."

But that wasn't happening in Jovan's case. Although Jovan saw Korb every few months in court, the case was stagnant, with continuances each time. Finally, Korb recommended that they file a motion with the court. It was Jovan's understanding that the motion was to quash his arrest. But to Jovan, Korb seemed less than impressed by their chances for winning, and his approach to the case appeared spiritless, as if he didn't care much. Jovan had heard other inmates call their PDs "Penitentiary Dispensers" or "Public Surrenders."

When faced with such accusations, public defenders generally explain, *It's not that we don't care, it's that we don't have enough time to show we care or do too much of anything.*

According to *Defending the Damned,* a stunning 80 percent of all murder defendants in Cook County are represented by public defenders.[100] One PD explained the immense workload like this: "For the defendants who are sitting in county, their case is the only thing on their minds 100% of the time. For us, it's like, 'Which file folder are you?' We're entirely overwhelmed."[101]

To pass the time in SuperMax, Jovan began to collaborate with a few other inmates on a rap song. Jovan had grown up on rap—usually the kid rappers like Kris Kross and Another Bad Creation. He remembered how he had done his first rap himself when he was about fourteen. He'd been sitting around with some guys doing freestyle folly rap, and he'd taken a shot and kept it going for a minute and thirty seconds, straight off the top of his head. If you couldn't think of something to say, you just threw in a curse word to give you some time. Some of the lyrics were about guns. His brother Michael heard him and laughed. "What do you know about a Glock?" he said.

At the beginning, the lyrics Jovan wrote with the other inmates were violent, particularly against cops.

They performed a song for the guys in the day room. Some people liked it, but a number of inmates kept quiet.

One of them came up to Jovan. "How you go do folly rap and then pray to Jesus at the same time?" He shook his head and walked away.

Those words stuck with Jovan. He thought about them while he lay on his steel bed at night. One of those nights, he had a dream that God was speaking to him, and God said, *You can't praise me and rap like that at the same time.*

The next day, Jovan got the group together and spoke to them about changing the lyrics. The rap had to be about God. Some disagreed and left the group. Jovan found other members who were interested. "God's Mission" was their next song. In it, they used some of the lyrics from the old song, but instead of talking about killing gang members or the police, they talked about killing demons for the Lord.

Jovan started reading the Bible often. Soon, he was regularly the first to the prison chapel for Sunday service.

The membership of the rap group shifted as some got out and some went to the pen. Jovan got new members and soon they were writing all gospel rap. When Christmas rolled around (nine months after his arrest), a guard asked Jovan's group to be in the jail's Christmas program, a kind of talent show.

When he and the group got up to perform "God's Mission" for the officers and the other inmates, the deck went crazy. Everyone leapt to their feet, cheering and clapping. The group did one more song, got another standing ovation. As Jovan stood looking around the deck, everyone applauding, he knew it was times like this that would keep him alive, would keep him believing that he would get out of SuperMax. And soon.

But as the months passed and he rounded the end of his first year in SuperMax, he began to realize that he could be stuck there. Indefinitely.

18

"Who really cares about me if I'm locked up?"

Every hour in SuperMax felt like a week. And every day Jovan's routine was the same. The inmates were woken at three thirty a.m. Those inmates who did not have a court appearance were locked back in their cells after breakfast until seven a.m., when the officers gave them the chance to use the day room. If they chose not to, they stayed put until three thirty p.m. when the shift changed. Lunch, for those in the day room, was served around ten thirty a.m., dinner at five p.m. Inmates were locked back in their cells at night at nine thirty. No college classes or other rehabilitative efforts were made available because the county jail was merely a holding facility for those awaiting trial.

Jovan continued to collaborate on gospel rap lyrics. On his own, he wrote poetry. Part of one poem read:

Why I Cry

Staring up into the sky;
Wondering why;
So I cry.

Watching cars passing by;
Wondering why;
So I cry.

Once he read the entire poem to a guard named Lisa Taylor. To Jovan's surprise, she dropped her head in her hands and began to cry. She asked if she could copy the poem. She wanted to take it to her church.

Jovan felt good about that—felt good that he had touched someone in some way, that maybe someone on the outside would hear about him. He prayed about the case constantly. One day, as he prayed in his cell, he heard a voice as clear as day say, *They cannot find you guilty.* The voice was so authoritative, so sure. He began to repeat the words in his head. And they kept him going for a while, gave him an optimistic boost whenever he used them. But then the mantra started to lose its magic and as another year slipped by, and then more time, Jovan hit a wall of apathy. In the two and a half years since he arrived at county, there had been twenty-four continuances in his case. His court visits seemed increasingly futile.

Edwin Korb, meanwhile, was going by the book, delaying a trial in a multiple-defendant case. He was also hoping to interview Jori Garth after she turned eighteen, so he could speak with her without the presence of her police officer father. From what Korb understood, Jori's testimony could go either way—she might say Jovan had been involved, she might not. "The State of Illinois's attorneys knew what was going on. If they thought I was going to demand trial and this case was being pushed, they would have gotten to that girl. This is based on my experience. And it would have been very harmful for our case. I think that she could have gone either way with the right kind of preparation."[102]

Korb did not know that Anton Williams had identified Jovan in a lineup, but only as someone who hadn't taken part in the beating. Instead, the summary of the lineup given to Korb said only that Jovan had been "identified" by Anton.

Jovan told Korb that during the interrogation he had been isolated for a long time and intimidated into confessing. Unfortunately, Korb had heard these complaints from clients many times. "In Jovan's case . . . there was no glaring police misconduct, because yelling and hitting, to be honest with you, are things I hear all the time."[103] Jovan's interrogation had been mild in comparison.

Jovan wrote another poem, this one entitled "Who Cares?" A line read, *Who really cares about me? If I'm locked up.*

As years passed, he found that nothing mattered to him. If his mother sent money so he could buy something from the commissary, fine. If she didn't, who cared? If the guards were nice to him or vicious, it didn't matter. If someone came to him with gossip from the halls of SuperMax, he would cut them off with a curt, "Don't bring me that. I don't want to hear that."

Jovan later realized he'd been intensely depressed. But there was no treatment for depression in SuperMax.

Meanwhile, the violence in the jail escalated, and when he didn't see it, Jovan would hear its rumblings from the guards. The guy who usually delivered razors to the men on the Christian Deck was a little round Mexican guard known as Rodriguez, and Jovan began to look forward to his visits. It was through Officer Rodriguez that he got a lot of his news about what was going on at other decks in the prison, and somehow Rodriguez always made it entertaining.

"Big fight," he would say, pantomiming the actions of the prisoner and guards.

Jovan knew that, technically, he was lucky. He made no trouble for anyone, and many guards grew to know and respect him as the years passed.

And despite his foul mood, Jovan was relieved that he was on the Christian Deck. Though violence occurred, the deck was relatively peaceful. Lawrence "Red" Wideman was transferred to the Christian Deck, for example, but because he fought often with other inmates he was transferred out.[104] Marvin Treadwell moved to the Christian Deck too, and for a while he and Jovan were roommates.

For much of the time he lived with Marvin, Jovan wasn't aware of Marvin's video statement to the police (in which Marvin had vaguely said that "we all" threw some punches). No one had ever shown Jovan his police records or those of the other guys. Finally, Frad and Red's attorneys provided these records to their clients, and after court one day, the guys showed Jovan the transcript of Marvin's statement. Red also told him that Marvin had taken the police to Jovan's house.

When Jovan got back from court, he confronted Marvin. Marvin told him he didn't want to get Jovan in trouble, so he took the cops to Jovan's old address, because he'd heard Jovan no longer lived there. He'd been scared, he said, and Jovan understood that. He'd been scared by the cops himself. Ultimately, he decided he couldn't blame Marvin for landing him in SuperMax. Jovan also found it hard to be angry with him because Marvin wasn't very good at the prison game. When he could convince the guards to bring him extra food, Jovan would share it with Marvin. Eventually, though, Marvin was kicked off the Christian Deck for fighting, just like Red.

Jovan also deeply appreciated the Christian Deck because there were rules for the deck, and those rules were not governed by the gangs. In fact, you could help make and enforce those rules, not through gang violence but through your reading of the Bible and teaching that to others. So Jovan learned to guard his spot on the Christian Deck. If you acted up, if the guards were in a capricious mood, they'd transfer you just because they could, and just like that you'd be at the whim of the gangs and the nastier guards and cellies who might be even nastier.

Once, during a lockdown, Jovan's side began to ache. Badly. When he lifted his DOC shirt, he saw that a boil as wide as a baseball had formed on his flank. He had no idea what had caused it. He called for a guard, but she accused him of trying to scheme his way out of his cell.

An hour later, as the boil grew, stretching his shirt, Jovan called the guard again. She yelled, "You're not getting out of your cell during lockdown!" and stormed away.

When it become so painful he could hardly stand it, Jovan once again rang for the guard. She was pissed off this time, but Jovan was near tears, and seeing this, she called a nurse.

The nurse was a tall, heavyset woman named Nurse Cannon. She looked at the growing boil. "Have you been living with that for all this time?" she said. The lockdown had been going on for days, during which no one had been let out of the cells.

"Yeah," he said.

Nurse Cannon glared at the guard, who was staring at the size of the boil.

They sent Jovan to Cermak Health Service, where medical personnel used huge needles to drain the boil of fluid. The explanation for the boil seemed flimsy ("either a spider bite or too many cold cuts"). It was nice to be out of SuperMax, though, in a spotless hospital bed so much more comfortable than the one in his cell. Yet the whole time he was there, Jovan kept his eye on the clock, waiting to go back to SuperMax. He'd heard about inmates who'd gone to the hospital for just a night, or even for a shift change, and come back to find they were in a different deck. He couldn't risk getting moved from the Christian Deck. Finally, Jovan took the van back to SuperMax and, finding his quarters unchanged, crawled gratefully back into his bunk.

19

"I need to get my son out of jail."

Delores Mosley stopped outside the massive stone building on South Drexel Avenue, her eyes drawn upward by its soaring columns, stopping at the top where a plastic sign hung: OPERATION PUSH. NATIONAL HEADQUARTERS. DR. KING'S WORKSHOP. She nervously straightened the skirt she'd worn just for this meeting. Well, it wasn't actually a meeting. She'd been calling Operation PUSH, and calling and calling. She had heard that the Reverend Jesse Jackson might be able to help Jovan. She had been told he helped with this kind of situation all the time. But every time she called, she was transferred, and all her messages stayed unreturned.

She had thought about calling the lawyer Jovan had worked for during high school, but when she'd asked Jovan, he'd told her that the lawyer only did personal injury work and that his relationship with the lawyer had consisted solely of "conversations" like, *Jovan, get me a split-pea soup and have it in my office in ten minutes.*

So she'd come directly to the center to ask the Reverend Jesse Jackson for his assistance. She didn't know if she could take it much longer—watching her innocent son spend so much time in prison, no end in sight.

Delores had visited Jovan every single week during the years he had been incarcerated. Visitation days were Wednesdays at first, then Tuesdays, then Sundays. Rain, sleet, snow, it didn't matter, she was there.

The first visit had been the worst. She arrived at two-thirty, and a guard told her she'd have to wait. And so she waited and waited and waited some more. *When can I see my son?* she asked, and a female guard who had inky black skin and dark eyes told her to just wait. Six hours passed and she began to weep in the waiting room. When the guard saw Delores crying, she said she'd forgotten to get Jovan. *Forgotten.* Delores didn't buy it, but soon she got to see her baby. And that was when the day got worse. He was behind a plastic shield. She couldn't touch or hug her child. They talked through phones set into the plastic wall. He was doing fine, he told her, but she could see the jail was wearing on him.

She could see it in court too, even though she never got to talk to him. She'd been to every court appearance, and seen every continuance.

And now? Now time was just flying by, and she needed to do something.

She walked into the building, into a large room with linoleum floors and couches and chairs to the right.

She took a deep breath and stepped up to the desk in front of her, smiling at the woman behind it. "I'd like to see Reverend Jackson."

The woman behind the desk did not return her smile. "He's not available."

"Please, it's about my son."

"Reverend Jackson's agenda is full."

"Ma'am, I just want to tell him about how much time my son has been in jail without a trial. I need to get my son out of jail."

The woman said nothing.

"Could I make an appointment?" Delores asked. "Even if it's in a few days or a week or a month?" A wave of bleakness hit her as she realized that Jovan would probably still be there in a month, probably longer.

Still the woman did not respond.

"Do you want my number?" Delores asked. "Maybe someone could check about an appointment and let me know."

The woman responded this time. She shook her head no.

Delores left with angry tears in her eyes. But she wouldn't give up. A few weeks later, Delores got a real meeting, this time with Congressman Danny Davis. She dressed up once again, even putting on high heels this time.

When she was escorted into the conference room where the congressman sat waiting for her, she felt as if her heart would burst out of the cage she'd kept it in since Jovan was arrested. *Finally,* she thought.

Congressman Davis wore a double-breasted suit. His eyes, when they landed on her, stayed there. His Afro, cut short, was gray, as were his eyebrows. He was a dignified man with a deep, deep voice.

She sat, and quickly told the congressman Jovan's story—the fight, the arrest, the confession. She told him how Jovan's case, if you could call it that, had continued to crawl, continued to be continued, nothing happening at all. The original state's attorney had just died of cancer, she explained, forcing the case to be reassigned and time given for another state's attorney to get up to speed. But wasn't something supposed to happen? Wasn't her son at least supposed to get a trial? He'd been in there for years, after all.

The congressman listened, really listened. He explained that he was involved with reform that would help offenders when they were released from jail.

But Jovan wasn't an offender, she told him.

He looked at her kindly. He told her he was sorry, but he didn't think he could help. In his deep voice he explained how she might have better luck with a local law school, some of which had free legal clinics.

She blinked, fighting back the tears that came as her hopes for freeing Jovan were dashed yet again.

Justice eluded Howard Thomas's family as well. Howard's daughter would later write in a statement for the court, *The murder of my father (Howard Thomas Jr.) has affected my life in many ways. . . . Since my father was abruptly and tragically taken away from me, all of my happy memories are mirrored by the way he died. I want to drive around 71st or 75th and Calumet. I can't bear the sight of those six feet tall sidewalk lights that are on Calumet, near the sight [sic] of where my father died. All of those things and more remind me of the horrific death of my father.* The family had gotten some measure of relief when the boys who killed Bug had been arrested, but they were still lounging around in county jail when they should be put away for good.

20

"Jovan just wanted to save people's souls."

Four years after he arrived at SuperMax, Jovan met Marsha Adger in the chapel on the Christian Deck. It wasn't much of a chapel, really, just a room with folding chairs and a makeshift stage, but it was the place where members of local Christian churches, like Marsha Adger, came to preach.

Marsha, a member of the Triedstone Full Gospel Baptist Church, was a tall, gracious black woman with a beaming smile. She was a woman who could seemingly take on anything. She would talk about the injustice facing people in prison (she didn't care whether they were innocent or not) and the current statutory law regarding expungement, then turn around and explain that the best way to make caramel sauce was to boil and then gently heat a can of condensed milk for approximately forty minutes. ("After you've done this a few times, you'll get the hang of it.")

Triedstone, located on West 104th Street in Chicago, was an active church that hadn't let the technological advances of the world pass it by. If SuperMax had allowed computers, the inmates could have visited the Triedstone Web site and seen videos of Bishop Simon Gordon's fiery, captivating sermons. CDs and audiotapes of the sermons were sold in the church. The speaker system was state-of-the-art to support the pack of musicians who played at the two services each Sunday. Like many churches, Baptist or not, Triedstone had a plethora of groups and outreach programs its followers could join. Marsha Adger was an elder at the church and for a time she led the group's prison outreach program. Marsha and Bishop Simon Gordon were some of the very few outsiders allowed into SuperMax. Through Triedstone's contract with the county, they were permitted to preach to the prisoners.

The best thing about Marsha, Jovan found, was that she was real. He had come out of his funk and regained some of his optimism, thanks mostly to his Bible studies, but he still wanted people to tell it like it really was. Some of the other church members who came to preach at SuperMax promised all the inmates they would be going home, or gave the everything-will-be-all-right speech. Jovan began to look forward to seeing Marsha, who never said things like that, only preached the Bible and talked to the prisoners about the little things, as if the prisoners were just like everyone else.

Jovan was inspired by Marsha and the way she taught the Bible. As his own propensity and passion for reading the Bible grew, Jovan became an elder on the deck and began to teach Bible classes a few times a week.

He befriended Michael Whitted, an inmate who had helped organize the Christian Deck. Michael had been in county for around two years, allegedly for murder. He was handsome, his skin deep black, his beard short and well-groomed.

Michael watched Jovan reading the Bible, preaching. He would later say, "Jovan just wanted to save people's souls."

Jovan's PD, Edwin Korb, eventually filed the motion he had recommended—the only paperwork Korb would ever file on behalf of Jovan. Korb then left the public defender's office to run for judge, changing his name to Edward Flanagan in order to sound more Irish. This kind of ruse had worked before in Cook County, which is heavily Irish, but it failed for Korb, who is now a solo practitioner.

Meanwhile, there was one person who hadn't given up on Jovan. His mom. Jovan was always happy to see her—it was a break from his otherwise monotonous week. Although Jovan and his mom were able to talk with phones at first, inmates kept breaking them, so now they had to lean close to the plastic shield and talk through mouthpieces. Although *talk* wasn't the right word. The mouthpieces didn't work well, requiring everyone to shout to be heard, so that the room was filled with bellowing family members and friends. Sometimes he got fifteen minutes with his mom, sometimes thirty minutes, depending on the mood of the guards.

One afternoon, though, his mother looked like she wasn't doing well—her skin was sallow and her eyes jumped from one thing to another.

He asked what was going on.

"Terrible headaches," she said. "I can't think straight."

"Have you seen a doctor?"

"They said it's the stress."

He felt guilty. It was because of him she didn't feel well.

She told him how intense the headaches were, how she just wanted them to stop. She got worked up as she talked, not letting Jovan say anything, and then suddenly she opened her mouth as if to scream, but no sound came out. Her eyes began to track the ceiling, as if looking for something up there.

"Ma!" he yelled.

No response.

"Ma!"

Still nothing.

His mother, an epileptic, was suffering from a staring seizure, something he'd seen once before when he was nine years old. It had been one of the scariest moments of his life, and yet he'd been able to help to her then. He could touch her, guide her, hold her. Now he was trapped behind this plastic wall.

"Put your head down," he told her.

Still her eyes moved back and forth.

"Ma!" he shouted. "Put your head down."

Finally, she did, lying slumped over for a while. He wanted to help her up; he wanted to hold her by the shoulders and look her in her eyes. When she finally sat up, he asked, "Are you okay?"

Her voice came out tiny. "Yeah. No. I don't . . ."

Not knowing what else to do, he directed her to breathe, to put her head down again. When she finally sat up she was better.

When she left, Jovan asked Officer Dizzette, whom everyone called "Dizzy," to keep an eye on his mother on the way out.

He watched her leave, knowing he would now worry about her epilepsy all the time. Finally, he turned around and walked back to his cell, useless.

21

"The years dripped by."

When he was finally assigned a new public defender, a guy named James Fryman, Jovan couldn't help but get excited. He might finally have someone on his side who would believe him and fight for him.

The day of their first meeting arrived. Jovan walked into the meeting room and stopped as if he'd hit a wall. Across the table were photos—photos of Howard Thomas, dead, grossly beaten.

One photo depicted Thomas's swollen-shut eyes, another his wholly displaced nose and grossly battered cheekbones. There were photos of bloodied teeth on the street. Others showed Thomas after he had been treated by paramedics—a ventilator was in Thomas's mouth, a hard collar on his neck. Most of his face was obscured by gauze wrapped around it but the gauze had turned so bloody it looked like a red turban. And then there were the autopsy photos showing Thomas's swollen brain.

Jovan looked at the guy standing next to the photos.

Jim Fryman was a brown-haired man, trim, wearing a suit. "The jury is going to see these."

"And?" Jovan said.

"They won't like 'em. I think you should take a plea." The man looked at the photos and shook his head sadly.

"I'm not taking a plea. I didn't do it." Jovan explained that he had been cuffed to a wall, that he had been threatened. They told him if he signed the statement saying he'd thrown two punches, he could go home.

But Fryman had heard such things from defendants before. Especially the part about being able to go home if they sign something. He again recommended a plea bargain.

"I'm not signing anything," Jovan said.

Francis Wolfe, who spent years working in the PD's Office and just about as long reflecting on the process, says, "PDs are overwhelmed by the volume, and so you don't spend the time and trouble or get too involved. . . . Sometimes you want to recoil from your own defendants when you're reading the charges, like someone raping a two-year-old. You get the feeling that your clients are wired differently than you are." Which is why, Wolfe says, "When you first start, you can smell it when they're innocent. Or at least you think you can. . . . But you invest so much energy at the beginning in so many bad guys that it's soon hard to get it up. It's hard not to get cynical. . . . You start thinking, He probably did it or the cops wouldn't have arrested him." The state's attorneys are no different, Wolfe says, in terms of their reliance on gut feelings when prosecuting a case. "The state's attorneys have fits when they lose," he says. "It's a problem because they think they're agents of God and they are out to do good." But this leaves no room for doubt once a prosecution has begun.

And if an innocent goes to prison and it's revealed later? "They just apologize," says Wolfe, "and let a guy out after he spent fourteen years behind bars."

In fact, the issue of forced confessions, wrongful convictions, and the ability to "remedy" such things with a mere apology was not just an issue in Chicago but around the country. It had become prevalent enough to be the subject of jokes. A 2008 comic strip by Rob Rogers in the *Pittsburgh Post-Gazette* showed an FDA investigator talking to a box of tomatoes (following accusations that a salmonella outbreak based on tomatoes turned out to be false). *You've been exonerated by DNA evidence,* the investigator says to one tomato. *We're sorry for falsely imprisoning you and destroying your reputation. You are now free to go.*

Jerry Miller, a Chicago man imprisoned for twenty-six years before DNA evidence exonerated him for crimes he didn't commit, appeared on *The Colbert Report* after his release. In the segment, Stephen Colbert presented him with a card that read, *We're really sorry!* and on the next line, *Sincerely, Society.*

Making matters worse for the already overloaded PDs, promotions in the field are based on the number of cases a PD handles, as well as the number of jury trials. In other words, the number of cases "disposed." Verdicts of not guilty, however, are never taken into account, so there is little professional incentive for a PD to vigorously defend a client.

While Jovan was in Division 11, prisoners were granted one hour in the library once or twice a week. As he began years three and then four in SuperMax, and his depression began to lift, Jovan began spending every minute he could in the library. He'd always wanted to be a lawyer, and he liked his job at the law firm during high school, but now the stakes were much higher.

During each visit to the library, a prisoner was allowed to copy a maximum of thirty pages, but only case law, no statutes. (The reason for this was never explained.) When Jovan found a case with an interesting statute, he would furiously scribble the statute number and wording on a piece of paper.

Jovan began reading the books that report on Illinois appellate and Supreme Court cases. He searched for cases concerning coercion, forced confessions, police manipulation, codefendants, and the accountability law. When a case he liked cited to another case, he searched for it, but often reporters were missing and it was difficult to locate information about whether a particular case had been overturned or compromised other cases. In other words, the county gave inmates enough to wet their tongues but not enough to drink.

When faced with the situation of a missing or outdated reporter, Jovan asked the librarian to order it, or to at least find the case or statute he was seeking.

"You can't order that right now," was the usual response. As if the librarian might do it tomorrow or the next day. Jovan began asking other inmates to use the hour in the library to copy cases for him.

There were no computers in SuperMax, nowhere for Jovan to compile his research, and so the stacks of cases in his cell began to grow. He filled up notebook after notebook with his interpretations and questions about the case law. He spent his nights rereading cases.

Sometimes Jovan read the headnotes in the case, those that quickly summarized the court's rulings at the beginning. Often he was thrilled at what he found there, but many times when he read through the entire case he noticed that the facts weren't the same as his, or the ruling was limited in some way.

He enjoyed the process, though, especially getting into the library for his hour, in part because the pressure was always there. The time was ticking. He couldn't peruse leisurely. He had to hunt. And the up-to-date books were always placed in the oddest corners or on the lowest shelf.

Jovan developed a way of reading cases quickly. He began to wonder if maybe he could represent himself. He'd heard that a lawyer who argues his own case has a fool for a client, but he felt he couldn't be any worse off than he was with the attorneys he'd had.

At night, in the dark cell, he imagined being in front of a judge or jury on his case. He played out in his mind how he would question the cops, what he would ask Anton and Jori. He wondered if the judge would allow him to put himself on the stand and question himself. He considered and then rejected the possibility of bringing in another inmate to question him.

When Jovan's PD Jim Fryman visited SuperMax, Jovan asked him questions about the law based on the cases he'd read. To Jovan, Fryman seemed a little nervous about such questions. Which only made Jovan spend more time in his cell reading.

James Fryman eventually argued and lost the motion that the first public defender had filed. After that, he met with Jovan every few months, always bringing the autopsy photos. Over and over he spread them across the table, pointing to Howard Thomas's grossly bloated face, his eyelids blue and swollen to the size of eggs, his lips split and splayed. Fryman pointed to photos of Thomas's bloodied teeth strewn about the street and to those of his brain, which had been battered about in his skull.

"You'd be better off with a plea," he told Jovan over and over.

"But I didn't touch that man," Jovan said, tired of hearing those words coming from his mouth and having the same lack of effect. "I. Did. Not. Touch. That. Man."

Fryman explained to Jovan the risks of going to trial. He told him that he'd spoken to the ASAs numerous times about reducing the charges, possibly to aggravated battery, but they were unwilling. The state offered to give Jovan eighteen years for a murder plea bargain. "I would take it," Fryman said.

Jovan declined again. Fryman said he would file a motion to suppress Jovan's "confession." But he persisted in showing the photos of Howard Thomas at every meeting.

Finally, during one such visit, Jovan hit the limits of his patience. He stood over the table and said to Fryman, "Don't bring those pictures here again. I won't look at them."

Fryman stopped bringing the photos, although he continued to recommend a plea bargain. No other options were discussed. To Fryman, the evidence against Jovan wasn't rock-solid, but there *was* a confession. As Fryman told Jovan, "You're the state's star witness against yourself."

Also, Fryman knew the state wins most criminal trials at 26th and Cal. For the state, says Steve Bogira in *Courtroom 302,* "winning is an expectation."[105] He reports that between 1996 and 2003, felony defendants in Cook County were convicted of at least one charge in 74 percent of the jury trials that ended in a verdict.[106] Add to that a signed confession, and a defendant is looking at serious consequences.

The tricky thing about written confessions, however, is that neither the judge nor the jury (nor the public defender, nor the state's attorney) can tell what conditions were present when the person signed that confession or agreed to sign it.

So Jim Fryman didn't know what the time before Jovan's confession was like. Neither did ASA Andy Varga, now assigned to the case, or even ASA Alan Murphy, who took the statement. Under current Illinois law, a confession such as Jovan's would now have to be videotaped to be admissible, a rule that aids in preventing forced confessions but which brings about its own problems (such as when the entire interrogation isn't recorded or when you can only see the face of the interrogee).[107]

Jovan and Fryman went to court, and continuances kept being granted. Flipping through the record of the case, the court orders are striking largely because they say nothing, each merely noting a new date for Jovan to appear in the future. Ultimately, Jovan's case would be "continued by agreement" seventy-five times, a very high number.

Fryman would later explain that many factors contributed to the length of time it took for Jovan's case to go to trial. "It was a capital case . . . there were four codefendants on the case. And there were retirements of at least one to three key players in the course of the trial." (The original state's attorney died and a new one, Andy Varga, was assigned. Judge Reyna was transferred and replaced by Judge Dennis Dernbach. Edwin Korb left, to be replaced by Fryman.)

But in reality, continuances are frequently granted—whether requested by one side or another—because everyone in the courtroom has to work together every day. The judge, the state's attorneys, and the public defenders are assigned to one courtroom, where, professionally, they live with each other. They see each other all the time, and so they're quick to help each other out if needed, to grant a continuance when it's suggested. Often the judges come from the state's attorney's office. Judge Denny Dernbach, a well-liked jurist, had been an ASA and the supervisor of the Felony Review Unit.[108]

There's another reason for the continuances. As Steve Bogira explains in his book, "If a judge always schedules only the cases he definitely will have time to hear in a day, he'll often be left with little to do, given the inevitable cancellations. Even the simplest 'status hearing,' in which the lawyers update the judge on progress toward trial or a plea, requires the presence of a defendant, his lawyer, the prosecutor, the judge and a court reporter. A trial or a hearing on a motion usually requires the presence of witnesses as well. Lawyers frequently get delayed in other courtrooms, witnesses get sick or arrested, and mix-ups in the jail sometimes result in a defendant not being sent over for his court date."[109] In short, a trial, particularly a felony trial, isn't a small thing to put together.

In the meantime, as Jovan described it, "the years dripped by." For the first time in his life, he read a book from cover to cover. The novel, by Donald Goines, was called *Daddy Cool.* It featured characters named Shaft and Foxy Brown, and it showed the wisdom that came from weathering the cruelty of black urban life. Jovan couldn't wait to get back to his cell to read it. He had no idea that reading could be like that. He was hooked, and he continued to read any books he could get.

———————

Jovan kept befriending the guards (also called COs, for "corrections offi-cers"), people like the sympathetic Lisa Taylor, who had wept at his poem. At his request, he was soon granted small jobs to perform. His duties included sweeping and mopping the halls, cleaning the guards' bath-rooms, and handing out trays during meals. The bathroom cleaning was the worst. Still, for six hours of work, he was given a dollar a day that went into his commissary bank. (If they remembered to pay him. Sometimes he had to beg them to do so.) More important, though, Jovan *wanted* to work, to do something with his time. He wanted to forget the grief and frustration that rose up and overtook him.

Jovan also got the guards to look the other way when he made certain adjustments to his cell, like fashioning sheets into a curtain around the toilet. Sure you could still hear your cellie taking a shit, but at least you couldn't see him. Jovan also worked to get more than one uniform. He'd always been interested in his own personal style—especially anything fea-turing the color orange—so it was killing him to have only one change of clothes in a drab khaki. And sometimes the laundry people wouldn't show up to give inmates a change of uniform or sheets. They might not show for weeks, or even a full month. The guards, when a prisoner would ask them, said, "I don't control them."

And so Jovan smiled and chatted up the laundry workers when they came to hand out clothes. He pointed at the one where the DOC on the shirt was still black, rather than a charcoal-gray. He angled for the pants that were crisper, and not as much like pajamas. Soon he had four pairs of pants and a few shirts. He missed his watches, but then again, in Super-Max time was kept by someone else. Eventually Jovan had eight changes of clothes in his cell. Not having to wear the same thing every day gave Jovan a boost, made him feel, just a little bit, like himself.

But it could all disappear in a minute. Once, after a brutal fight in which two guys were stabbed, the guards did a sweep of all the rooms, looking for weapons and taking issue with everything else that wasn't protocol.

"Who's in 310?" Jovan heard one of the guards yell while they were inspecting his room.

Jovan went to the cell door and identified himself.

The guard was throwing into the center of the room the extra sheets and blankets Jovan had begged off the laundry people. "Why do you need all this stuff?" the guard demanded.

"Because we're sleeping on sponges, man," Jovan said.

"You've got enough stuff here to open a hotel."

But a few minutes later, that wasn't true. Jovan was back to one pair of scratchy sheets for the sponge on his bed, one coarse wool blanket full of holes, and the one uniform he already wore on his back.

Jovan made friends with the inmates, too, who started to call him Big Orange, after his favorite color. They all knew that Jovan was often slow at mealtime. Food was something that he had always derived pleasure from, and even though the food at SuperMax was deplorable, he often wanted to sit and simply revel in it.

But usually that wasn't possible. Often the guards would decide that everyone needed to be in their cells immediately after a meal. "Let's go, let's go," they'd yell. "Anyone still out here is going to the hole."

"The hole" was the solitary confinement deck, a place where Jovan had never been and never wanted to go. He'd heard that the walls of the day room there, which you got to use for exactly one hour a day, were painted electric yellow (just to mess with the minds of the prisoners). The lights were intentionally glaring and bright. There was no clock, no TV, nothing to read, nothing to do. After the one hour alloted in the day room, an inmate spent the remaining twenty-three hours in his cell, alone.

The lockdowns at SuperMax continued to follow the frequent, brutal fights. Inmates might be kept in their cells for days, sometimes weeks, but Jovan's efforts with the guards paid off, and they'd let him out for a few hours, allowing him to hand out trays or sweep.

The guards even looked the other way when Jovan began making what came to be his specialty—apple pie—which he made by saving scraps from his meals. The pie was cooked on the metal table in his cell. He set a stack of milk cartons under the table and set them alight. They burned slowly from the top down, turning the table surface's into a passable stovetop.

Jovan's apple pie dough was made from old bread mixed with water or milk. He had to hustle for the bread, asking inmates to give it to him from their lunch or dinner trays, promising those who donated bread a small portion of pie when it was done. The pie filling consisted of lunchtime apples peeled with a plastic knife (this took a *long* time) and then cut into wedges. These were mixed with honey, sugar, and sometimes crumbled brownies from the commissary. Tortillas from the commissary formed the top of the pie—laid across the concoction and covered with honey. Inmates would line up outside Jovan's cell when they heard it was apple pie time. His usual recipe made enough for fifteen people.

At his request, a guard might bring him a hamburger from McDonald's. Once, he told a guard how much he missed eating rib tips, and the next time that guard arrived at work, she handed him a carry-out box. Full of rib tips. A whole order.

Jovan was so excited he pretended to cry in a jokey way. The guard laughed. For her it was simple kindness; for Jovan it was a gift from the heavens.

Jovan also worked to put a structure in place on the Christian Deck. He developed regulations that mandated Bible study (he remained one of the instructors) and general rules for the deck. For example, if someone was caught gangbanging, that inmate would be transferred from the deck. There were other rules too, like a prohibition against certain things on TV, such as *Jerry Springer,* talk shows, or soap operas. Jovan also became the go-to guy for dispute resolution among inmates.

But no matter how much control he exerted over himself or the goings-on at SuperMax, Jovan had no control over one thing: when his case would go to trial.

On the mornings he knew he had a court call, Jovan would jump out of bed at the first click of the door at three thirty a.m., not requiring the whole series of *click, click, clicks* to get him moving. If he'd been able to collect more uniforms, he would pick out the freshest one, and he would get on the bus, ready, excited, because today might be the day it would change.

Standing in the bullpens was interminable, but there lingered a sliver of hope because he was going to court. Each time he went to court he had read more cases, more statutes. Each time, he knew more about the law than he had during his last appearance.

But invariably Jovan's dream would crash, painfully. His public defender never asked whether he minded that the state's attorney wanted a continuance (or maybe the judge did, or maybe the PD himself did). It didn't matter who wanted the continuance. It was always granted, and the entire "hearing" would last mere minutes. And then it was back to the bullpen, back to the waiting.

22

"Tell that kid to have his mom call me."

The 2004 Christmas season rolled around. Jovan had been in Super-Max for nearly five years. His hard-won optimism and his hopes of getting out of there had begun to wane again.

He was sweeping the halls one day when he heard hollering. He saw a woman, obviously a lawyer, standing with a briefcase, shifting uncomfortably back and forth as prisoners who were going to and from the rec room yelled at her. And from down the hall, other inmates, who weren't supposed to be out of their cells, were slowly but surely heading her way, stalking her.

The lawyer was Catharine O'Daniel. She was in SuperMax to visit a client, a guy who had allegedly shot someone point-blank outside a 7-Eleven. He had given fourteen statements to the cops admitting to the crime. It was going to be a tough one.

After the meeting, the guards led Cathy's client back to his tier, telling her they'd return to escort her downstairs. But they didn't right away. For some reason, the guards had left her alone in one of the most violent places in Chicago.

The inmates continued to shout at Cathy, the ones on the same floor shuffling around her. In the tier above her, other inmates joined in, hanging over the railing, calling down to her. Some told her what they'd like to do to her sexually if given the chance. Others called out that she should be their lawyer, trying to ask her questions about a motion to suppress or public defenders they hadn't heard from. Still more were coming down the hall.

An occasionally trash-talking woman, Cathy could usually handle her own, but as the inmates swarmed her, she began to worry that her life would end at SuperMax. To make matters worse, she looked up and saw an inmate coming down the hall pushing a broom. In a place like SuperMax, a broom makes a great weapon.

But the inmate only approached her respectfully, keeping a distance of a few feet, then stood between her and the other inmates, giving them a shake of his head.

And at that, everyone went silent.

Cathy looked around, surprised at the responsiveness of the crowd to this inmate with the broom—a fit-looking black guy with fair skin, huge eyes, and long eyelashes.

He looked at Cathy, pointing to a wall. "If you move over there, they won't be able to see you from above."

Cathy did as he said. He was right. Once she'd moved, she could no longer be seen by the inmates on the upper tier. The ones who'd been surrounding her, shockingly, had dissipated.

She studied the inmate who'd helped her. He looked like a gentle giant. There was something about him that made her think, *This guy doesn't belong here.*

"Thanks," she said. "What kind of case are you fighting?"

"Murder."

Cathy nodded, unimpressed. "How's it going?"

"I'm not sure." Worry flitted across his features.

"Who's your judge?"

"Dernbach," the inmate said.

"He's a good guy. When's your trial date?"

"Don't have one."

"Sure you do. You should ask your lawyer."

"I have asked him." Now a look of frustration moved across his face, then disappeared just as fast. "There's no trial date."

"How long have you been here?"

"Almost five years."

Cathy almost laughed. "No, I mean here." She pointed at the ground.

"Almost five years," the inmate said, distinctly sounding out his words.

Cathy was shocked. In her practice, big cases like murder might take almost two years, but she'd never seen anything take longer than that.

"Did you go up and come back?" Meaning, *Did you get your case tried, file an appeal, have your case overturned, and wind up back in county?*

The inmate shook his head.

"What's your name?"

"Jovan Mosley."

She looked at the kid, wondered if he was a little crazy. Or maybe he was lying. *No one* was in county for five years waiting for a trial. That didn't happen in the American justice system.

She glanced around. The guards still weren't there. She decided to ask another question. "What's been happening in your case?"

Jovan told her about the motion that had been litigated, the motion to suppress his statement that was still on file. He told her about all the continuances, about the recommendation that he sign a guilty plea. He told her that he'd refused.

Standing there, Cathy felt compelled by how articulate and intelligent the guy was. In her years of practicing criminal defense law, Cathy had heard it all. She didn't get emotional about her cases. But something tugged at her gut as she listened to the inmate. If he was telling her the truth, if he'd been in there that long, the situation was deplorable. And yet she didn't notice any bitterness in his attitude.

"Where's your family? Isn't there anyone out there screaming for you?"

"I got my mom," he said. Jovan spotted a guard up the hall and waved. "Can you escort her out?"

The guard, rather than seeming put off by being directed by an inmate, nodded, said, "Sure," in a congenial way.

On her way out of the jail, Cathy stopped the guard. "What's the story with that kid? Has he really been here five years?"

The guard nodded. "And he's never given us a bit of trouble."

Cathy gave the guard her phone number. "Tell that kid to have his mom call me."

"I don't know what you did," a guard said to Jovan.

Jovan was in the day room, reading something he'd copied from the law library. He looked up, asked the guard what he meant.

"I don't know what you did to that lady lawyer, but she liked you. She said to give you or your family her phone number."

Jovan sat up straight. "For real?"

For the first time in a long, long time, he felt real hope soaring up within him and filling him up.

He went from the day room to the cells and found the guy who the female attorney had been there to visit. "What's up with your lawyer?" Jovan asked.

"She cool. Why? You thinking about going with her?"

"She gave the CO her phone number for me."

"Well, she expensive. She's charging me one hundred G's on one charge and sixty on the other."

Jovan lost that fresh hope. His family had no money. Even if they could somehow scrounge up something, it wouldn't come close to $100,000.

Still, when his mother visited the next day, he told her about the attorney.

Cathy jogged from her desk to her printer, muttering, "Let's go, let's go."

She tapped the toe of her patent leather pump and tried not to scream at the printer. She had to file this motion soon, at five o'clock, or the judge wouldn't allow it.

Cathy did all of her own paperwork, but she shared about one-tenth of a receptionist with some of the civil lawyers from whom she rented an office space.

The receptionist buzzed now. "Phone call."

"Can you tell me who it is?"

"Not sure."

"Ask, please."

They had this conversation every time.

A pause, then the receptionist came back on. "Delores Mosley."

"Yes!" Cathy said, talking to the printer, which had just finished cranking out the motion.

The receptionist thought she meant the phone call and put it through.

Cathy swore under her breath and picked up the phone with a rushed, "Catharine O'Daniel."

"Mrs. O'Daniel, the attorney?"

"Yes?" She grabbed the stapler, shoved the motion inside, and gave it a satisfying *bam* with her fist.

"Mrs. O'Daniel, this is Delores Mosley. I'm Jovan Mosley's mother."

The names didn't register right away, but Cathy had received calls from mothers of defendants before. "What's he charged with?" She stuffed her motion in her briefcase and started to search for her coat.

"Murder," the woman said. "But he didn't do it."

"Mmm-hmm. When is the bond hearing?"

"It was a long time ago."

"How much was it?" Cathy found her coat and shrugged on one sleeve.

"One and a half million."

That stopped Cathy for a second. That was a large bond, even for murder.

"We can't afford the bond," the woman said, "or a lawyer."

Cathy grimaced a little, felt bad. Never in her career had she taken a pro bono case (one that an attorney works for free). As both a solo practitioner, without an assistant or an associate, and a mother of two, she had no extra time. The lawyers she knew who did pro bono work were in big firms, where pro bono work was not only encouraged but required, and where support staff and other attorneys were plentiful.

"Mrs. Mosley," Cathy said, shrugging on the other sleeve, "I'm sorry, but I don't generally take pro bono cases."

"But my son met you. You gave him your card."

Cathy pulled her hair from the collar of her coat. And she remembered the guy from county, the one with the broom. She remembered that overwhelming feeling: *This kid doesn't belong here.* She had even talked to her sister about him after they'd met.

"He said that you gave him his card," Mrs. Mosley repeated.

"That's right."

"I just know you're going to bring my baby home!"

Whoa, Cathy thought.

"Thank you, God!" the woman continued. "I thank the Lord for you. He didn't do what they say he did."

"Well, let's talk about this. What did happen?"

"He was walking around with some boys. . . ." She told Cathy the story.

And in the same way, Cathy was touched again, felt the difference in this case from the others, from Jovan and the other inmates and defendants she'd met over the years.

She got Delores's number. "I'll look into this."

"We couldn't pay anything."

"I understand that," Cathy said. Jovan had been in county for so long, she felt an obligation to do something other than sit back and let it happen. "I won't charge anything," Cathy said. Then, to reassure Delores, she said again, "I'll look into this."

But over the next few days, Cathy regretted her promise to Delores Mosley. She was already insanely busy, not only with her legal practice but with the holidays. The pre-Christmas season was something Cathy enjoyed when she had time for it—enjoyed the shopping, the Christmas card production, the bedecking of her suburban home with thousands of lights. But she didn't have time that Christmas, and so she sprinted through her holiday preparations, ordering gifts from Amazon at three in the morning, tacking on stops to Toys "R" Us after a one-day trial on a prescription fraud case, and thinking sardonically, *Yeah, this is all about the baby Jesus.*

Every time she thought about Jovan Mosley and how she'd said she'd look into the case, she thought, *I've got a fucking bull's-eye on my back.*

And yet Christmas gave her pause. She turned the phones off, she baked, she set her table with her Lenox Christmas dishes. And as she watched her beautiful, blond children play under the tree in her beautiful home, she couldn't help but think of Jovan. What was his Christmas like at the county jail? She went over and over in her head the account of his arrest and confession. She didn't know if she believed it or not. But she knew she had the ability to do something for the kid. If she was just about clients who could give her money, what did that say about her? Right then she knew she couldn't turn her back on him.

23

"Something is really wrong here."

After the holidays, while on other business at 26th and Cal, Cathy stopped into the courtroom of Judge Dernbach, who now had Jovan's case. Cathy knew a few of the state's attorneys and a few public defenders who were assigned to Judge Dernbach's courtroom, as in most other courtrooms at 26th and Cal. So she knew someone could tell her something about Jovan's case.

Andy Varga, the lead state's attorney in Judge Dernbach's courtroom, was there. He was an excellent lawyer, well-liked around the courthouse.

"I met this kid at county," Cathy told Andy. "Jovan Mosley."

Andy, a slim, attractive guy in his thirties with prematurely gray hair, said nothing.

"He says he's been there for five years," Cathy said.

"Yeah."

"Yeah? How in the hell did that happen?"

Andy ran a hand over his face. "The case used to be in front of Reyna, but he got transferred. And before I had the case someone else did." He told Cathy about the first assistant state's attorney, who had died.

Cathy nodded grimly. She remembered the woman, who had been talented and widely respected.

"And Korb had Mosley first," Andy said, mentioning the public defender who initially had Jovan's case. "Then he ran for judge, and then Fryman got the case, and then . . ." Andy gave a helpless shrug.

"So what's the trial date?"

He shook his head.

"No trial date?"

Another shake of his head. Andy explained that a motion to suppress Jovan's statement had been filed, but it had never been litigated.

Cathy asked Andy Varga a few more questions: What were the facts of the case? How many defendants were involved? She learned that the death penalty had been dropped but the charges were still murder one and armed robbery.

That same day, Cathy called Jovan's current public defender, Jim Fryman. "Look," she said, "I'm not a bleeding heart, but I met this Mosley kid at county. And I've never taken a pro bono case before. But I'm taking this one from you."

Cathy received Jovan's file in early February 2005, just about five years after he'd arrived at SuperMax. She expected a mountain of paper, because usually a case that has been investigated for seven months after the victim dies, leading to a suspect being interrogated for almost two days, will produce reams of reports, especially General Progress Reports, or GPRs.

Cathy sat down in her immaculate home office, ready to analyze the file. But it was a mess. "It looked like it was shuffled," Cathy said, "then put on the back of a pickup truck, driven to Vegas and back, and handed to me."

And yet, as she went through the file, she realized that most of the papers were copies of documents from the other defendants' cases. The actual file for Jovan Mosley was nearly empty—unheard-of in a case in which a suspect is kept in custody so long.

Decades ago, Chicago police detectives used to keep notes on just about anything handy—scraps of paper, matchbook covers—but once such notes were made, there was no efficient way to keep them in the file.[110] And the truth was, the police were keeping two files—a street file with all those random notes in it and the official file that was turned over to the prosecutors, containing notes that usually showed only evidence of the guilt of the defendant. After a lawsuit in the early eighties revealed the deficiencies in the record-keeping process, the department created the GPR form for any notes or memoranda that the detectives might make,[111] and they also ended the "doubling filing" technique and required that detectives turn over everything, even exculpatory information that could show the possible innocence of the defendant.

So GPRs are essentially the notes that police officers take during the course of their investigation—notes they're required to take. The GPRs reflect detectives' initial thought processes and show the officers' progress on the case. The officers might note who they talked to, what that person said, a description of a scene. Many will recount when they read Miranda rights to a subject.[112] They will often detail exactly how a suspect was treated while in custody—when the suspect ate, when he went to the bathroom, what he was given to drink. And so, most important, GPRs are the means detectives use later during court proceedings to show the quality of treatment a suspect received, and, if a confession is involved, the degree to which it was voluntary.

Generally, a GPR is handwritten and kept by a detective until the detective has the opportunity to put it in the office file.[113] As a matter of course, the original GPRs are then kept in the office file. The time they were placed into the file would be noted at the bottom.[114] Detectives usually kept copies of the originals, depending on the type of investigation.[115]

But as Cathy waded through Jovan's file she realized that Jovan Mosley had no GPRs. Not one.

Cathy also expected to find supplementary reports. Usually called "supps," such reports are typically typewritten summaries of the investigation, created by using information from the GPRs. Once a supplementary report is completed, it's sent electronically to the sergeant for review.[116] When approval is given, one copy is placed in the office file and another sent to the computerized records department. In addition, any detective who had authored the supplemental would usually keep a copy,[117] as would the supervisor. Detectives also often kept such reports in their desk drawers, even after their cases had closed.

At a minimum, then, three copies of an approved supp should be available.[118] If an investigation leads to charges being filed, all GPRs and supps get copied and turned over to the state's attorneys, while the originals are stored at the station. When a defense attorney accepts a new client, the attorney, in turn, is provided with copies of all these documents.

Jovan's file had only two supps, again a very small amount for a murder investigation with someone held in custody for a long time.

Cathy separated what little there was in Jovan's file from the copies of the other defendants' documents. All she had then were Jovan's arrest record, the confession written by ASA Alan Murphy, a supp authored by Detectives Hill and Williams, and only one other supp, which was essentially a lineup report. She took a closer look at the first supp. It indicated that it was a final report regarding the interrogations of Jovan and Marvin Treadwell. Treadwell's lineup was summarized, which was standard, but there was no mention at all of Jovan's lineup. Even stranger, the supplementary report hadn't been authored contemporaneously with Jovan's interrogation or even shortly afterward, which would have been standard. Instead it had been created three and a half months later.

Cathy then studied the supp that described the lineup and realized it had been created *a year and a half* after Jovan had been in custody, even though there was a photo taken of the men in the lineup. Cathy had seen a lot of lineup reports in her career, but she'd never seen one created that late in the investigation. Like GPRs, lineup reports are generally authored at the time of the investigation. In fact, department procedure requires lineup reports to be submitted to the supervisor within ten days.[119] Chicago cops are taught how to write those documents when they are in the academy, and as with other reports, the original lineups are placed in the office file and a copy sent to the records department.[120]

But as she scrutinized the lineup more, things kept getting stranger. The report had, she realized, been prepared only in response to the motion filed by Edwin Korb, Jovan's first public defender, and only, the record said, because no original lineup reports existed in Jovan's file.

Cathy reviewed the other defendants' lineups. Were those reports concerning Frad, Marvin, and Red authored at the time of their interrogations? They were. Even more curious, those lineup reports, unlike Jovan's, listed *exactly* what each of those defendants had been identified as doing in the beating of Howard Thomas. Jovan's lineup, however, stated only that he had been "identified" by Anton Williams. Nothing indicated what Anton had identified Jovan as doing, if anything.

Cathy began to organize the mess of papers, separating into additional stacks the documents having to do with each of the other defendants. All of their files, she found, contained numerous supplementary reports and even more numerous GPRs. GPRs even existed for the interrogation of Fetta. In fact, in what seemed like a hard slap in the face to Jovan, Fetta had *handwritten* his own GPR, waxing poetic with statements like, *Jason [sic] you really didn't do anything but passed a couple licks maybe God will forgive you.* And *Anton and Jory, I'm sorry you had to witness this just as well as myself but look at the bright side I got hit y'all didn't. (Laughs.)*

Cathy looked out the window of her office. It wasn't much past five in the afternoon, yet it was already dark. She picked up the phone and called a few cops and lawyers she knew. Had anyone ever seen a GPR written by a suspect? she asked, telling them about Fetta's self-written GPR. The answer was a resounding no. How was it possible, she kept asking herself, that Jovan Mosley didn't have a single GPR in his file and yet Fettuccini Alfredo or whatever they called him, had gotten to write his own? It was unbelievable. All of it, absolutely unbelievable.

24

"If I lose this case, he's going to disappear for good."

Jovan Mosley was woken at three thirty a.m., just like any other day. But today he had court, and so it was easier to get up. He still had hope enough to endure the strip search, to stand in the bullpens shoulder to shoulder with hundreds of other inmates for hours, to wait for his case to be called, to step into the courtroom. It was only when he usually heard, *Continued by agreement,* that his optimism was drowned.

But something was different this time. Someone extra sat at the tables in front of the judge. It was that lawyer. Catharine O'Daniel. He felt his heart quicken.

A few minutes later, his case was called, and the blond lawyer stood from the table. "Your Honor," she said in a clear, loud voice. "Catharine O'Daniel appearing on behalf of Jovan Mosley."

Afterward, she made her way over to him. "Congratulations," she said, shaking his hand. "You're my first pro bono case."

Jovan had tried not to smile for years. Too much emotion on display in SuperMax could get you into trouble. But he couldn't help it now. He couldn't stop grinning.

Cathy and Jovan began meeting regularly over the next few months. She was the first attorney, he felt, to treat him like a human being. She was the first to actually provide him with his file, meager as it was. She also gave him the other defendants' complete files. She told him she was perform-ing the laborious task of collecting evidence, analyzing the files of all four defendants, and talking to potential witnesses five years after the fact. She asked what had happened to the other guys who were there that night when Howard Thomas died.

Frad was still at SuperMax, although on a different deck, so Jovan rarely saw him.

Marvin and Red, meanwhile, had both been found guilty of first-degree murder. Jovan had no idea what had become of Fetta.

By that time, I had been fortunate enough to publish five novels. My sabbatical from the law had been great initially, just a small break. But then my firm was bought out by a larger one and I had a decision to make—go back into big firm life, which would leave little time for writing, or cut myself loose. I was scared as hell, but I decided to keep writing, keep trying to get published. As time stretched, the long sabbatical seemed rather pitiful. But luck came in the form of a cocktail party at a writers' conference, where I would meet an editor who would buy my first (and, ultimately, next six) books. I started calling myself a "lapsed lawyer," although I was an adjunct professor at the law school of my alma mater, Loyola University Chicago.

During the first half of 2005, I researched my sixth book, *The Rome Affair*, a novel about a trip to Italy that leads to blackmail and murder. Ultimately, a Chicago society couple in the book is charged with murder, taken to the Belmont Police Station, and interrogated. My fictional detectives attempt to force the couple into confessing using lies and subterfuge. I had already interviewed homicide detectives, and they confirmed that detectives frequently lie to suspects, but I wondered if I was overplaying the interrogation in the book.

In the meantime, a mystery bookshop called Centuries & Sleuths held a book signing for my most recent book, *Look Closely*. The truth about book tours and signings is that occasionally they are glamorous: when my first Italian-translated novel was released, I found myself in Milan, where the front windows of huge bookstores were devoted to my book and designed by an Armani stylist. But book events can be humbling too. An example: the same book that landed me in Milan also put me at the opening of a grocery store in South Bend. I was placed near the frozen foods, where I shivered and gazed at the "massive PR" I'd been promised, which consisted of a tiny head shot of me in the weekly coupon handout (right below an ad for 45-cent green beans).

Everyone in my life had heard book-tour tales of woe. Wanting to spare herself another one, my friend Beth Kaveny rounded up people to attend the signing, which happened to be in her hometown. Included in that group was Cathy O'Daniel, with whom Beth shared her office space.

I was flattered that Cathy came to the signing. During the few times we'd met, I'd been enamored of her brash-talking sense of fun, her terrific confidence, and her hilarious, self-deprecating humility.

After the signing, four of us went to dinner at an Italian restaurant. During dinner, Cathy and I sat next to each other. She asked what I was working on, and I told her about *The Rome Affair*. I asked her if the cops ever really coerced someone into confessing. Although allegations of brutality by Jon Burge and other detectives at Area 2 had been reported in Chicago, forced confessions or wrongful convictions weren't making a lot of current headlines, and I had a hard time envisioning how a forced confession could happen. If someone was trying to force me into a murder confession, I reasoned, there wouldn't be anything they could do to make me say I did it.

"So really," I said to Cathy, "do forced confessions ever happen?"

Cathy shot me a sympathetic look at my apparent naïveté. "Oh, honey, do I have a forced confession story for you."

She gestured at the waitress for more wine and, glass in hand, turned to me, giving me the bare bones of the story—she was representing a kid named Jovan who had been present for part of a fight but not involved in it. The cops had taken into custody all the kids there that night, and they'd chained Jovan to a wall for nearly two days until he said he threw two punches. They told him two punches wasn't murder.

"Then what happened?"

"They charged him with death-penalty murder and put him in Division Eleven. It's a campus of criminality. All the . . ." She paused. "All the *allegedly* worst criminals in the city are there. His arrest was over five years ago, but he's still there."

She took another sip of her wine, looking across the table as one of the other women propelled the group into another story. Meanwhile, I sat there unnerved by the thought of the kid in the holding cell.

When we were into our second bottle of wine, I commandeered Cathy again, asking her more about the forced-confession case. "When is the trial?"

"I'm pushing for it ASAP, but I have to litigate the motion to suppress his statement first. I'd love to get the confession thrown out and get him out of there without a trial. If that doesn't work, it should be set for this summer." She went on to describe a big case, such as a murder trial, as "a chess game that will give you the worst diarrhea you've ever had."

"What happens if you lose?"

She closed her eyes for a minute and shook her head. "Imagine. I have this kid who doesn't have a fucking thing in his life, and he's stripped down to nothingness. He's barely hanging on. If I lose this case, he's going to disappear for good."

The story of Jovan Mosley stuck with me, and so did the concept of forced confessions. I kept working on that part of the story in *The Rome Affair*, imagining my characters pitted against seasoned detectives. A few months later, I was working on the book in a coffee shop, and I stepped outside to call Cathy. When she answered I told her I had more questions about forced confessions, such as, how do they actually get someone to confess to something that isn't true?

Cathy told me the cops used a host of tactics—outright lying, seclusion of the suspect, sleep deprivation, lack of food and water. She told me about Jovan in particular, about how he was cuffed to a wall for at least a day and a half, probably more, by a ring around his wrist. (It was hard to tell the timing, she said, because the police records were so meager).

As she spoke, I looked across the street at an idyllic park where people ran their dogs and chased their kids.

"He didn't eat, sleep, or use the bathroom that whole time," Cathy said. "And now he's *still* in jail."

"Jesus." In the park, a group of teenage boys began a softball game. "Do you take a lot of pro bono cases?"

"I'm a virgin." She laughed. "He's my first." Her laugh disappeared. "He's the one client in my entire career that I believe in fully. I mean absolutely one hundred percent."

"So how do you represent those other people? The ones you don't believe in completely?"

"Everyone is entitled to a fair arrest, a fair interrogation, a fair trial. Someone has to be in place to make sure that happens."

"But what if they're guilty?"

"A lot of times I don't ask that question. That's what people forget when they think about criminal lawyers—we weren't given the power to determine guilt or innocence. The Constitution gave that job to the judge or jury. The lawyers are simply there to make sure both sides get a fair trial."

Cathy explained that many people think ill of criminal defense lawyers for representing people who might be guilty of the crime charged. But the point of criminal defense representation is not necessarily to find people you think are innocent and then fight for them. And it's not to find people you think are guilty and get them off. The point is to fight for their rights, the due-process rights all of us have. If we didn't have those rights, Cathy believed, we as a society would have very, very little. Even those who appeared to have been involved in a crime in some way deserve those rights. We can't dole out such rights only to people who might be innocent.

And after working on Jovan's case, Cathy said, she knew Jovan had received few, if any, of his rights. The worst part, she reiterated, was that she believed in him. "There's nothing more stressful than representing someone you think is innocent." Thinking about it some more, she added, "They come along almost never."

"And a murder trial can't be a small feat."

She sighed. "It's not." She described how much work was involved, how hard it would be to convince a jury to say "not guilty" to a guy who'd signed a confession. She told me how overworked she already was. With no secretary, no associate, Cathy was a one-man band.

"I'll do some research if you need it," I offered. "Maybe write your motions."

I tried to think of what other assistance I could give her. The legal world was so specialized, particularly in urban areas like Chicago, that a civil litigator like myself would likely never have the occasion, or the skill, to work on a complicated criminal matter like a murder trial.

"I could write the jury instructions too," I said.

"Sold." Cathy got off the phone before I could change my mind.

The "practice of law" truly is a practice; it requires paying attention every single day, during every single case. So many areas of law exist that no one can know them all. Even experts find their fields of law constantly in flux, sometimes subtly, sometimes not, and often very different from state to state or from federal court to county court.

I was reminded of this when Cathy called me a month or two later saying she was ready for some research on the Jovan Mosley case. The first issue, she said, was about the people who wanted to testify for Jovan—his boss from a job in high school, neighbors from his old neighborhood, friends of his family, and Marsha Adger, the woman Jovan knew from prison ministry. Could we use these people? she wanted to know. What was the state of the law in Illinois on bringing character witnesses into a murder trial?

She also needed the current *Batson* cases, she told me, meaning any Illinois cases interpreting the U.S. Supreme Court opinion that says, essentially, potential jurors can't be excused solely on their race. *Batson* "objections" are always tossed back and forth during jury selection, and so she needed to know what any recent courts had said.

I asked Cathy if the trial was still scheduled for the summer. It was nearly June by then, and Chicago was just starting to wake up from a long winter that had, inevitably, bled into spring.

She told me the trial wasn't set for the summer. The motion to suppress the confession that Cathy had litigated had eaten up a lot of time, because it was essentially a mini-trial, requiring that the detectives who were subpoenaed all be available to testify on the same day and the lawyers and judge be available too. The judge had denied the motion, but she wasn't surprised. They were tough motions to win, she said, especially in Cook County.

In *Courtroom 302*, Steve Bogira says, "Through the years, Cook County judges have largely . . . suppress[ed] confessions only when the evidence of coercion is overwhelming—and often not even then."

So now the trial was scheduled for the fall, Cathy said. And she also needed help on certain jury instructions. Jury instructions are written guidelines that are read to a jury at the close of evidence and sent back into the jury room with them, telling them exactly what they need in order to find someone guilty or to let that person free. While basic instructions exist for different criminal charges (or different types of civil lawsuits), in Illinois those instructions are slightly tailored at the end of each trial based on the individual case. Hence the submitting and arguing of instructions is one of the most important things a trial lawyer does. This meant that if Cathy could get an instruction that would make it even a little harder to convict Jovan, it would help. But lawyers have to be ready at the *beginning* of a trial to argue their proposed instructions to the judge because they have to try and prove those instructions during the course of the trial.

Given my civil background, an instruction called "the accountability instruction," was one I couldn't quite get my head around.

"If you're in for a penny, you're in for a pound," was how Cathy explained it. "So if you took an action that in any way, even a very small way, led to someone's death, you're still accountable for the whole of his death."

"So if the jury believes Jovan's confession that he threw two punches—"

"He's cooked."

I hadn't even met this Jovan guy, but something hard formed in my stomach at Cathy's words. When I represented doctors, the actions of defendants were essentially apportioned. If one doctor amputated the wrong leg on a patient, for example, and later a different doctor prescribed an antibiotic, causing a rash, both doctors could be found guilty. But the jury would probably hit the first doctor with a massive verdict, while the doctor who had only contributed a four-day rash would likely be found liable for a much, much smaller amount of money. So in civil cases, we were always looking for how much a person contributed to an injury. Even the plaintiff could be found negligent and contributing to his own injury, which would reduce the verdict.

But when considering the horrible death of Howard Thomas, the jury wouldn't be asked to parcel out who caused more damage. If a man had something to do with that fight—whether he swung a bat fifty times or a landed a single punch somewhere benign like on the man's calf—the accountability instruction said that person would be guilty of murder.

———

Cathy and I began talking frequently on the phone. In addition to discussing Jovan, we talked about our lives, the many other things we were working on. I loved hearing about Cathy's cases. She was negotiating an international crisis surrounding a kidnapping and murder in Mexico. Her case, concerning a well-respected businessman accused of stealing prescription pads from his doctor's office (and writing lots of them), was heating up. The criminal arena Cathy ran in seemed like the Wild West, and Cathy was the one out there in the dust, wearing the handmade boots and the stylish cowboy hat.

The more we talked about Jovan's case, the more she threw out comments like, "You should try this case with me."

I laughed whenever she said that. Except for teaching, I'd been on hiatus from the law for five years. I hadn't been in front of a jury in all that time, I told Cathy, and although I had tried civil cases, on the criminal side of things I'd never even handled a parking ticket, much less a murder.

"You can do it," Cathy said. "You never forget how to try a case." She seemed to be likening a jury trial to riding a bike.

"I'm telling you, I don't know the criminal system at all. What would I do?"

"You're an expert on the medical stuff, so you could cross-examine the coroner. You could also question potential jurors, argue the motions, put lay witnesses on the stand."

She had a point. It had taken years of legal practice, but now I could do those things well. Still, I said, "I don't know . . ." I thought about it. "Don't you need a certification to try a murder case?" I'd heard that to obtain that certification, the court required an attorney to have at least eight felony trials, including two murder cases, under your belt.

"Only the lead attorney needs that. And don't worry. I've got it." When I didn't say anything, she kept talking. "I need help. Really. This is my first pro bono case. I've got so much other shit going on."

Although I was helping Cathy by writing her motions and the proposed jury instructions, Cathy still had to prepare for every single witness who might be called at trial. And according to the disclosure she'd gotten from the state's attorney, that could be just about anybody whose name appeared in any police file about Howard Thomas's death.

I thought about my schedule. I'd turned in *The Rome Affair,* but it still needed to be edited. I was under contract for *The Good Liar*, but it still needed to be written. I'd sold article proposals to *Lake* magazine, and those articles also needed to be written. And I needed to teach my law school class. But the fact was that with the exception of the class, which was once a week, my schedule was mine to set. I could write in the middle of the night if I wanted. I could also, I realized, with a lot of shuffling, work into my schedule the preparation and trial of a murder case, something I'd *never* have been able to do if I'd still been practicing civil law. I was a writer; my time was my own.

And the story of Jovan Mosley was impossible to ignore.

"Yeah, okay," I said finally. "I'll try it with you. But just remember that this is different from what I'm used to dealing with."

"Yeah," Cathy said in a wry, mischievous tone, "you'll find out that things work just a little different in criminal courtrooms."

Understatement. Massive understatement.

25

"I believe in him too much.
I need you to do it."

Without really thinking it over, I'd agreed to second-chair a murder trial. If I *had* thought about it, I might have mulled over the reality that I had no real understanding of what a murder trial entailed. I might have contemplated the fact that I'd left the law for a very good reason—I liked it, but I didn't love it. Writing, I loved. And I had lots of writing to do. Instead, I found myself researching the law of accountability, poring over Howard Thomas's autopsy records, and studying my old *Fundamentals of Trial Techniques.*

The more I thought about Jovan's situation, imagining myself in a windowless room for almost two days with no food and no bathroom, I found it wasn't that difficult for me to believe Jovan had been coerced. I'm a mess if I get only six hours of sleep a night, I go to the bathroom fifty times a day, and if I don't eat every few hours I feel faint. If you put *me* in a room for two days with no sleep, no food, and no bathroom, I realized, I'd probably tell you that my mother killed Kennedy.

But for me, the hurdle was the police records. Not Jovan's, necessarily, since there was almost nothing in his file. It was the records of the other defendants that threw me. They reminded me that in matters of memory, nothing is certain. There is no science to back you up.

The police records were a maze—an absolute mass of notes and typed text and summaries of he-said, she-said, they-said, all filtered through the cops' biases, judgments, preconceived notions, authoritarianism, and genuine desire for justice.

And everything in the Howard Thomas files conflicted. Some witness said three guys were fighting with Thomas, others said four, still others said several or between three and five. Sometimes the witnesses contradicted themselves. There were a number of people around at the time of the incident, but no one seemed to remember it straight. Certainly, no clear picture emerged from the witness statements. One thing that was evident was that none of the independent witnesses (those who were innocent bystanders during the fight) said that Jovan (or anyone who looked like him, etc.) had done anything.

As for the other guys who'd been in the fight, again the reports were confusing. One indicated that Frad didn't place Jovan in the action. In another report, according to detective notes, Frad said "everyone" had been in the fight. In his final statement, the confession taken by the state's attorney, Frad said nothing about Jovan whatsoever.

Lawrence "Red" Wideman identified the boys who were in the fight as Frad, himself, and Marvin. He didn't describe Jovan as being part of it. As I studied Red and Frad's confessions, I noticed both were written by the same state's attorney, both almost word-for-word the same. Neither mentioned Jovan being in the fight.

But according to Marvin Treadwell's video confession, "my guy," a guy named "Jason," was part of the group and everyone in the group, he said, had hit Howard Thomas a few times. Other than that general comment, there was no mention of Jovan or of the few punches he'd supposedly taken.

During Marvin's and Red's cases, both of them had filed motions that required the detectives—the same who had interrogated Jovan—to testify in court.[121] I read the transcript for Red's hearing. Detective Howard testified that Red was "asked if he wanted to take a polygraph." They told Red that "what he was saying didn't add up" and "a polygraph would help clear up some of the issues." Officer Bartik also testified about Red's polygraph. They had given it to him, he said, because Red was denying participation in the death of Howard Thomas. "Mr. Wideman was not acknowledging any participation at all [in the death of Howard Thomas], and that is the reason why he was there, to take a polygraph."[122]

I went over that testimony more than once. Interesting, because Jovan had requested a lie detector test but had never been given one.

―――――――

There's an old joke that asks, *Why is procrastination like masturbation?* Answer: *It feels good while you're doing it, but in the end you realize you're fucking yourself.*

Procrastination and the art of screwing oneself are two things every trial lawyer is acquainted with.

Trials are essentially live theater. Like theater, trials require preparation, which attorneys often put off until the last minute, and yet such theater also requires constant improvisation and great bluster. And existing alongside all this—always, always—is the knowledge that any minute you might make a misstep and find you've completely ruined yourself. But unlike theater, trials are productions in which fortunes can be lost. Or in this case, Jovan's life.

In civil cases, nearly every witness—from the big ones (the surgeons who cut off the wrong limb) to the small (the janitorial worker who carted the leg away)—is deposed ahead of time. And usually those depositions last for a long time (so long that state courts in Illinois had to adopt rules mandating that depositions last no longer than three hours unless expressly agreed to by the parties or ruled upon by the judge). The point is that when those witnesses get to court, civil trial lawyers know nearly everything a witness is supposed to say.

So when I told Cathy I could cross-examine the coroner, I'd assumed there would be a deposition of her.

"Nope," Cathy said.

"Well, how am I supposed to know what she's going to say?"

"You've got her report."

"Yeah, but you should have been able to grill her about that report in a dep."

"You don't get to do that in criminal cases."

I blinked. "Seriously?"

"Yeah, there's no pretrial discovery in Illinois for criminal cases."

"Well, then how am I supposed to get ready to cross her?"

"She did testify briefly at the trial for Marvin and Red."

"Yeah, I've seen that. There's barely anything there."

"Yep."

In Loving Memory
of

Howard Thomas, Jr.

WEDNESDAY, AUGUST 11, 1999

Wake 10:00 A.M.   Funeral 11:00 A.M.

SOLID ROCK TEMPLE CHURCH
7757 South Greenwood
Chicago, Illinois

Rev. John R. Thomas

The program for Howard Thomas's funeral.

A bungalow, near 73rd and Calumet, where the fight happened.

Howard Thomas's fast food bag at the scene of the fight.

Blood found at the scene of the fight.

Frad Muhammad.

Marvin Treadwell.

Gregory "Fettuccine Corleone" or "Fetta" Reed.

Frad Muhammad (far left in "Paco Sport" shirt) and Lawrence "Red" Wideman
(third from left), Gregory "Fettuccine Corleone" or "Fetta" Reed
(third from right in plaid shirt).

Jovan Mosley around the time of his line up.

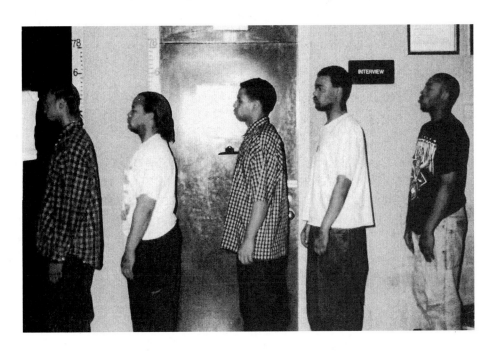

Jovan Mosley line up.

Jovan Mosley in younger days.

A few days after the Mosley verdict. From left to right:
Laura Caldwell (author), Jovan, and Catherine O'Daniel.
Photograph courtesy of the author

Laura and Jovan at a Loyola Law banquet, where Laura received
an alumni award, in part for her work on the Mosley case.
Photograph by Lucy A. Kennedy/Kennedy Photography

The groomsmen at Jovan's wedding, along with Laura as Best "Man."
Photograph by Joseph Gordon

Jovan and Andrea Mosley at their wedding, along with the foreperson
of his jury, Andrea Schultz. *Photograph by Joseph Gordon*

"Doesn't the other side have to tell you what testimony they expect from her?" In civil cases, we not only took a pretrial deposition of every witness, we were also required to summarize for opposing counsel, before the trial, the testimony we intended to get from those witnesses.

"Nah. They just say she'll testify to cause of death, and that's it."

"So no deps, no testimony disclosure, nothing." Again I imagined Cathy in those cowboy boots with the cool hat. "What is this, the Wild, Wild West?"

"Something like that."

I started telling people I was second-chairing a murder trial. My old attorney friends were concerned. Did I still have a license? they wondered. Did I even remember how to pick a jury or cross-examine a witness? I began to worry along with them. The truth was I was a little foggy on my trial skills.

When my husband, Jason, learned I'd be representing Jovan, he nodded, always supportive. He thought it was atrocious that Jovan had been in county jail as long as he had, and as he said, nearly every high school guy had been near a fight and decided not to get into it. I began to feel better and better about having Jovan Mosley as a client.

Then I made the mistake of seeing the movie *Capote*. I hadn't heard much about it, although I knew it dealt in some way with Truman Capote's writing about the murders that led to his book *In Cold Blood*. I assumed, however, that in addition to the tragic story of the Clutter family from Holcolm, Kansas, there would be a lot of writing-life-in-Manhattan kind of stuff. I anticipated witty literati and fabulous parties. Instead, I got a gritty movie about a writer who gets involved in a murder trial and whose life skids off the rails, never to publish another book because of it. I put my popcorn on the floor and nudged it away, wondering if I was somehow witnessing my own future.

When I left the movie it was gray and rainy outside. I stumbled up the street thinking, *Why in the name of all things holy have I agreed to defend an accused murderer? I don't know how to try a criminal case. I don't want to be invested in someone whose friends beat the shit out of a fifty-one-year-old man. Even if he didn't do it, why do I need to get involved with this?*

And then I started thinking about the cops. The truth is I'm a cop groupie. I think that cops, and the Chicago PD in particular, are amazing people who do an amazingly hard job. The cops in Chicago have always been great to me. Many of them hang out at the 7-Eleven across the street from my house, and I spend lots of time over there, picking their brains for information I can use in my mystery novels. So it was hard for me to believe that the brethren of the cops I knew would keep a nineteen-year-old kid locked in a room for a couple of days and force him to say he was in a fight when they should have known he wasn't.

I arrived home from the movie full of doubt about Jovan Mosley, whom I'd never met and now seriously doubted whether I wanted to meet at all. I felt as if everything in my life was about to change, and not for the better. I attributed this oncoming desolation to the murder trial. I probably should have been looking a little closer.

Cathy called early one morning. "I'm planning a visit to the jail," she said. "I have to get Jovan ready because he wants to take the stand."

"How do you get him ready?"

"Cross-examine him the way a state's attorney would at trial. Problem is, I don't think I can do it. I'm too involved. I believe in him too much. I need you to do it. Are you in?"

"Hell, yes." With my Capote depression still coursing through me, kicking up despondent thoughts, I relished the task. I had lots of questions now about Mr. Mosley and his case. And if I didn't believe him, I'd have to excuse myself from representing him. I understood now the reasons why Cathy worked as a criminal defense lawyer, but I knew I wouldn't be able to handle the case if I couldn't truly get behind our client.

I heard Cathy's young son say something in the background about losing his magician's cape and wand and about needing to bring them to school.

"I have your wand," Cathy said to him. "I'm taking it to court to try to get a woman out on bond who beat the crap out of her husband *and* the cops."

Silence from her son.

"Kidding," she said. "It's in your superhero box."

26

"I'm here to see a client."

For my visit to the jail, I dressed in a tan suit, heels, and a pink wool coat. No matter that this was a jail visit, this was a potential client, and I'd been taught to dress up for client meetings.

I'd been to the courthouse at 26th and Cal only once before for jury duty, but I'd quickly been dismissed. And yet it was impossible to forget the feel of the air there. Its atmosphere was cruel and zingingly alive. Within a block of the place now, I felt it again, felt my pulse quicken.

Across the street from the courthouse was an abused cement parking garage. Cathy had only told me that Division 11 was at 26th and Cal, so I parked in the garage and went inside the courthouse to ask where the jail was.

A bored bailiff pointed to a smaller brick building to the right of the more utilitarian side of the courthouse. I went there and got in the security line behind about eight other people. I threw my leather bag on the conveyor belt and walked through the metal detector, just the way I did in civil court, picking up my bag on the other side.

A sheriff stood on the other side with a clipboard. He gave me a friendly smile and asked where I was headed.

"I'm here to see a client." The words gave me a strange thrill. I used to visit my clients—physicians—in the well-appointed offices of their medical practices. This was a whole new world.

"Client's name?"

"Jovan Mosley."

The sheriff consulted a document on a clipboard. He flipped a few pages back, then forward again. "M-o-s-l-e-y?" he said.

"Yes."

"He's not in here."

I could feel my brow furrow. "He's been here for forever."

A shrug. "Maybe somebody posted bond."

"No, the bond is like a million dollars. He's about to go to trial."

Now it was the sheriff's turn to make a confused face. "What's he in for?"

"Murder one and armed robbery."

"Whoa. Then he's definitely not here."

"I was told this was the jail."

"Yeah, it's one of them, but he's in Division Eleven. We keep those guys apart from everyone else. You know the white building?"

"No."

"When you leave here, look to your right and you'll see it. That's where your client is."

I looked at my watch. I'd been exactly on time for the meeting, but now this whole thing had made me late. "Thanks." I sprinted out of the facility, looking right as directed.

I was surprised I hadn't seen it on my way in. There in the distance, across a few empty blocks, was a monolithic building with no windows. In contrast to the rest of the dingy neighborhood, the building was an odd, almost gleaming white.

"You're late," Cathy said congenially when I walked in. She was dressed in jeans and a sweatshirt, no makeup on her face, and her blond hair in a ponytail. She had brought Eddie, her husband. He was also in jeans, and he waved hello.

I apologized and told her about ending up at the wrong jail.

She laughed, then looked me up and down once. Then again, stopping at my pink coat. "What in the hell are you wearing?"

Apparently one didn't dress for one's clients at SuperMax.

I lied and said that I'd had a lunch meeting with some other law professors.

She chuckled. "Go." She pointed to an area with metal detectors and other high-tech security machines.

In addition to the usual screening of bags and coats and such, a visitor also had to step into a tunnel known as the Puffer. You stood still, arms outstretched, while the Puffer shot noisy gusts of air all over your body. My hair flew up and out, my coat billowed around me.

A technician sat at the end of the tunnel, reading a screen. After about a minute of feeling like I was on the roof deck of the Hancock Center, the tech said, "You're fine."

I made my way through the now-silent tunnel, trying to smooth my hair and my clothes. "What was that machine?" I called to Cathy.

"It puffs air into your skin and clothes, then pulls it back in and analyzes it for gunpowder or signs that you've been drinking or doing drugs in the last twenty-four hours. If you've got anything like that in your system, they'll put you through tougher screening in case you're trying to smuggle something into the jail."

I thought back to the bottle of wine I'd had the other night with a friend. Thankfully that had been forty-eight hours before.

A guard searched my bag, then eyed it. "You're not supposed to bring bags in," she said.

"But I need it," I told her. "We're meeting a client, and I've got my notes in there." I was also thinking about my bottle of water and my lip gloss, neither of which I liked parting with for too long.

The guard glanced at my pink coat, shook her head at me, and waved me through.

"They let you in with that bag?" Cathy said in amazement when I reached her at the elevators.

I shrugged.

Cathy, Eddie, and I were escorted into an elevator by two armed guards. There were no buttons in the elevator, and our arrival was announced via an intercom, through which a request was made to take us to the third floor. Once we reached it, we were escorted into an anteroom and locked in. The other side was then opened by more armed guards, who led us down a hallway and into another elevator, where the process was repeated. The guards said nothing, just eyed us.

With each foray deeper and deeper into the bowels of Division 11, I grew more and more nervous. I had never been in a prison before. And although I'd been looking forward to questioning Jovan Mosley and flexing my trial skills, now that I was *inside,* anxiety coursed through me.

By the time we reached the intended floor, I was entirely discombobu-
lated. Months later, I would marvel when six inmates escaped from Division 11. I couldn't have made my way out of there with four grenades and
a map.

The final set of guards led us into a recreation room with an old pool
table. "All the meeting rooms are taken," one said. Then they locked us in.

When they were gone, Eddie eyed two cue sticks across the room.
"Those would make great weapons."

I gulped and felt my body temperature drop. In my head, I heard the
high-toned, pithy voice of Truman Capote saying, *What are you doing, you
silly, silly girl?*

Cathy shrugged. "The guards trust Jovan."

Just then the door opened, and Jovan Mosley stepped inside.

My first thought when I saw Jovan, dressed in county-issue baggy tan
pants and a shirt reading DOC, was, *What a sweet kid.* He had fair almond
skin and wide round eyes with the kind of long curly eyelashes girls love.
In the police photo I'd seen of him, he'd sported an Afro, but now his hair
was cropped close to his head. A trim beard rimmed his jaw. He wasn't
tall—probably only five-nine or so—but he was a big dude, easily wearing
an XXL shirt over his broad shoulders. Yet when he smiled at Cathy (sort
of a sad, I'm-so-happy-to-see-you smile) he just seemed like a big kid. He
shook hands with me, giving me a shy nod.

Cathy asked Jovan how he was doing.

"Okay," he said.

None of us believed him. I looked around the linoleum-clad room
thinking of how long he'd been in this place.

Cathy introduced Eddie. Then pointed at me. "She's helping me out on
your case. She's going to try it with me."

Jovan's gaze held mine. "Thank you," he said softly.

Then Jovan asked the questions. He asked Cathy about the trial,
about witnesses who might be called and evidence he thought should be
excluded. He had clearly scrutinized the file from front to back, along with
the files of the other guys he'd been with that night. I remembered hearing
from Cathy that Jovan had always wanted to be a lawyer, that he'd actu-

ally worked for a firm during high school. Most kids I knew worked at the Dairy Queen during high school, if they worked at all. I was impressed with him. I was swayed by his intellect, I admit. But I still didn't know if I believed that he hadn't thrown a couple of punches in that fight.

So when Cathy told Eddie and me to "go ahead," meaning question the hell out of him, neither of us held back. Did Jovan expect us to believe that he just stood there watching a fight while all his buddies were in it? we asked. And if he *was* just standing there, why not try to stop it, why not call the cops? And why was he walking around with kids who were carrying bats? Why did someone need to carry a bat? Did they drink that night? Were they drunk? Had they done any drugs?

Jovan answered each of our questions with a frustrated but calm demeanor. We had to understand his neighborhood, he said. Fights happened on a regular basis, and *everyone* watched. It was just how it went. Jovan pointed to the witnesses in the case—two brothers in their fifties, a young woman and her boyfriend—all of whom had watched the fight. No one had called the cops, except the brothers, and they didn't call until the fight was long over. No one had tried to stop it. That's how it happened in that neighborhood.

Yes, they'd had a few beers, he'd told us, but that was it. And his buddy Frad always carried a bat. Again, it was that kind of neighborhood.

"I didn't touch that guy," Jovan told us, just as he'd told the cops that night. He had seen only the beginning of the fight, then when the bat came out he walked over to the porch where Jori and Anton sat, his back to the fight. When he realized it wasn't going to end soon, he thought, *Someone is going to get into trouble,* and took off. The guys caught up to him after a few minutes. And that was that. "I didn't touch that guy."

We kept questioning him for hours. It got heated, it got ugly. Eddie and I scoffed when he said he hadn't hit Howard Thomas. We nitpicked every recollection he had, purposely confusing him about certain details and eventually making him cry.

But Jovan never wavered about one thing. "I didn't touch that man," he told us over and over.

I searched his eyes for some indication that this was just a story he had told himself. I saw only pure conviction.

Three hours later, as we stood to leave, Cathy peppered Jovan with a series of instructions about how he needed to prepare for the trial, what he needed to wear.

"And I need you to shave that," she said, pointing at his minimal beard.

"What?" He put a protective hand on his jaw.

"I know you're twenty-five years old, but I want the jury to see you as you were when you were nineteen—a nice kid who wasn't in that fight."

"Nah, I can't cut it."

Cathy shrugged. "It's your life."

That seemed to stop Jovan. He rubbed his beard like he was thinking hard about it.

When we got out of the rec room and the guards were leading us into one of the many elevators, Cathy pulled me aside. "Did he do it?"

I shook my head no.

"You believe him?"

I nodded.

27

"Put your seat belt on."

The day after the lawyers visited him, Jovan flipped through a stack of legal cases that he kept in the corner of his cell. Something one of the lawyers had said the day before made him want to reread one.

He found the case, started to read, but then closed his eyes for a second, thinking about yesterday when Cathy, Eddie, and Laura had come to see him—three lawyers in a room, all there for him. For some reason—a reason he couldn't ascertain—they wanted to help. It was like a dream team, like the one O.J. had, but better. Because the facts were on their side. He wasn't guilty, and he could tell that the lawyers believed him. For the first time in years, someone actually believed him.

Cathy and I stepped up the work on Jovan's case, talking frequently on the phone about witnesses and evidentiary issues, e-mailing, *Don't forget to ask this . . .* and *Let's do a motion for that . . .*

Philosophically, even though I was now one hundred percent into the case, I sometimes still struggled with representing Jovan. The way I saw it, the cops had gone too far, deciding who was in that fight with Howard Thomas and then creating evidence and pushing for a confession to prove their theory. Was I any better, though? In order to represent Jovan, I ultimately had to do the same thing the detectives did—make a decision based on what was in front with me and go with it. I had decided that Jovan was innocent, and I was helping to create a defense to show that. Unlike the cops, I believed I had much more than a gut instinct. But whether or not that was true, having to make the decision to represent him helped me understand the detectives' motives. They were trying to right a wrong too—the death of an innocent man—and they went after the people they had decided killed him.

It occurred to me that the best chance we had of showing that Jovan's confession was forced was to get the cops to admit the conditions in which they'd detained him. Cathy laughed at this. The cops would never, never admit it, she said. I did some research and found she was probably right. In two studies, completed in 1987 and 1992, a law professor assessed a group of Cook County officers, judges, prosecutors, and public defenders.[123] He found that the Chicago police lie "pervasively" while on the stand, as well as "throughout the investigative process," and further stated that lying on the stand is "nurtured by prosecutors and tolerated by judges."[124] In one part of the study, 92 percent of narcotics officers said police lie at least some of the time when responding to motions to suppress evidence (such as a motion to suppress a confession).[125]

That year, as we prepped for Jovan's trial, I was teaching a class at Loyola Law School called Advanced Writing for Civil Litigation. It was mostly attended by third-year law students who were about to graduate and had suddenly realized that while they were perfectly equipped to memorize whole portions of the RICO statute, they actually knew very little about how to practice law. In my class, we talked about the basics of writing motions and complaints, answering discovery, and arguing at hearings.

I'd been talking a lot about Jovan Mosley too, telling the students about his plight, asking them what they thought about the actions of the detectives and other facts of the case.

As Jovan's trial approached, I realized this was a great case for law students to work on, and it would help clear off my large workload. So I made the decision to pimp the law students.

"Remember Jovan Mosley?" I said one day in class.

Many of the students struggled not to roll their eyes. How could they forget?

"The trial is starting soon, and we need help with research and motions. It's a great opportunity to put into action some of what we've been working on in this class. Anyone interested in chipping in?"

The students shifted in their chairs. Silence.

"It's also an amazing opportunity to help someone," I said. "Really help someone. Remember, this is why we go to law school, to do what's right, to make sure the system works properly."

A few eyes darted around the room. No takers. Not one word from the class.

"The other thing," I continued, "is that you'll be able to say you worked on a murder trial. This will look great on a résumé."

Five hands shot into the air.

The day before Jovan's trial, I knew Cathy was still playing with different versions of her opening argument.

"If you've got any thoughts," she said to me on the phone, "send them to me."

I sat down at the computer, opened an e-mail to Cathy, and wrote:

The detectives want to solve crimes, and they want to close cases. That's their job. But in this case, in their haste to do that, the detectives prejudged Jovan Mosley. They prejudged him because of where he lived; they prejudged him because of his race; they prejudged him because of his age; and they prejudged him because of the people he happened to be with for a few hours one summer night.

So when Jovan told them that first time that he had not struck Howard Thomas it didn't matter. They already knew what he had done. They didn't need him to explain.

When he told them the second, third, fourth and fifth time that he hadn't been involved in the fight, they still didn't care. They kept him handcuffed to a wall for days. They didn't care that they didn't give him food during that time. They didn't care that they didn't give him any liquid to drink, not one ounce, for all that time. They didn't care that he couldn't sleep or use the bathroom. They didn't need to. They had already prejudged him.

Ladies and gentleman of the jury, please . . . please . . . do not do the same thing. I ask you to listen. I ask you not to prejudge. I ask you to pay attention to everything so that this young man can tell the story that, until now, no one cared to hear.

Cathy and I e-mailed back and forth, discussing the opening statement, the motions we were filing, our strategy for picking the jury.

Finally, right before I went to bed, I e-mailed Cathy once more. I told her I was going to be heartbroken if we couldn't get Jovan a "not guilty."

She e-mailed me back:

As for your potential broken heart, my only advice is BUCK UP and PUT YOUR SEAT BELT ON, we are about to go for Mr. Toad's Wild Ride . . . All of my defense buddies have said, essentially, "Well, good luck with that." None of them thinks we have much of a chance for acquittal.

Part III

28

"Let's do this."

For the midwesterner, the weather is a person—one the neighbors talk about when they walk the dog or buy their morning coffee.

"God, this winter," one will say. "Absolute hell this year."

The other neighbor will nod sadly. "I remember when winter was so much easier."

Both neighbors then shake their heads in unison, murmuring things like, "It's so sad."

November in Chicago in 2005 was a very bad boy. On the morning of Jovan's trial, unable to sleep, I got up at four, went to my rooftop deck, and stepped outside. It was freezing, austere, and deep gray more than it was black. The lights of the Hancock Center and the Sears Tower, usually bright and visible from my deck, barely showed through the cold, murky fog.

I went back to my bedroom and began trying on suits. What did people wear to a murder trial? Cathy's what-the-hell? comment, upon seeing my suit and pink coat at SuperMax, played over and over in my head. Was the fashion of criminal litigation so different from that of the civil world?

I called Cathy, who I knew routinely awoke at five a.m. to work before her household came to life. "What suit should I wear?"

"What have you got?" she said.

I ran down the list—brown tweed, herringbone with peplum jacket, basic black, Jackie O–style with rounded collar.

"Wear the Jackie," Cathy said. "We're picking the jury today, and they need to love you. By the way, bring some of Jason's ties for Jovan, will you?"

———

The days before the trial had found Delores Mosley searching for something to wear to the murder trial as well. But it wasn't for her, it was for Jovan. The trial would be the first time in almost six years that he would be able to wear something other than his prison uniform.

She went down into the basement at her mother-in-law's house, where she'd stored Jovan's clothes and personal belongings. But in the space in the corner of the basement where she'd put his stuff—nothing. She looked around the basement quickly, frantically, but there was nothing of Jovan's there. All of it—his clothes, jewelry, shoes, Social Security card, other IDs, CDs, wallet, books, watches, photos, mementos, stereo equipment—all of it was gone.

Delores stood still in the basement, trying to work out what had happened. And then she remembered something. She'd seen one of Jovan's cousins wearing a shirt that was just like one Jovan used to have. It was, she realized now, actually Jovan's shirt. The cousins and other family members had slowly taken their pick of Jovan's property, and bled him dry. To them, since Jovan was in jail, he was as good as gone.

Delores went to Men's Wearhouse, and using money she didn't have, bought a dark gray suit and a white shirt for her son.

When I arrived at 26th and Cal, a huge security line spread from the courthouse door, through the plaza, and down the steps. I took my place at the end, checking my watch anxiously. I was supposed to be upstairs in fifteen minutes, but the line would take at least thirty.

A few minutes later, a guy in a suit and trench coat saved me, telling me lawyers didn't have to wait in line. The fact that he had picked me out as a lawyer cheered me.

When I found the majestic Courtroom 600 it was empty, save for a clerk sitting to the right of the judge's bench. A pale white light filtered through the tall windows on the right. The courtrooms at the Daley Center—the hub of civil, state-court litigation—were technically nicer. The wood there was polished and unscarred, the floors were carpeted and regularly groomed. But the courtrooms there were small, boxy, and utilitarian at best; there was no natural light, no character. Yet here was the courtroom every law student dreamed of. Legal books bound in dusty reds, blues, and gold lined the inlaid shelf behind the intricately carved judge's bench, which towered over the courtroom. The jury box to the left was slightly raised too, lending it an authority of its own. The ceiling soared. Instead of the few viewing pews found in the civil court, there were rows and rows of seats built for a population whose investment in the legal system was taken for granted.

I looked at my watch. I was a little early, but usually a courtroom on the morning of a trial is hopping with grim-faced, fearful attorneys readying exhibits, studying notes, and barking orders to their law clerks. But no. No one there. A few files sat on counsels' tables. The clerk looked decidedly bored.

My heels clicked out succinct taps as I walked the marble floor through the center aisle of pews.

"Um . . . ," I said to the clerk, "I'm here for the trial of Jovan Mosley?" My voice sounded timid. I pined for the days when I used to charge into civil courtrooms and call confident hellos to everyone.

The clerk jerked a thumb at the doors that led to the judge's chambers and sheriff's room.

"Um . . . ," I said again, unsure. In civil courtrooms, you didn't go behind the curtain. Okay, maybe you did if you were in trouble, or maybe if the judge wanted to negotiate a settlement in his office, but even then you didn't enter unless specifically invited, and then you were usually escorted.

Silent, the clerk jerked her thumb again.

I tiptoed around the bench and tentatively pushed open one of the doors. It led to a short hallway. At the end was an open door, and from it bounced friendly laughter. As I came closer, I saw a sign that designated it as the sheriff's office. When I reached it, I stuck my head in the room and blinked at what I saw there.

No one noticed me at first, so I just kept watching and blinking, my mind scuttling after explanations, finding none.

Cathy, wearing a black suit, peered in a small, cracked mirror that hung crookedly from the wall while she spritzed her blond hair with spray. Six guys sat around her, all talking loudly.

Two of the guys were in uniform, and were, I realized, the sheriffs. The other guys, dressed in suits, were clearly lawyers.

"Oh, for Christ's sake," Cathy said to one of them, smiling in the mirror and spritzing some more. "The judge told me not to take a bench. I *had* to take a jury. And you know what? I got an NG."

"Whatever," one of the suits said, laughing. He was lean and handsome, his hair graying. He rolled his eyes at Cathy.

The other guys were arguing about the Bears.

"Orton is never going to do it," one of the sheriffs was saying, practically shouting. "Never!"

A younger guy in an olive suit nodded fast. "Exactly. We need Rex."

"Rex is *never* going to get it done," the sheriff bellowed.

The conviviality in that room was something you wouldn't see in a civil courtroom in Cook County. In the moments before a trial started, opposing sides were usually much less than "civil" and they didn't sit around together primping their bangs and arguing about the Bears as if these things were more important than what was about to happen in the courtroom. And although the attorneys were often cordial to the sheriffs, everyone kept their distance.

Cathy clapped her hands when she saw me and introduced me to the suits, three of whom were Andy Varga, Jim Lynch, and Ethan Holland, the assistant state's attorneys who would be trying the case. Varga was the slim guy with graying hair whom she'd originally talked to about Jovan's case and who happened to live in Cathy's neighborhood. Jim Lynch, the second chair, was a tall guy with an amiable demeanor, who wrote plays on the weekends. The third chair, Ethan Holland, was a shorter, good-looking guy with auburn hair. In short, they looked like three guys you'd want to hang out with.

The other man in a suit was Jim Mullinex, the public defender representing Frad Muhammad. Frad's case hadn't been tried yet either, and the judge had decided the cases would be tried at the same time with two different juries.

Once the introductions were over, Cathy went back to working on her hair, and the guys resumed their rowdy conversation about the Bears.

"Are you all ready?" I heard.

I turned and saw a black man standing behind me in a dress shirt, tie, and slacks.

"You got it," one of the state's attorneys said.

"Whenever you are," a sheriff said.

He left. No one moved from his seat, and the conversation rolled on.

"Who was that?" I asked Cathy.

"Judge Brown," she said.

Once again, I was surprised. A civil judge probably wouldn't have strolled casually into the room, and if he had, everyone would have leapt to their feet.

"He took over for Denny," Cathy said.

"Denny?"

"Denny Dernbach. You know, the judge who used to have Jovan's case. He's out for a while."

She took lipstick out of her purse and applied it, then turned around to face the other attorneys as if they were all members of the same singing group about to take the stage together. "See you guys out there."

The camaraderie and lack of formality was, I would come to find out, common in Chicago's criminal law world. And as I'd seen in Courtroom 600, it existed not just between opposing attorneys but also between the judges and attorneys. When I asked criminal lawyer Brian Sexton about this phenomenon, he said, "It's a foxhole thing. We've all been in the same war."

This theory—the criminal justice system as a unique war that only other soldiers can understand—is widespread. "But there is also a great deal of professionalism and civility amongst PDs, states attorneys, and judges," says Jim McKay, an assistant state's attorney. "People are genuinely kind to each other, and we'll go out and have a couple of beers together after trial."

McKay suggested another possible explanation for the amiability among the players—"It's a volume thing." There aren't as many people in the criminal system as there are in the civil. And they work in groups—one set of characters: prosecutors, public defenders, judges, and sheriffs, assigned to their courtrooms for all their cases. "I'm still going to see you the next day and the next day and the next," said McKay, "and guess what?

It's a hell of a lot easier when you roll with the punches, don't hold grudges, and have fun with it."

Judge John Fleming, a former prosecutor turned 26th and Cal judge, agreed with the volume explanation. "The criminal court system is a smaller pond." And, he said, "Civil lawyers charge a fee, and that changes everything."

When I pointed out that criminal defense lawyers charge fees too, he said, "Yeah, but it's different. Criminal lawyers charge a flat fee, not by the hour and not on contingency based on the outcome. In civil, you're either charging hourly or you're getting a contingency fee." Therefore, he said, in the civil system, how you perform in the case—such as a plaintiff's lawyer getting a third of whatever award you bring in or a defense lawyer raising hell about something, thereby billing a ton of hours—translates into money.

"And when there's money involved, there's a lot of fighting." As a result, Judge Fleming said, "You'll find more lawyers acting 'civil' in the criminal arena than you will in civil law."

In the hallway Cathy turned to me. "You want to see Vizzle?" It took me a minute to realize she was referring to Jovan. (One of the witness statements indicated that some guys in the neighborhood called Jovan by the name "Jovizzle." Cathy thought this was priceless and proceeded to call him Vizzle as a matter of course.)

"Where is he?"

"The bullpen."

She led me from the sheriff's room down a glazed concrete hallway. While we walked, Cathy told me she was having a bad hair day. She'd been so nervous that morning that she'd forgotten to wash off her conditioner. I stopped her and tried to fix her lank hair with my fingers. I halted when I realized that we were being watched. By about fifty men. We were just short of the bullpen, a nice word for a cage, which was packed with prisoners and located only fifty or so feet from the office where Cathy and the guys had been shooting the shit. All the prisoners wore tan pants and DOC shirts.

As we came closer, the smell of testosterone overwhelmed us. The men were so crowded into the cage that most prisoners were standing with little room to move. When they saw us, many pushed their way to the bars and leered at us, describing various sexual feats.

I was freaking. Cathy was completely unperturbed.

"Mosley!" she yelled at the pack. The sea of tan-clothed men parted until we could see a bench at the side of the cell. There was Jovan, sitting on the bench and dressed in the dark gray suit and white shirt his mother had found him. His beard had been shaved. He looked up at us, and his eyes said, *Help.*

One of the inmates near me turned and looked at me in a whole different way. "You his lawyer?"

I looked at Jovan. I nodded, finding myself proud of that nod.

The guy moved closer, dropped his chin, and said in a low voice, "Get that kid out of here. He doesn't belong."

The other guys backed off when they knew we were there for Jovan. A few actually raised their hands, as if to say, *Hands off these two.*

"Seriously," the guy said, still looking at me. "He. Does. Not. Belong. Here."

It was exactly what Cathy had thought the first time she met Jovan.

I nodded again and looked past the other guys to Jovan, sitting on that bench, and when he met my eyes I gave him a small smile, hoping he'd understand I was trying to tell him it would be okay, but the truth was, I didn't know that for sure.

"Let's do this," Cathy said.

29

"Two white girls representing a black guy? We should be all over him."

A sheriff led Jovan from the bullpen. Jovan had done this walk before, but this time it was different. This time he barely noticed the handcuffs.

In his mind he repeated the prayer he'd been saying for months. *God, lead me in choosing this jury.* Tears sprang to his eyes. He looked up at the high, vaulted ceiling of the courtroom as he walked in, hoping to get the tears to roll back inside his eyes.

It was starting. Finally, it was starting. That was the only other thing Jovan could think: *Thank you, God, that it is starting.*

Jovan and Frad were brought into the courtroom together. They looked entirely different. Frad was tall, with a large Afro and dark Malcolm X glasses. He was thinner than he had been before he'd been in county. He wore casual clothes—pants and a blue cotton shirt that was striped white and checkered with little squares of red. He also wore the bland expression he would maintain for the rest of the trial.

Jovan, on the other hand, was alive with energy. And fear. You could see it in his unblinking brown eyes that kept welling up with tears. You could see it in the way he tugged at the sleeves of the foreign gray suit.

Cathy and I pulled out the raft of ties we'd brought with us, holding them up to Jovan and his new suit.

"We have to pick the best one," Cathy said. "He's going to be wearing this thing for the next week or two."

I was holding a tie with yellow stripes, wondering if it was too presidential. I looked at Cathy. "I thought we brought all these so he could wear a different one every day."

Cathy shook her head. She glanced at Jovan. "Sorry, my friend," she said, "but you have to live in the same suit, shirt, and tie for as long as this trial goes on. The jury won't be able to hear that you've been in SuperMax for almost six years waiting for your trial."

"Why?" I asked.

"It's considered prejudicial. They don't want the jury to make their decision based on time the defendant has already served. I don't want them to think he's been out on bail. So he's wearing the same thing every day." She held up a gray and white diagonally striped tie. "What do you think?"

Jovan and I nodded.

"Congratulations, it's yours," Cathy said. "A gift from Eddie."

Jovan fumbled trying to put on his tie. I wondered how often he had worn one. Once it was on, I stood in front of him and straightened it, trying to make the knot smaller, as I always did with my husband.

"Thanks," he said.

"Let's go, counsel," said Judge Brown.

As the horde of prospective jurors took their seats, I felt that fluttering, nervous stomach that always hit me before a jury. But when I glanced over at Jovan, the fluttering turned into all-out churning. There was so much at stake.

I turned. Whispering to Cathy, I asked her how she wanted us to act with Jovan in front of the jury. Should we consult with him? Was it acceptable to touch him?

She thought about it for a second. "I'm usually pretty detached from my clients, but I want to humanize him. Two white girls representing a black guy? Yeah, we should be all over him."

30

"Yes, Your Honor. I can."

Andrea Shultz was a white woman with brown hair cut short. As she walked into Courtroom 600, she wore khakis, a cardigan sweater, and rectangular wire-frame glasses. Andrea Schultz had been a voter for three decades, but until now she'd never been called to jury duty. And yet she had a sense about people charged with crimes. Basically it was, *If you're arrested for something, chances are you did it.*

Although Andrea lived in a suburb (which fell just within the Cook County borders), she had grown up in Chicago. Ultimately, her family had moved out of the city as part of the white flight from the Roseland neighborhood.

Andrea had been married three times. Her third, and present, husband, Bill, was a former cop. Yet when she filled out the juror's questionnaire, she had dutifully listed Bill's current job as the Supervisor of Special Investigators for the National Insurance Crime Bureau (NICB.)

From the gallery, Andrea searched the courtroom until she found the defendant. Although he was a black man, he looked white with fear. She didn't know what he was charged with, but the sight of him made her feel vaguely emotional.

The next thing she noticed were the two female lawyers sitting next to him. And as the judge began to talk and then to call potential jurors to the box, Andrea noticed that those female lawyers weren't just sitting there—they were talking to the defendant, consulting with him, clearly respecting him.

What's going on here? she wondered. She knew then that she had to be on the jury.

When it was her turn to be questioned, the judge and lawyers asked her some questions about the NICB and she answered them. But as with the questionnaire, no one asked her what her husband had done before that, and she didn't tell them that he had been a detective with a local police department for fourteen years.

She answered the lawyers' and the judge's questions properly. When the judge asked her whether she felt she could be unbiased, she answered in a clear, loud voice, "Yes, Your Honor. I can." And she meant it.

31

"God put you two in Jovan's path."

The sight of the jury made Jovan emotional. He teared up again, and we shot him glances and shook our heads. Cathy had mentioned to him that he shouldn't cry or stare at the jury. They could take stares in a threatening way. One tears could present as guilt.

As the first panel of jurors was seated, Cathy leaned toward Jovan. "Dude, this is your jury," she said. "Anyone you want to kick off, you let us know. Any you want to keep? Tell us."

Jovan nodded and gave her a grateful smile.

As we questioned the jurors, Cathy and I scribbled notes to each other and to Jovan. We wrote stuff like, *She never said she could be impartial*; *His son is a police officer, let's get him off*; *What the hell is up with this dude?* When Cathy was pleased with a juror, she drew a huge smiley face, which always made Jovan crack a smile of his own. If she didn't like someone, she drew a frown on the face. If she wasn't sure, the mouth was a flat line. We asked Jovan about every juror before we made our final decisions, and he had very firm opinions about everyone. One juror described being mugged by a group of black kids a few years earlier. Jovan looked at Cathy and said one word: "No." One woman made long eye contact with him, which he thought was positive, and he said he'd like to keep her. Another juror looked like the state's attorney, Andy Varga, so Jovan shook his head, rejecting him.

There were two jurors he was adamant about keeping—Alfonzo Lewis, a young black guy, and Andrea Schultz. One of the last jurors was a Chinese gentleman. He'd been mugged before, he said. Cathy and I didn't like it—the experience might make him overly connected to the victim in our case. But Jovan said he wanted him on the jury.

"Are you sure?" Cathy and I said to him. "Are you *sure?*"

He was. Jovan said that the juror didn't seem bitter about being mugged, so it was okay. Cathy and I shrugged our shoulders. There is no real science to picking a jury, no matter how much we'd like there to be. We kept the juror.

When the court took a break for lunch, I sat in the courtroom and worked on my edits for *The Rome Affair*. My editor had called over the weekend and said, essentially, *Yeah, I know you've got this murder trial, but we need the manuscript as soon as possible.*

The previous weekend had been so packed with trial prep, I hadn't tackled the manuscript at all. This lunch break was the only time I had.

The courtroom was empty. Jovan was brought back to the bullpen for each lunch hour and Cathy was with Eddie. Being in that vacant courtroom, reading over that manuscript, was surreal. For one thing, *The Rome Affair* was the book that had landed me in Jovan's world as his lawyer.

What was also bizarre was that my main character, after being charged with murder, had to appear in a courtroom at 26th and Cal, essentially the same courtroom in which I sat. When I thought the manuscript needed detail, I simply looked up, let my eyes fall on something in the courtroom—the way the light came in through the high windows, the scrolling woodwork below the judge's bench—and all those details went into the manuscript.

After lunch, we finished picking the jury within an hour. The final twelve jurors, plus two alternates, ended up being a good mix of races and sexes.

When the judge gave the jury a break before the start of the trial, Cathy looked over my shoulder at the gallery. I followed her look and saw a woman sitting on the left side of the gallery, gesturing toward Cathy.

Cathy smiled at her and mouthed, *One minute.* She turned to me. "Here is one of your biggest jobs on this trial. Helping Delores."

"Delores?"

Cathy nodded at the woman. "That is Delores Mosley, Jovan's mother. The poor woman has been watching her kid go through this nightmare for six years without any help. We might call a few character witnesses on behalf of Jovan, and she might be one of them. But she's going to require prep."

"I can do that."

"And get a number from her for Anita, Jovan's boss at the law firm where he worked during high school. Work with those two to get them ready to testify. You'll do the direct exams." She stood. "Come on, I'll introduce you."

As Jovan was handcuffed and taken back to the bullpen for the break, Cathy and I approached Delores.

Delores stood when we reached her. She was a woman of medium build, her hair in cornrows, wearing a skirt topped by layers of sweaters. Her jacket, hat, and other outerwear sat on the bench next to her.

She came out of the row and launched herself into Cathy's arms. "I can't believe this day is here," she said breathlessly. "I had to take four buses to get here. It took me three hours and then I had to wait outside an hour to get in."

Cathy hugged her back tight.

"Thank you so much," Delores said.

"Don't thank me for anything yet." Cathy pointed to me. "This is Laura Caldwell. She's a professor at Loyola Law School, and she'll be helping me try this case."

"Oh, bless you." Delores grabbed me into a hug now. "God put you two in Jovan's path."

"I have to check on something," Cathy said, "but Laura will answer any questions you have."

As Cathy walked away, Delores looked over my shoulder into the courtroom. "What I want to know is if I can go back there and talk to my son."

"No, I'm sorry. I'm told they only allow attorneys and court employees."

Her eyes looked anguished, but she nodded before she turned to a woman sitting next to her on the bench. "Have you met Frad's mother?" She introduced us.

Mrs. Muhammad stood, and we shook hands. For some reason I was startled. I hadn't expected to see a family member of Frad's. The evidence against Frad seemed so clear that for some reason I thought he might not have any supporters present.

"Nice to meet you," she said softly, smiling at me.

I looked into her eyes, wondering if she understood that the chances of Frad going to jail were very, very good. I glanced from her to Delores.

Although I felt terrible for Delores, at least she had hope. If Mrs. Muhammad comprehended the situation, she would probably have little or none.

I turned to Delores. "Can I talk to you? We want to discuss possibly putting you on the stand as a character witness for Jovan."

Delores nodded vigorously.

I looked over my shoulder and saw one of the state's attorneys glancing at me. I gestured to the door. "Let's talk outside."

But outside, the halls were packed with people pouring in and out of other courtrooms. There was one trial rule I was sure was the same whether in a civil or criminal case—never, never, never speak to a witness about his or her testimony unless in absolute privacy. You never knew who could overhear.

I spied a women's bathroom down the hall and led Delores there. The bathroom was empty. Like the rest of 26th and Cal, it had the look of something once grand gone to ruin—the place had marble floors but no toilet seats and everything was scarred with cigarette burns and graffiti.

I leaned against a wall and looked at Delores. "Do you think you can testify for Jovan as to his good character?"

Delores's worried expression ruptured into pain, and she burst into tears. "Jovan was the son who was never in any trouble. I had trouble with my other sons. But Jovan always came home. He was never in a gang. He's never had any problems with the police. When he called me from the station and told me that he had signed some papers . . ." A new flurry of tears sprang from her eyes. "Of course I'll testify for him. I'll do anything for him."

Over the weekend, my husband, Jason, and I went to our cabin in Indiana. On Saturday night, Jason made dinner, while I ran over my jury notes, asking for his impressions on the people we'd chosen. We had both been busy and distracted lately, and that night was the most connected we'd felt in months.

Our conversation was interrupted when I got a call from a book club in Ohio. They had read my latest book and arranged to talk with me by speakerphone. I was on the phone for almost an hour. When I finished, the kitchen was clean, and Jason was asleep on the couch.

Monday morning, Jason left for a guys' golf trip to Mexico that he'd had planned for months, while I set off for another foreign country—26th and Cal.

When I visited the bullpen, Jovan looked wan.

As he and I stood at the bars, most of the men behind him backed up to give Jovan room.

"Hey, I gotta question for you about my case," one of the guys said. He started making his way over to me.

Jovan threw a stern glance over his shoulder and gave the man a short shake of his head. The guy stopped in his tracks.

"C'mere." Jovan waved me toward the far right side of the cage.

As we made our way to the end of the bullpen, the men continued to draw away in deference to Jovan. By the time we reached the corner, they had given us as much space as possible. It was only about a two-foot space because there were so many men in there, but I was struck by their kindness. They had all shoved themselves, shoulder to shoulder, into one mass toward the other side of the bullpen. Jovan they had respect for, that was clear, but me? They were eyeing me like bait, and the scent of testosterone and unwashed bodies was potent.

I met their gazes and tried to shoot a casual hail-fellow kind of look. This was met with disdain by a few (and lascivious glances down my body by more than a few). I felt distinctly nervous.

Jovan must have sensed my unease. He looked over his shoulder at the group and gave another shake of his head. This time, most of the inmates turned away. That was the only kind of privacy Jovan and I could get.

"How was your weekend?" I asked, focusing on Jovan. Immediately I regretted the question. It was the kind you asked someone in your office, expecting an answer like, *Not bad. Watched the Bears game. Got a lot of sleep.*

Jovan, on the other hand, clearly had not been blessed with a great deal of sleep. There were faint half-moons of charcoal-gray under his eyes and a flatness to those eyes.

"Not good," he said simply. He'd spent most of the weekend in the day room just sitting and thinking. Some of the guys had asked him how the trial was going, but he told them he didn't want to talk about it. He said he hadn't been able to eat for days.

I noticed his suit jacket seemed looser than it had last week, his pants baggier. "You have to eat. It'll make you think better. You'll be able to concentrate."

He nodded briefly.

"Have you seen Cathy today?" I asked.

"Yeah."

"Did she tell you what's going to happen?"

He gave a single nod.

"Are you ready for openings?"

"I think so."

"You have to be ready mentally. You have to be prepared for the state's attorneys to stand there and hammer at you, to say that you did it. And you can't react in any kind of grand fashion, okay? The jury is going to be watching you, and if you look really pissed off, some of them might think, *Okay, he did it.* And if you get upset, they might think the same thing. You really can't win unless you stay as emotionless as possible. Just listen intently. Pay attention. Tell us if you hear anything in their opening that you want Cathy to respond to, then we'll go from there. Got it?"

This time he nodded. And nodded. And nodded again. I bobbed my head along with him.

Andy Varga opened for the state. He was unflinching and ardent. In short, Andy was a pro, a seasoned veteran, the kind of authoritative lawyer juries love.

He started out talking about Dr. Nancy Jones, the medical examiner, who, he said, "is unlike any physician that any of you know, any of us have ever seen for a checkup or for emergency care or for any kind of health care. . . . She sees her patients once, because Dr. Jones is a forensic pathologist . . . and when she sees her patients, that person is dead. And her job is to figure out . . . what killed the person who is before her.

"I would venture a guess," Varga said, "that when Dr. Jones saw Mr. Thomas she didn't think, Oh, my goodness, this is going to be challenging. Because when she saw Mr. Thomas he was lying on that stainless steel table, he was nude and his nose wasn't in the middle of his face, it was over a cheekbone.[126] His head was deformed as though it was caved in on the sides and in the back. His mouth had been cut."

Varga went on describing Mr. Thomas's injuries in detail. "And what you will [also] hear over the next couple of days is what brought Mr. Thomas to that table. You will learn that on the night of August sixth, Jovan Mosley, this young man seated here in the suit, Frad Muhammad and a couple of their other buddies, a gentleman named Lawrence Wideman and Marvin Treadwell, were out for the evening. They had been out drinking and they ran out. They wanted to get some money to come up with some more liquor and to come up with some marijuana.

"Rather than pooling their money, because apparently they didn't have anything between them, rather than borrow it from someone, rather than come about it by any kind of honest, law-abiding means, they decided to find somebody to rob."

The group of boys, Varga said, including Gregory Reed, who went by the nickname of Fetta, walked around and spoke to some people sitting on the front porch of a house. At that moment, Mr. Thomas, who lived on the next block, strolled by carrying a couple of grocery bags and "he was set upon by Mr. Mosley, Mr. Muhammad, Mr. Wideman, and Mr. Treadwell."

Varga told the jury that Frad and Red had both used a bat, that they had kicked and punched Mr. Thomas even after he'd fallen to the ground, and that a car was used as a brace by one of the boys to stomp on him.

Marvin Treadwell came away from the fight, Varga said, counting a couple of dollar bills, money he didn't have before the beating. Lawrence Wideman, also known as Red, came up to the group holding a bottle of pop, and all the boys shared in the bottle of pop.

"Seven dollars and a bottle of pop," Varga said. "That's what Mr. Thomas died for that night."

I glanced at Judge Michael Brown, then I wrote a note to Cathy. *Judge very attentive.* She looked at him and nodded her agreement.

Varga brought up the concept of accountability. "I don't think you're going to hear any evidence in this case from anyone who's going to put the bat in [Jovan's] hand. . . . I don't anticipate you hearing any evidence that Mr. Mosley struck Mr. Thomas in the torso or in the head with the baseball bat. The evidence you're going to hear is that Mr. Mosley, at most, got in maybe two punches to the torso. Nevertheless he knew what the plan was, he participated in the plan and he shared in the proceeds, even if that sharing amounted to nothing more than a bottle of pop.

"Accountability," Varga said, "basically means if you go out to commit a crime with your buddies, you're responsible for everything they do. They're responsible for everything you do."

Varga turned toward the state's table and gestured at his co-counsels. "At the end of this case . . . we're going to ask you to find [Jovan Mosley] guilty of murder and armed robbery."

As he took his seat, I wrote a note to Cathy: *Curious. Not much mention of Fetta.* She wrote back, *Fetta KILLS state on Muhammad.* It was true. In Fetta's rambling statement he'd said that Frad was a mere witness, that it was Red who had the bat the whole time. No one else who'd seen the fight backed up Fetta's recollection, but still, it would make for great evidence for Frad.

The judge peered over his glasses to our table. "Any opening statement by the defense?"

Cathy stood with a determined look on her face and straightened her suit jacket. "Yes, sir."

She walked to the center of the jury box and looked up and down at the faces of the jury, standing silently for a moment to build up anticipation.

Instead of talking about the day of Howard Thomas's fight, Cathy said, "On March sixth of 2000, Jovan Mosley was a nineteen-year-old boy."

She told the jury that Jovan was a high school graduate, that he'd worked at a well-known law firm downtown and at a packaging firm in the northern suburbs. "On March sixth, around four o'clock in the afternoon, two cars pulled up in Jovan Mosley's neighborhood. Those cars were filled with Chicago police detectives and officers, seven to eight in total. Those detectives and police officers . . . asked him what his name was, and he told them Jovan Mosley. They got out of the car. They handcuffed him behind his back. They put him in the back of a detective car and they drove him away."

When they got Jovan to police headquarters, she said, they "took all of his personal things away. They kept him in the handcuffs and they took him into . . . an interrogation room."

About the room, Cathy said, "It's eight feet by eight feet. Not a large room. It has no carpet, it has no windows, it has no clock on the wall. It has no bathroom, it has no water fountain, there's no food in there, and there isn't a telephone either."

She took a breath, glanced over her shoulder at Jovan, and then glanced back at the jury. "You're going to learn that that's the room Jovan Mosley spent the next twenty-seven, twenty-eight hours of his young life." The time between Jovan's arrest and signing the confession had most likely taken more than two days, but Cathy was referring to the roughly twenty-eight hours he'd spent in the one interrogation room.

"The detectives cuffed Jovan to a ring on the wall of that room," she continued, then they "shut the door and locked it from the outside." During the entire time he was there, Cathy said, "Jovan was not given anything to eat, he was not given anything to drink, he was never even told what time it was, and you're going to hear that he wasn't ever offered the chance to use the telephone."

The jury was rapt.

Cathy detailed exactly what Jovan had been through when he was interrogated and before the confession was signed. I looked over and saw tears running down Jovan's face in thin rivulets.

Instinctively, I put my arm on his shoulder and patted it. I didn't think once about what Cathy had said about being "all over him." I just wanted to console this young man who had been through so much.

Jovan shot me a surprised look. It was probably the first time in years he had been touched in an affectionate way. He blinked a few times, then mumbled, "Thanks. Thanks."

Cathy continued. "You will learn that . . . teams of detectives working in shifts visiting Jovan Mosley in that little room. Always in that little room. . . . Jovan made several denials to the detectives . . . [and] after three or four, maybe five denials to the detectives (and now we're in about the twenty-fifth hour of Jovan's custody in that little room) you're going to learn that Detective Porter comes onto the scene."

She described how Porter got in Jovan's face, calling him a liar, telling him that if he just admitted he threw two punches, he could go home.

"That's how Detective Porter got Mosley's statement."

She told the jury how once they got Jovan to say he would admit to two punches, "things got a little better." He was taken out of that room and taken to a larger room with carpeting, a table, chairs, a drink. She told the jury how ASA Allen Murphy had written Jovan's statement and that no one ever offered Jovan a pen to do it for himself.

Then Cathy got into the missing police records, and her words were scathing. "You will learn that every detective in this case wrote general progress reports. There were quite a lot of them." Cathy held up Jovan's meager police file. "Every single general progress report relating to conversations with Jovan Mosley is missing. They're just gone. Not for anybody else in the case, but his are just gone. We believe that will speak volumes to you, ladies and gentlemen, about the credibility of the investigation."

The police, she said, "already had their minds made up. They knew what they were going to do without hearing one word of evidence. Well, ladies and gentlemen, that's why you are here, because you have made a commitment and you promised that you will fairly try the facts of the case and that you will listen to all of the evidence before you draw your conclusions. . . . You've promised to uphold the concept of presumption of innocence."

Finally, Cathy told the jury that Jovan had no burden of proof, none whatsoever, and no duty to take the stand on his own behalf. "He doesn't have to bring in witnesses, he doesn't have to give physical evidence, and most importantly, he doesn't have to testify. He does not have to testify, but you will hear from him. He has been waiting six years to tell you what happened."

When she sat down, I wrote on her notepad, *RIVETING*. She wrote back, *I ♥ you for doing this with me.*

32

"It's just me, you, and Jovan."

The state called Howard Thomas's daughter as their first witness. A striking woman with broad shoulders, she walked proudly to the stand in front of both Jovan's jury and Frad's. For reasons of economy, if a certain witness was needed for both cases, the juries viewed that testimony together.

As she reached the witness box, Cathy and I glanced at each other uncomfortably. We had talked a great deal about the fact that there were so many victims in the case—Howard, Jovan, and both of their families. We were acutely aware that for Howard Thomas's family, answers had been long in coming. Jovan wasn't the only one who had waited nearly six long years for justice.

Thomas's daughter raised her hand and was sworn in. Ethan Holland asked her to introduce herself to the jury, then directed her attention to August 5, 1999. "Was your father alive on that day?"

"Yes, he was."

"Who is your father?"

"Howard Thomas, Jr."

"And do you know where he lived on that date?"

She testified that he lived in Chicago, that she'd seen her dad around eleven in the morning the day he was killed.

"And for what purpose did you see him if you remember?"

"I had just come back from San Diego, so it was like my first time seeing him in a while."

"Directing your attention, ma'am," Holland said, "to August sixth, 1999, the next day. Did you receive a phone call?"

"Yes." She told them that her aunt had called her. She'd gone to Cook County Hospital and learned her father had been killed.

Holland showed her a picture. "Who is that a photograph of?"

"That's a picture of my father, Howard Thomas, Jr."

The photo was shown to the jury. In it, Thomas wore a blue baseball cap with a red bill, large wire-framed glasses, and a big smile. Holland asked the judge to admit the photo into evidence and all attorneys agreed.

"Any cross-examination?" the judge asked the defense attorneys.

"No, thank you," we all said. No one wanted to mess with what must have been the immense amount of grief this woman had, what her whole family had. She looked at us lawyers with disgust, and I couldn't blame her. She and her family probably hoped Jovan would be convicted; they might even wish him dead. I probably would too if my father had been killed and I believed that some punk had done it. Even if she didn't believe Jovan was the perpetrator, he'd been walking around with the guys who'd done it. And not done a thing to stop the beating.

But I knew Jovan. And I now understood how Cathy could represent the clients she did.

"Thank you," the judge said to the witness, "you may step down. The court is adjourned for lunch."

In the bullpen, Jovan sat on the bench, his regulation bologna sandwich next to him on a white paper plate. He stared straight ahead, as he'd been doing for the last half hour. At the other end of the bench, Frad had already eaten his sandwich and was sitting with his arms on his knees, his head down.

Although they hadn't said anything to each other since they'd returned from the courtroom, both of them digesting the start of the trial, Jovan finally turn to Frad. "How did you pick those people?" he asked. He meant the jury.

When his jury had been brought out at the same time as Frad's, he had been shocked. His own jury had all sorts of people on it—Asian, black, white, Polish, Hispanic—and they were all different ages too, with a relatively equal number of men and women. But Frad's jury seemed to be mostly white men. That couldn't be good.

When Frad didn't answer, Jovan said, "Seriously, how did you pick those people?" Still, Frad had no answer. He didn't seem to care.

Then Jovan knew Frad had essentially given up. He didn't really understand the proceedings and didn't necessarily want to. Jovan had noticed over the last few days in court that whenever the judge heard motions or objections, he invited Jovan and Frad to listen. It was only Jovan, however, who took part in those discussions. Frad would always sit at the table or return to the bullpen.

Jovan stared straight ahead again, thinking of his jury, then said a silent prayer that they would do what he trusted them to do.

Cathy and I, along with Eddie (who'd been watching the trial), huddled in the law library over cartons of soup, trying to figure out who the state might call next. In a civil trial, the judge would have made the attorneys script out exactly what witness was coming when. But here at 26th and Cal, we only had the massive overly inclusive list of everyone the state *might* call. We speculated about when the state would introduce their doozies—Fetta's expected testimony that Jovan had thrown a couple of punches, the detectives' testimony about the interrogation, and the state's attorney's testimony about the creation of Jovan's signed confession—the most difficult obstacle to overcome, especially in Cook County. Walking the hallway to return to the courtroom, people called hello to Cathy at every step. The sheriffs, the lawyers, the court reporters, even a few people who appeared to be defendants, gave her a nod or a wave.

When she saw a short black lawyer, she called to him in a friendly voice, "Hey! How in the *Stan Hill* are you?"

I look at her quizzically.

"Great guy," she said. "His name is Stan Hill, kinda like Sam Hill. Isn't that priceless?"

Stan Hill gave her a good-natured wave in return.

When Cathy and I got back to the courtroom, we chatted with the state's attorneys and then the bailiffs.

As we turned back to our counsels' table, I commented to Cathy, "I feel like we're outnumbered."

"All the guys?"

"Yeah, the state's attorneys are male, the judge, the PD, Jovan, Frad, the guys in the bullpen."

"You're right. We need some girly stuff." Cathy's face took on a mischievous glint. "Like potpourri in a nice cut-glass bowl."

"Scented candles," I said. "This courtroom is kind of musty."

"A table runner would be nice." Cathy gestured with her hand down the length of our table.

We went on about other things we'd add—colored and scented paper for the motions we filed with the judge, a bowl of breath mints, tiny bottles of hand lotion—starting to laugh now. The state's attorneys, overhearing us, shot us looks and rolled their eyes but said nothing. They knew as well as we did that trials were intense animals, living breathing monsters that could devour you at any turn. Sometimes a smile or a laugh was the only way to battle the tension of a trial.

We were still giggling when the deputy led Jovan into the courtroom.

"Ready, Vizzle?" Cathy said, sending us into another peal of laughter.

I told him about our mock plans to *girlify* our table.

"You two are crazy," Jovan said. And yet even he cracked a smile.

Before the state introduced their next witnesses, I flipped to a new piece of paper on my legal pad and wrote a crib sheet of common objections—*compound question; asked & answered; leading; form; foundation; assumes facts not in evidence; hearsay.* It had been so long since I'd tried a case, I didn't completely trust myself to remember them all.

The state called Derek and Ronald Barnes, brothers who lived on Calumet Avenue. Derek Barnes testified that in the early morning hours of August 6, 1999, he had just come from a construction job and was unloading things from his pickup truck. A group of four or five African-American men walked by, about six feet from him. They were roughly between the ages of eighteen and thirty. He described their varying complexions.

One state's attorney asked if he recognized anyone in the courtroom from that night, and Derek Barnes pointed to Frad Muhammad. Frad sat, slightly slumped, next to his public defender, wearing the same pants and a blue-checkered shirt, along with his Malcolm X eyeglasses. Derek Barnes testified that he "maybe" recognized Frad as being a part of that group.[127] He had noticed that one of the guys had something like a bat in his hands when he walked by.

Shortly after the men passed, Derek Barnes was joined on the street by his brother, Ronald. Seconds later they heard "hollering" from down the street—"Noises of pain, 'Ow, stop, stop, don't kill me.'" They looked up the street and saw a group of guys around a car and the motion of a bat going up and down, but Derek couldn't see the person who was being hit. The other men in the group were looking down, and they were kicking or participating. He couldn't tell how many people were involved. All this activity lasted for two to five minutes.

Then the group scattered. Mr. Barnes and his brother walked over to the car and saw a badly beaten man.

On cross-examination, Cathy, in a kind, respectful voice, pointed out to Mr. Barnes that at the trials of Marvin and Red, he had testified that the men were twelve to fifteen feet away when they walked by him, not six. He admitted that if he had said that, that was true.

She also pointed out to him that he had spoken to the police right after the event. She asked if, at that point, he had mentioned to them that he had seen a bat. From the way Cathy asked the question, it was clear she knew he hadn't.

"I'm just saying I'm getting flashes now that those are the things that I see," Mr. Barnes responded. He admitted he wasn't sure if he'd had those same flashes the night it happened.

Cathy gently reminded him that he had just testified that the fight up the street lasted two to five minutes, but at the trials of Marvin and Red, he had testified that it "lasted about twenty, thirty seconds."

Mr. Barnes admitted that might have been the case. "It was a long time ago."

Finally Cathy asked Mr. Barnes, "Did you see any punches thrown?"

"No."

"You didn't see anybody going through any pockets or belongings, correct?"

"No, not that I can remember."

Derek Barnes was excused.

Ronald Barnes, his brother, was the state's next witness, and his testimony mirrored that of his brother. As for the fight, he said, "I couldn't see any exact faces. I just saw shadows."[128]

Andy Varga asked, "Was there something blocking your view of the person on the ground?"

"Well, I think there was an automobile in the path of the—in the sight path."

"Now, Mr. Barnes, you said you were able to see silhouettes of the people that were standing by the car."

"Yes."

"How many people did you see over there?"

"I saw three to five. At least that number."

"How many people did you see, of those three to five, did you see swinging the bat?"

"I saw one person swing."

"What did the other people in the group appear to be doing, if anything?"

"To be honest, it's kind of hard to tell, to remember that far back. . . . Commotion, I guess is the best way I could describe it. I saw commotion."

"Now, Mr. Barnes, the car that was blocking your view of the victim, was that car also obstructing your ability to view any part of the bodies of the other people standing around?"

"No, no, I could see the bodies of the people standing around. I could see the silhouettes of them and their activity, movements and whatever they were doing."

I wrote a note to Cathy, *Hit the fact that he didn't see anyone's face.*

When she got up to cross-examine him, she did. He couldn't identify any of the attackers, he testified. And no, he didn't see anyone going through anyone's pockets. He didn't hear anyone saying, *Let's get his money,* or anything like that.

Ronald Barnes was excused from the witness stand.

Cathy and Jovan and I huddled together at the counsels' table. "What did you think?" Cathy asked.

"They didn't hurt us," I said. "They couldn't identify anyone but Frad and all they remember about Mr. Thomas's beating was a bat. They didn't see any punches being thrown at all."

Cathy and I looked at Jovan, waiting for him to weigh in.

He returned our looks, blinking, blinking, then blinking again.

"What do you think?" Cathy said.

He looked surprised. He would tell me later that until then no attorney had asked him what he had thought of any proceedings, not once during his whole ordeal.

"It went good," he said, his voice almost a whisper. He cleared his throat and repeated, "It went good."

Cathy and I went to the cafeteria for lunch. I decided to try the salad bar, and immediately regretted it after I'd paid and was in front of it. The lettuce was limp and pale, with brown edges. The "salads" like macaroni salad or tuna salad seemed to be comprised predominantly of mayonnaise.

I put a couple of florets of what were allegedly broccoli on my plate along with a few cubes of cheddar that looked fairly harmless.

I sat down next to Cathy, who was studying notes. "What are you going to get for lunch? Stay far away from that salad bar."

She shook her head. "I can't eat. I'm too nervous."

"You didn't look nervous when you were crossing those brothers."

"I'm not nervous when I'm doing it, when I'm in the courtroom; it's the rest of the time. And this case is killing me. I couldn't sleep last night."

"Me either. I was up all night tossing and turning."

She pushed the notes away and gave me a small smile. "Did Jason want to kill you?"

"He's in Mexico."

"That must be hard."

"What do you mean?"

"Well, you're on trial. A *murder* trial. I mean, I always want to talk to Eddie whenever I'm doing anything in court. And this is a big one."

"He's got his cell phone. I'm not sure if it'll work down there, but I'm sure I'll talk to him."

She nodded.

"Besides," I said, "I've got you. And really, no one else understands this whole case. It takes too long to explain to someone."

"I know." She pulled her notes back toward her again. "It's just me, you, and Jovan."

"Your Honor," Andy Varga said, "the people would call Jori Garth."

A short, curvaceous young black woman took the stand, held up her hand, and was sworn in.

Ms. Garth testified that she was twenty years old and a freshman in college.[129] She worked as a legal assistant for Exelon Corporation doing administrative work.

In August 1999, Jori had been fourteen and living with her mother and brother on 73rd and Calumet. Her father, a Chicago police officer, did not live in the house, as her parents were going through a divorce. She had a boyfriend named Anton Williams, who was sixteen. On the night of August 5, 1999, she and Anton had gone to a bowling alley until it closed and then walked back to her house, where they sat on the porch and talked. Eventually, they were joined by some friends. A little after midnight five or six boys, around the ages of eighteen to twenty, came up to the house. She recognized Fetta and Marvin but didn't know the others. She and Anton spoke to Fetta, while the other boys stayed at the bottom of the porch.

A man came walking down the street, and one of the guys at the bottom of the porch said something like, "There goes that motherfucker right there." Jori had told this story before—at the grand jury and the murder trials of Marvin and Red—and she recounted it again in a flat voice.

At this point in Jori's testimony, Andy Varga paused. "Jori," he said, "before we go any further, could you stand up and take a look around the courtroom and let us know whether or not you see this afternoon any of the boys that were there in that group at the base of your stairs?"

Jori didn't look pleased about it, but she complied and stood. "The guy in the glasses." She pointed to Frad.

"Your Honor," Andy Varga said, "let the record reflect in-court identification of the defendant, Frad Muhammad."

"It shall," Judge Brown replied.

Andy didn't ask any questions about Jovan, but rather asked Jori to continue with her story.

Some of the boys went toward the man, Jori said, and started fighting. "It was like three of them," she said.

Two of the boys punched and hit the man and later kicked him. There was one person with a bat who hit the man in the upper torso. Initially, the man fought back. Then, when he was getting hit by the bat, "He was saying 'Stop' and 'No.'"

One of the boys slung the man against a car. "He slid down the car," Jori Garth said, "and two guys, they kept kicking him and hitting him and then they started jumping on top of him." They were holding on to the hood of the car while they did this.

After he was on the ground, the man continued to get hit with the baseball bat between five and ten times about the torso and head. Then the guys walked away.

Andy Varga stood with his arms crossed, a finger on his chin, studying his witness. Finally he asked the big question. "Who had the bat?"

"Mr. Muhammad."

"Mr. Muhammad had the bat?"

"Yes."

Jori had not met Frad Muhammad before that night, she said.

After the beating stopped, Jori and Anton went in the house and told her brother what had happened. Eventually, they went back outside and saw the man still lying by the car, with blood on his shirt and face. She also saw teeth on the ground and a "food bag" with chicken in it. The man's backpack or satchel was on the ground as well.

Jori went back inside the house again before the police came. She didn't tell her father or any other police about the fight until months later, when her dad brought her and Anton to the station.

"I didn't want to get involved with it," she said. "I was scared. I just didn't want to say anything."

In fact, when the detective first on the scene interviewed her, she told him she was in the house when the fight happened.

Andy Varga thanked his witness and sat down.

Cathy stood and pleasantly cross-examined Jori about a few details of the group of boys who had walked up to the Garth porch.

"Okay," Cathy said, "now at some point you saw an individual that wasn't part of the group coming down the street, is that right?"

"I just heard the comments and then they ran off and [Fetta] ran down the stairs and that's when I saw the man."

"Okay. The comment you heard was, 'There goes that motherfucker right there,' correct?"

"Yes."

"You didn't hear [any] comments about let's rob that guy, did you?"

"No."

"And you didn't see anybody trying to get his money away or anything . . . ?"

"No."

"In fact, you never saw any of these boys take a bottle of pop from him, did you?"

"No."

Cathy asked a few more questions, moving slightly closer to the witness. "[The] fight involved three individuals, correct?"

"Yes."

"And two of those individuals had braids in their hair, isn't that correct?" She said, referring to Marvin and Red.

"Yes."

"And the other one was the person that was holding the bat, correct?" she asked, meaning Frad.

"Yes."

A few questions later, still discussing the man with the bat, Cathy asked, "Was he a taller guy?"

"He was taller than the other two."

"And you were able to identify him, correct?"

"Yes."

"And you were also able to identify Marvin, correct?"

"Yes."

"And when you made those identifications, you identified those people as having been involved, correct?"

"Yes."

I looked at Jovan, who was studying Jori so intently he didn't see my glance.

As Cathy looked at her notes, I realized I was holding my breath, and I tried to breathe. So far, we'd survived two witnesses—the Barnes brothers—who'd been at or near the scene that night, and no one could identify Jovan as having done anything.

Cathy brought up the fact that Jori had eventually told the truth to the police about the incident after she was taken to the station for questioning. "And when you were talking to those detectives again, you told them about three people being involved in this incident, correct?"

"Yes."

"And you also gave them physical descriptions of some individuals, correct?"

"Yes."

"You talked to them about Fetta, correct?"

"Yes."

"You talked about Marvin, correct?"

"Yes."

"And you talked about the taller guy who had the bat, is that right?"

"Yes."

In every cross-examination that rolls nicely, as Cathy's was, there is a moment—a moment when the attorney has to decide, *Do I push it with one more question or do I leave it alone?*

Cautious, by-the-book lawyers will tell you, *Never ask one more question. Be happy with what you have. Shut your mouth and sit down so you don't risk blowing the whole thing.*

The more renegade litigators would say, *Fuck it. Ask it. Roll the dice.*

But Cathy was, and is, the best kind of litigator—the kind that trusts her instincts and refuses to have a hard-line policy. Rather, she lets her intuition guide her and decides her course at that heightened moment, when the cautious elements of the attorney's personality battle against its more daring traits.

The courtroom was silent, waiting as Cathy pretended to examine her notes. Although Jovan remembered meeting Jori that night, in large part because he had found her attractive, Cathy knew from Jori's testimony in other cases that she couldn't recall him specifically.

I looked at Jovan. This time he met my glance. Jovan had mentioned that he wanted to be a lawyer, and I could see as the trial proceeded that he had great instincts about the process. That had been evident in the jury selection and in his insistence on taking the stand but also in his careful attention to Cathy's performance.

I saw Cathy roll her shoulders back. She cleared her throat and looked at Jori Garth. "Jori, you had a good view of this incident as it was happening, didn't you?"

"Yes."

"And, in fact, this was something that would have really caught your attention, is that fair to say?"

"Yes."

Cathy took a step away from her notes, looked at Jori Garth, and crossed her arms. "You *never* met Jovan Mosley. . . ."

"No."

"Thank you very much," Cathy said. "No further questions."

The judge looked at Andy Varga. "Is there any redirect?"

Andy paused, gave a short, disappointed shake of his head, then gave the same answer as his witness. "No."

At the end of the day's testimony, Jovan was led away. Back to the bullpen to await his return to SuperMax.

Cathy and I were walking from the bullpen when the bailiff appeared. "Laura," he said. "Judge wants to see you."

My eyes shot to Cathy's. *Why?*

Cathy shrugged. *No idea.*

Fear flamed inside me. I felt, distinctly, like I was getting called to the principal's office, and like a fifth-grader, I started frantically searching my mind for something I'd done wrong so that I could mount a mental defense.

The only thing I could imagine he might ask was, *What in the hell do you think you're doing here, representing a defendant on a murder one trial?*

The only response I could think of was, *I have no clue.*

I stood outside the judge's open chamber doors. He sat behind his desk, still in his robes.

He looked up at me and with a blank expression on his face said, "So I hear you're an author."

"Yes, your honor," I said in a small voice. It sounded like he was working up to asking me the exact questions that I feared. "I'm also a law professor," I tossed in for good measure.

A beat, then, "What do you write?"

"My most recent book was a mystery," I said.

"Is that right?" he said, and his composed judge's appearance disappeared. "I enjoy a good mystery."

I peered more closely at him, trying to divine his expression. If I read it correctly, it was the first time Judge Brown looked even remotely impressed by me. We chatted for another minute about writing, never talking about the case (which would have been prohibited), and then I left when it was clear there was nothing else he wanted to discuss.

At night, alone in my townhouse, I worked on Jovan's case and called Anita Owens, who had been Jovan's boss at the law firm during high school. I prepped her to be a character witness. When we got off the phone, I called my husband, but no luck. We kept missing each other: when he had time to talk, I was in the middle of the trial; when I had time, he was in the middle of a golf game or out with friends.

Next, I phoned Delores Mosley to see how she was doing. "Laura," she said, her voice full of anxiety. "I think it went good today. Do you think it went good?"

"Definitely. No one put Jovan in the fight."

"I thank God for you and Cathy. You two are going to save my Jovan."

I thought of what Cathy had told me while we were working up the case—that signed-confession cases almost always resulted in a guilty verdict—and fear gripped me.

"I don't know, Delores," I said, desperate not to let her expectations get out of hand, any more than mine had. "This kind of case is very hard to win."

"Oh, I know it will be okay. The Lord brought you and Cathy to Jovan. It's in the Lord's hands."

"You're right about that."

I hung up the phone and pulled out my old medical reference books, prepping for my cross-examination of the coroner. When I went to bed at two a.m., all I could do was think of Jovan. Was he lying in his bunk at SuperMax? If I was this scared—no, this *terrified*—about losing his case, what was he feeling? I never slept that night.

33

"I don't remember him hitting him or nothing."

Anton Williams testified next. Anton was a small guy with short hair. He wore dark, baggy jeans and a jacket to court.

On the night of Howard Thomas's beating, he testified, he was sitting on the porch at the house of his girlfriend, Jori Garth. He and Ms. Garth were still in a relationship today. They had one child together.

He's a decent witness, I wrote in a note to Cathy.

"Yeah," she said softly.

After sitting on the porch for a while, Anton said, four or five guys came down the block. Anton recognized three of them—Frad, Fetta, and Marvin. He did not recognize anyone else at the time.

A minute later, assistant state's attorney, Ethan Holland, who was handling the direct examination of Anton, stopped and asked Anton if he recognized anyone in the courtroom whom he had seen that night. Anton pointed to Frad and described what Frad was wearing. Then he pointed to Jovan and said, "I recognize him, but I don't know his name."

Anton testified that after the guys came up to the porch, they started talking about some guy who they said had robbed someone's uncle. Then a guy in his fifties started walking down the street, and somebody said, "There go the guy right there." The next thing Anton knew, "everybody that was out there" rushed him. Specifically, he said, Frad, Marvin, Fetta, Red, and the other guy rush toward him. He saw Marvin, Frad, and Red punch and kick the man. They were hitting him in the upper body area. Then "a bat came out." Frad was holding it, and he started hitting the man with it.

The man fell to the ground, "covering up." Three people were attacking him at that point—the one with the bat and two others. They kept punching and kicking him in his face and upper body. Marvin held on to a car and stomped on the man. Frad kept hitting the man with the bat while he was on the ground. The fight took approximately five or six minutes.

"What were you and Jori doing while this was going on?" Holland asked.

"We was sitting on the porch."[130]

After the fight, the guys walked toward Calumet, and Anton and Jori went inside the house and told Jori's brother what had happened. Then they went back out to see if the guy was all right.

"What did you see when you looked down?" Holland asked Anton Williams.

"Blood, teeth."

"I will stop you. Where did you see teeth?"

"Seen them on his face."

"They were on his face?"

"Yes."

"Not in his mouth?"

"No."

"Where else were they?"

"On the ground."

Anton testified that they asked the man his name. He wasn't able to respond, but they felt through his jacket, where they found a letter with his name on it. They looked in his bag and found a Bible.

When the police arrived, Anton did not speak to them because he didn't want to get involved with what had happened. "I was scared the guys might come back at me or something, you know."

Six months later, in February 2000, Jori's father, Walter Garth, brought them to the police station, and Anton finally spoke to officers about the matter. At that time, he was asked to view a lineup.

Ethan Holland asked the judge for permission to approach the witness and showed Anton a photo of men in a lineup.

My stomach clenched. Was he viewing Jovan's lineup photo? What testimony would he give? It was impossible to know, since the lineup record in the police file had been made years after the actual lineup, and only then in response to a defense motion filed by one of Jovan's lawyers. And since no depositions are taken in a criminal case, we really had no idea what he was going to say.

Jovan clasped his hands on the table and leaned forward, listening intently to Anton. Cathy and I looked at each other.

What's going to happen? I asked her with my eyes.

She shook her head brusquely, as if to say, *Don't ask. Don't even think about it.* Then she turned her head back to the witness.

"I will hand you a black marker and ask you to place an X over the heads of anybody that you identified on that day," Holland said, handing the witness a marker.

Anton studied the photo, then marked an X over three men in the lineup photo. He then named each of them—Frad, who had hit the man with the bat, Red, and Fetta. He had not seen Fetta hitting the man, but did see Fetta get hit accidentally by Frad with the bat. When that happened, Fetta came back to the porch where they were sitting.

Anton was then shown another lineup photo—one that included Marvin Treadwell, whom he identified as being one of the individuals beating the victim.

Then Holland identified and brought out Jovan's lineup photo from March 6, 2000. I swallowed at what felt like a hard pellet in my throat.

"Did you identify anybody in that lineup?" Ethan Holland asked Anton.

"Yes."

"Who did you identify?"

Anton pointed at the picture. "Him right there."

"Let the record reflect that the witness has pointed to the middle individual in the five-person lineup." He nodded at Anton. "Please place an X over the head of the individual that you identified to the police."

Anton complied.

"Was he out there that night too?" Holland asked.

"Yes."

"Did you see him participate in this beating?"

The jurors swung their heads to Anton. There were more people in the gallery now than when the trial had started, but no one spoke or moved. I could feel the tension spreading from Jovan's body, as if in waves.

"No," Anton Williams testified. "As I remember, I think he was standing over to the side. I don't remember him really hitting him or nothing. He had kind of stepped off."

I looked at Jovan. His eyes shot to the ceiling, and he looked as if he were deep in prayer—a prayer of thanks, a prayer that said, *Finally, the truth.*

Cathy and I exchanged relieved looks. The state's own key witness—an independent witness who'd seen the whole fight—had just testified that Jovan had had nothing to do with it.

Frad Muhammad's second public defender, Dawn Sheikh, asked Anton on cross-examination, "Mr. Williams, you said that you were sitting on your porch back on August sixth, 1999, correct?"

"Yes."

"And you watched a man being beaten?"

"Yes."

"You're saying it was for several minutes, correct?"

"Yes."

"And you didn't call the police."

"No."

"You just sat and watched the entire incident, correct?"

"Correct."

"You didn't even go back into your house until the entire incident was over, correct?"

"Correct."

She asked him then about the different hairstyles the group of guys had. Frad's was short, he said. Marvin had braids. He couldn't remember Red's hairstyle. Jovan's, he said, was "low."

"Sorry?" the public defender said.

"Short."

"You said that when you saw the group surrounding the man that you just saw Jovan standing off to the side, right?"

"Yes. As I remember the fighting was going on. I don't remember him hitting him or nothing. I think he had kind of stepped off to the side, like."

"So you didn't see him doing anything at all?"

"No, not as I remember."

Dawn Sheikh changed topics and confronted Anton with his grand jury testimony, during which he'd said, "While we [he and Jori] were sitting on the porch, some of my associates walked up."

"Yeah," Anton said. "If you say I said it, I said it."

"So you have referred to this group of men in the past as your associates, correct?"

"I knew them from the neighborhood. I wouldn't call them a friend or nothing. But you know, I knew them. I talked to them."

Cathy was up next, and she had two main goals for her cross-examination. The first was to reinforce the fact that Jovan had nothing to do with the fight. She had to make sure that the jury had heard and understood that part of Anton's testimony. But this kind of task is always treacherous because there's a chance that the witness might waver or hedge and erase the effect of his direct testimony. And if she asked too many questions, she might open the door for the state to delve further into any ambiguities on redirect.

The second goal was the most important. And Jovan's life hung, in part, on whether Cathy could accomplish it. She needed to show the court that the cops *knew* Jovan had no involvement and yet had forced him into a confession, thereby discrediting the confession Jovan had signed.

"You saw three people head over to the victim, is that right?" Cathy said, taking on goal number one.

"Yes."

"And you identified those as Red?"

"Yes."

"Marvin?"

"Yes."

"And who was the third?"

"Red, Marvin, Frad."

"And you said that Mr. Mosley just kind of stepped off to the side, right?"

"Right."

Cathy put her notes on the podium, then strolled toward Anton. "You also told us that Mr. Mosley didn't attack this man, correct?"

"Not that I remember, no."

"You had a good view of all these events, is that right?"

"Yes."

"No trees in your way or cars?"

"No."

"Streetlights made things pretty visible, is that right?"

"Yes."

"You had no trouble seeing this encounter from the beginning to the end, is that correct?"

"Yes."

Goal number one: accomplished. Cathy turned and picked up her notes from the podium. Time for goal number two.

"Now when you talked to the detectives," Cathy said, "they were taking notes, weren't they?" She held up her own notes as if to give an example.

"Yes."

"Writing down all the things that you were saying?"

"Yes."

"During the course of those conversations, you described the three attackers, correct?"

"Yes."

"And you also tried to describe the roles of everybody that was out there, didn't you?"

"Yes."

"In fact . . ."—Cathy paused—"you told them that Jovan didn't do anything." Another pause. "Correct?"

The judge turned his body toward the witness. You could feel the courtroom waiting for the answer.

"Yes," Anton said.

Cathy nodded. "They asked you to view a lineup on March the sixth, correct?"

"Yes."

"And you were already shown the picture and you drew an X over Jovan, correct?"

"Yes."

"*That's* the person you identified as having been out there," Cathy said," but *not* having done anything, correct?"

"Correct."

I looked at the state's attorneys. All wore grim expressions. There they were, trying a first-degree murder trial, and not only had one of their big witnesses testified that the defendant hadn't done it, he'd also testified that he had told the cops just that.

"Let me ask you this," Cathy said. "At any time did you see them going through his pockets?"

"The guy that . . . that they was beating on?"

"Yes."

"No."

"Did you ever hear words to the effect let's rob this guy?"

"No."

"Did you ever hear words to the effect let's get his money?"

"No."

"Thank you very much, Mr. Williams. I have nothing further."

The judge looked at the state's table. "Any redirect?"

"No, Your Honor."

Walter Garth, Jori's father and a Chicago police detective, testified next about how he had learned, in February 2000, about an unsolved murder from the 73rd block of Calumet. He also learned that his daughter, Jori Garth, was a possible witness.[131] After meeting with detectives, Officer Garth brought Jori and Anton into the station to be interviewed.

During Officer Garth's brief, and relatively unimportant, testimony, I glanced at Jovan, then I wrote Cathy a note: *Jovan looks inordinately bored.*

Cathy elbowed him in the ribs. We would find out later that he hadn't slept in days.

But his attentiveness never flagged for the rest of the trial. Frad Muhammad, on the other hand, fell asleep numerous times. Cathy wrote me a note: *The dude is sleeping during his own murder trial!*

During a break, I stopped into the judge's chambers and gave him a paperback copy of one of my books, *Look Closely*. On the cover was a blue stiletto shoe with a spatter of blood under the heel—an attempt to tie my first four novels, which had been women's fiction, to my first suspense novel.

"It's a mystery," I said. "Ignore the high heel."

Next, Officer Lionel Dunem was called by the state. Officer Dunem testified that he was sent to a battery in progress in August 1999 on the 7300 block of South Calumet.[132] He was at the scene within two to four minutes of receiving the call and found the victim lying near a curb. There was a pool of blood around his head and splatters of blood on one of the vehicles parked at the curb. A bag of Harold's Chicken was near the sidewalk along with a couple of pieces of chicken.

Officer Dunem believed the victim was alive when he arrived. The ambulance arrived shortly thereafter. Officer Dunem stayed to secure the scene and waited until the detectives could get there.

Cathy's cross was quick but very intentional. She confirmed that the call Officer Dunem had received was for a battery in progress, not a robbery. Officer Dunem did speak with one gentleman named Joseph Saunders who had not been at the scene but had heard an argument on the street from his apartment. In a dig to the detectives, Cathy asked Officer Dunem if he had memorialized everything he'd done in a report. He had, he said.

Good job, I wrote on my notepad when she sat down.

Court was recessed early that day for Jovan's jury, because the state was ready to call witnesses who dealt only with Frad Muhammad.

As we packed our exhibits, notes, and records, I whispered to Cathy, "Where the hell is Fetta?"

The more we studied the police records and the more we heard from Anton and Jori, the more mystified we were that Fetta had never been charged. The same flimsy ties that initially existed against Jovan—like Marvin stating vaguely that all the guys had thrown some punches that night—existed against Fetta as well.

Cathy and I glanced over at the table where the state's attorneys were preparing for their next witness. I was struck with how much these guys had to handle—the prosecution of two murder defendants at once, not to mention their already bloated caseload. In the mornings, before our trial started, they were always arguing motions on other cases before Judge Brown and making calls about scheduling witnesses for their next trial, which would start shortly after Jovan's. They seemed almost superhuman (or superattorney) in their ability to handle so much work.

"Go talk to those guys," Cathy said. "Smile at 'em. See if you can get some information about Fetta. They won't give me anything. They'll know I'm fishing. But if you ask, they'll never see it coming."

A minute later, I threw my bag over my shoulder and sauntered over to the state's attorneys' table. "Who do you guys have the rest of the after-noon?" I asked.

They told me who the next witnesses were. Fetta's name was absent. We chatted about one of the alternate jurors whom the judge had dismissed for missing a day of testimony.

Eventually, Andy Varga and Ethan Holland turned away to grab some documents, and I stayed, talking to Jim Lynch. We were both writers, though he wrote mainly plays, and so we talked about that. Then I moved the conversation to the next few days of trial and the witnesses we'd see. "Is Fetta coming in tomorrow?"

Lynch groaned. "You have no idea how hard it is to get lay witnesses in for trial." He explained the difficulties that went along with that, especially those that went along with tracking down Fetta.

A minute later, I walked back to Cathy and whispered, "I'm pretty sure they can't find Fetta."

She clenched a fist. "Yes!"

As we did every day before we left court, Cathy and I visited Jovan in the bullpen to discuss the day's testimony. I was getting slightly more used to the vibe at the cage. It was especially easier at the end of the day when Jovan was the only one there, but at the same time it was heartbreaking to see him sitting alone, his suit hanging more loosely, it seemed, with every passing hour. He knew he would have to take the stand soon, and although he wanted this desperately, he was scared. Cathy and I were too.

"You haven't always held up well under questioning," Cathy told him that day, reminding him of his interrogation.

"Yeah, but I want to tell my story," Jovan said. "I *have* to."

Cathy shook her head. "I don't know. Unless they put on some solid evidence against you—hell, *any* evidence against you—I don't know if you should take the stand."

"But you told the jury in your opening that he would," I said.

"I know." Cathy's forehead creased. "And I've never, ever told a jury I would put someone on, or introduce some piece of evidence, and not done it. But I just don't see how it would help here." She looked at Jovan, her eyes growing concerned. "And I don't want to put you through it if we don't have to. You don't deserve it."

Jovan took a breath and kept quiet, as he often did when he was thinking hard.

Then a small smile broke his face. "Thank you, you guys," Jovan said. "Thank you for everything."

Though we drove home in separate cars, Cathy and I spoke on the phone, further analyzing the case. The evidence so far had been damning for Frad but left Jovan looking good. Maybe he shouldn't testify. Why subject him to a long and grueling cross-examination if the state couldn't put on one piece of independent evidence against him? We spent the rest of the night researching, preparing cross-examinations, sending each other e-mails with tidbits we'd found interesting. I spoke for hours to the character witnesses we considered calling to the stand.

The next morning Jason and I finally reached each other just as they were about to tee off for the day. He passed around the phone to the group of guys he was with, so that each one could tell me that representing Jovan was a good thing and that Jason was very proud of me. Jason had been talking about me the whole trip, they said. Jason got on the phone again. *Keep at it,* he said, but then he had to go, and I was left missing him, missing having someone with me in the house.

I kept hearing Jason's words in my head: *Keep at it.* And I did. For Cathy and me that week, it was all Jovan Mosley, all the time.

34

"Now, that's not a reference to talent, right?"

O n the fourth day of trial, on the way to the courtroom, I walked past the judge's chambers. He sat at his desk, in his robes, reading my book, the blue stiletto prominently displayed.

When the judge took the bench a few minutes later, he said that he had received a note with two questions from the jurors: (1) *What are the first and last names of the defense attorneys and prosecutors?* and (2) *Where has the defendant Mosley been since he was arrested?*

All the attorneys agreed that our names could be sent back to the jurors. They'd already been told our names during jury selection.

But the question of where Jovan had been? The state indicated that such information would be improper.

Cathy nodded her head. "I agree it is not proper." She dropped her voice and leaned over to me. "See? This is why he's got to wear the same thing every day. We've got them wondering if he's been in jail the whole time."

Allen Murphy, formerly an assistant state's attorney and now a judge, took the witness bench looking like the quintessential Chicago lawyer—a stocky, ruddy-faced Irishman with a smart but jovial demeanor.

He testified that in March 2000, he was on the Felony Review Unit. He explained that a Felony Review Unit is comprised of four teams of assistant state's attorneys who review violent-crime cases before they come to court. And they take statements from defendants "if the defendant wishes to speak to us, or chooses to speak to us."[133] One night, he was called to Area 2 with regard to an investigation into the beating of Howard Thomas.

When he first arrived, he spoke to Detective Hill and read the information about the case that was available. Then he spoke to Jovan in an interview room. He told Jovan that he was a prosecutor, which meant he wasn't his lawyer. From memory, Murphy rattled off the constitutional rights he had apprised Jovan of—he had the right to remain silent; anything he said could be used against him in a court of law; he had a right to have a lawyer present during questioning and if he could not afford a lawyer the court or a court of law would appoint a lawyer for him free of charge.

Murphy testified that he told Jovan they could memorialize their conversation in one of three ways—with video, a court reporter, or a handwritten statement created by Murphy and signed by both of them.[134] Mr. Mosley chose the handwritten statement, and Murphy had Jovan moved down the hall to a small office. He and Jovan sat down at a table.

There, he asked Mosley "how he had been treated by the police since he had been at Area 2, if he was hungry, if he had been fed."[135]

ASA Jim Lynch, who was directing Murphy, looked up from his notes. "Did he indicate to you that he had any complaints about his treatment?"

"He had no complaints at all."

"Did the defendant indicate to you that he had been told that he could go home?"

"No."

"Did he indicate to you that he had been promised that he would be a witness in this case?"

"No."

"Did he ever ask you about when he could go home?" Lynch asked.

"No."

"Did you then prepare a handwritten statement with the defendant?"

"Yes, I did."

Murphy testified that he wrote a summary of Jovan's statement, in which Jovan said he'd been in a fight and admitted hitting Howard Thomas twice and later taking a sip of his pop. Murphy read the statement into the record. At the end he'd written how Jovan had been treated well by the police.

I looked at Cathy, who gave a disgusted shake of her head. She had told me that the Felony Review lawyers always put the exact same language in confessions about how the subjects had been treated well, how they'd been advised of their constitutional rights, etc. It was essentially boiler-plate language. In fact, Edwin Korb, Jovan's first public defender, who had defended forty or fifty murder cases before being assigned to Jovan's case, would later say, "[The disclaimers about treatment] are always in the same place in each statement that I have seen. . . . That's how common it is. What you are saying about 'I have been treated well by the police and no threats or force used against me,' that is right at the end of the statement on every statement taken by a state's attorney. I have never seen one that's not like this."

On the stand, Murphy pointed to the three signatures on the confession—his, Detective Hill's, and Jovan's.

The state had no further questions for ASA Murphy.

Cathy stood to cross Murphy, determined to show that Murphy hadn't asked, and didn't necessarily care, what kind of treatment Jovan had received before he arrived there. "Had you been out to the area in reference to this particular investigation prior to that time?" she asked him.

"No."

"Had any of your brother or sister state's attorneys who work twenty-four hours around the clock been out to talk to Mr. Mosley at that time?"

"No."

She asked a few questions about *Miranda* warnings, getting Murphy to admit that no note indicated that Jovan had received *Miranda* warnings before he was given them by Murphy.

Then Cathy stopped as if struck by a different thought. "Now, you said that there are four teams of assistant state's attorneys that work around the clock."

"Yes."

"A team, B team, C team, D team."

"Yes."

"Which team were you on?"

Cathy had a slightly mischievous tone to her voice, and Jim Lynch must have caught it.

"Objection to relevance," Lynch said.

"Why is this relevant?" the judge asked.

"It goes to the investigation. It gives a background to the ladies and gentlemen." Cathy's was a pretty weak response, but the question seemed harmless.

The judge looked at the witness. "Mr. Murphy, if you recall, you may answer that question."

"If I recall, I was on the B team then."

Cathy put a confused look on her face. "Now, that's not a reference to talent, right?"

I coughed to cover a laugh. My eyes shot to Jim Lynch, who had a look on his face like he wanted to laugh too, like he wanted to say, *Oh, she did not just say that, did she?* I looked down and bit my lip.

ASA Murphy wasn't laughing, though. His face had reddened more.

"It's just a different group of state's attorneys?" Cathy prompted.

Through gritted teeth, Murphy said, "There are four sets of state's attorneys."

Cathy's cross rolled on, and she got Murphy to admit a number of points: he knew Jovan had been in an interrogation room for well over a day; he had no idea why the police reports were missing; he didn't know if Jovan had been in a lineup; he didn't know if Jovan had ever made any denials about the beating; he didn't ask Jovan if he'd been able to make a phone call or use the bathroom; he didn't know if Jovan had been crying or upset prior to his arrival.

Lastly, Murphy admitted that as a lawyer whose specialty was criminal law, he knew the elements that made up a crime, but he never told Jovan that if he admitted to being involved in the beating and taking a sip of pop he would be charged with murder and armed robbery.

In order to prep for cross-examining the coroner, Dr. Nancy Jones, I'd been studying her autopsy and the testimony she'd given during the trials of Marvin and Red.

In my old job representing physicians, I spent much of my time deposing doctors and studying medical records. And we always—*always*—employed another physician beforehand to coach us on how to question a particular doctor at trial.

But I had no expert here.

I had searched my mind for some coroner I'd deposed in the past. I had rifled through my old files, hunting for names. I located a few, but my file notes reminded me what the doctors charged for their help—$400 an hour, $600 an hour, sometimes even $1,000 an hour. Since Jovan had no budget, I had to think of something else.

During a break, I hurried through the halls of 26th and Cal, searching for a room where I could make a private phone call. Finally a clerk found me an empty meeting room, where I called Dr. Stuart Rice.

Stuart Rice is a neurosurgeon I'd met at a writers' conference in Hawaii. After the conference, Dr. Rice and I had stayed in touch and helped each other out on a few cases.

Dr. Rice is one of the busiest neurosurgeons in the state of South Dakota, and he can take months to return a call. But when I placed an SOS call to his secretary and mentioned the phrase "murder trial" a few times, he called me back on my cell phone immediately.

I told him the whole story and faxed him the autopsy report. When Dr. Rice had read all the injuries suffered by Howard Thomas, he said, "Even if your kid did do it, a couple of punches to someone's flank would never have caused those injuries. They wouldn't even cause any *serious* injuries. They would never have led to this death. You should bring out all the injuries, every one, to show how he couldn't have contributed to this death. Not even a little bit."

I explained about the accountability rule—if Jovan threw even one punch, even if he had just slapped the guy, he would be responsible for the whole of the crime. So I wasn't sure if I should be introducing evidence intended to show how minimal his involvement was. It didn't *matter* to the law how minimal his involvement was. If the jury believed he threw even one punch, if they believed he took a sip of that pop, then he was done.

A short time later, the state called Dr. Nancy Jones, the forensic pathologist and the assistant medical examiner who performed the autopsy on Howard Thomas. Dr. Jones had testified in hundreds of criminal cases, and she was appealing and polished.

Using the original file from the medical records department, Dr. Jones testified that Thomas had suffered multiple blunt traumas, including lacerations (on his forehead, nostril, corner of eye, chin, brain, mouth, and lips), abrasions (to his forehead, elbow, hands, and left cheekbone), bruises (on the upper and lower lids of both eyes, and on his chest, neck, head, and forehead), swelling (inside the skull and brain), bleeding (on and inside the brain), and fractures (of the right and left sides of his jaw, nasal bones, other facial bones, ribs, skull, and thyroid cartilage).[136]

Dr. Jones's examination also found bullets near Mr. Thomas's left shoulder blade and lumbar back. "These are old bullets that have been there for a long time," Dr. Jones said.

"Dr. Jones," Andy Varga said, "based upon your training and experience, did you reach an opinion to a reasonable degree of forensic pathological certainty concerning Mr. Thomas's death?"

"Yes, I did. . . . Howard Thomas died as a result of the multiple blunt trauma injuries due to an assault."

"Doctor, did you also render an opinion as to the manner of Mr. Thomas's death?"

"Yes, I did."

"What was that opinion?"

"The death was ruled a homicide."

Andy Varga paused a moment to let that word—*homicide*—resonate through the courtroom.

He gestured to his co-counsel, who then pushed a TV in front of the jury and also placed one at our defense table.

Suddenly an image appeared on the screen. One of the jurors gasped.

The image was a gruesome photo of Howard Thomas's dead face and torso, his eyes permanently swollen shut, his face cut and bloody.

Varga approached his witness, handed her a stack of photographs, and asked her if they accurately depicted "what Mr. Thomas looked like on the morning of August seventh 1999."

"Yes," Dr. Jones said, "they do."

I looked at Jovan. These were the same photos that his public defender used to show him while attempting to get Jovan to take a plea. As Jovan looked at the screen, his mouth hung open a little and he swallowed hard. He was fighting down emotions, I could tell, following our instructions not to give the jury anything to read into.

Varga asked Dr. Jones to leave the witness stand and step to the TV in front of the jurors. Once there, she explained all the photos—those of Howard Thomas's autopsy, those of him at the scene, those of him after being treated by paramedics.

The jurors were as stalwart as possible, but many dropped their heads into their hands. Others shook their heads or looked up at the ceiling for momentary escape.

Finally, Dr. Jones was asked to take the stand again.

"Doctor," Varga said, "with respect to the injuries that you just described in the photographs, would those injuries be consistent with being struck with an object such as a baseball bat?"

"Yes."

"Would those injuries be consistent with being punched or kicked?"

"Some of them would but not all of them."

"Would some of the injuries be consistent with being jumped on?"

"Yes."

"Thank you, Doctor," Varga said. "I have no further questions."

At the defense table, Cathy looked at me. "Go for it."

As I stood to cross-examine Dr. Jones, I was nervous. But the first rule of being a litigator is never to let them see you sweat. I walked to the podium and put down my notes. I looked them over for a moment, letting a pause settle into the room in an effort to dissipate the shock of those photographs.

Then I looked at Jovan, still trying to decide if I should take the cross in the manner Dr. Rice had recommended.

I thought of the fact that Jovan had initially been charged with death-penalty murder.

In Illinois, the death penalty can be sought when another felony takes place at the same time as a murder. At the time of Jovan's arrest, the death penalty was still in effect in Illinois, but since 2003 there had been a moratorium on executions. "We have exonerated not one, not two, but thirteen men from death row," Governor Ryan had said in a speech declaring the moratorium. He was referring to the men freed from death row using DNA, showing they never could have committed the crime. "They were found innocent. Innocent of the charges for which they were sentenced to die. Can you imagine?"

Sometime after the moratorium, the state had decided not to seek the death penalty in Jovan's case. But as I looked at Jovan, who was pale with grief from the coroner's testimony and the pictures, I knew that he would die if he ended up in prison. Yes, he had survived SuperMax, but if he was convicted, if he no longer had the hope of freedom, the kid would *die.* His body might survive, but it would only be a shell. The Jovan I knew would be gone.

And so, I figured, until the state's attorneys objected, I was going to use Dr. Rice's idea. I would bring out every little piece of evidence that showed only the most brutal attack would have caused Mr. Thomas's injuries, and that my client had not been responsible for any of them. Period.

I took Dr. Jones, in detail, through nearly every injury Howard Thomas had suffered, including those to his brain, his face, his lips, his eyes, his ears, his cheekbones, his jaw, his chin, his thyroid cartilage, his lungs, his ribs, his back, his neck, his elbow, his knee, his kidney, and his stomach.

No objections from the state's attorneys.

"Now, with respect to the photographs that you viewed today . . . ," I said, "those are photographs of the deceased's face, correct?"

"Yes."

"The injuries that you see that were depicted there are far too severe to be caused by just someone's fist."

"Well, some of them could be. Like the abrasions could be from that, but where the fractures are, especially the mandible because that is a really strong bone, would be inconsistent with just a fist." Dr. Jones stopped and cocked her head a bit. "Actually, depending on how hard and how big, we just had a football player who got a fractured jaw from another football player, so it can happen."

I told Dr. Jones that I was referring not to a hypothetical NFL situation but to the photographs she'd viewed today. "Those are injuries far too severe to come from someone's fist, correct?"

"I would agree with that."

"Doctor, those are the kinds of injuries that you see when implements are used," I said, referring to the bat.

"Yes."

"And with respect to the fracture of the facial bones, those were injuries that require a great deal of force, correct?"

"Yes."

"And it's more likely that those fractures were caused by an instrument rather than a fist."

"Correct."

I paused a second. I'd prepared a crib sheet of cases I could argue if the state objected. But they still hadn't. Maybe they thought my cross wasn't deadly enough to their case. Or maybe they were hoping the testimony would go over the jury's head, as it does some times with expert witnesses.

I moved on. "On your internal examination you found fractures of the three posterior ribs, correct?"

"Yes."

"Those are ribs nine, ten, eleven?"

"Yes."

"With respect to those kinds of rib fractures, in order for those types of injuries to be caused by a punch it would have to be a forceful punch."

"Correct."

"And generally, with respect to those kinds of rib fractures, that is the kind of injury that you see in instances where people have been struck with an object or in people who have been stomped or kicked, correct?"

"Correct."

"With respect to your internal exam and the photo today, you also found a laceration of the kidney, is that right?"

"Correct."

"How large is that?"

"The largest one—there are actually two—the largest one was one inch long."

"The kidney is an organ that is deep inside the cavity of the body, is that right?'

"It is all the way in the back of the body."

"It takes a great deal of force to generate the kinds of injuries that would cause these lacerations."

"That's correct."

"And in fact, the easiest way to understand—you mentioned football

players—and the easiest way to understand the kind of injuries to the kid-
neys, that is the kind of injuries that you see sometimes in football players
who have been tackled."

"That's correct."

"That's the kind of extreme force that you're talking about."

"Yes."

I glanced over at Cathy, who was nodding with approval. She held up
her notebook then, and I knew what she was getting at.

Trials are a performance, but they are not performed in a neat, chronological narrative. Instead, evidence is introduced piece by unpredictable
piece, testimony from witnesses is often given nonconsecutively, based
only on what witness is available in a particular week. It is the job of the
attorneys to eventually gather those pieces and in a closing argument make
sense of them for the jury. I knew that Cathy wanted to elicit from as many
witnesses as possible the undeniable importance of keeping careful notes
in order to highlight the utter lack of police notes.

"Doctor," I said, "when you're performing your autopsy . . . you said
the purpose of an autopsy is to get a detailed examination to find out what
happened to this person."

"That's correct."

"It's important for you to be as detailed as possible when you're making
your report?"

"Yes."

"Especially in a case like this where you know it appears to be a homicide or something with medical and legal potential. You know it is important to be detailed in your report."

"Yes."

I glanced at Cathy again, who gave me a single nod, as if to say, *Thanks,
that's all I needed.*

"Thank you, doctor."

Jovan, Cathy, and I waited, nervous, to see who the state would call next.
Fetta? The state's attorneys clustered together at their table.

Jovan reached up and, in a nervous gesture, tugged on his shirt collar,
but the truth was, it wasn't tight. He'd lost weight. A lot of it. And his face

had taken on a grayish tint from lack of sleep and food. Or maybe it was just fear.

But then the judge spoke. "We are going to start our lunch hour. All rise for the jury."

He dismissed the jury for lunch, then called us to the bench and told us to take care of any housekeeping matters, like any motions or scheduling issues.

Andy Varga asked for admission of certain photographs and documents into evidence and the judge went through them all, hearing any arguments against admission and then making a separate ruling as to each.

In the middle of this process the sheriff stepped forward. "Judge," he said, "can the gallery be seated?"

We all turned and saw, standing in the gallery, at least fifty spectators. We were a bit shocked. Over the course of the trial, word had gotten out about Jovan, about the kid who was in a holding cell for almost six years and was now on trial for murder. More and more spectators had appeared until there was a small crowd.

"Yes, I'm sorry," the judge said. "Please be seated."

Andy Varga turned back to the bench. "Your Honor . . . the people will be resting their case in chief."

Cathy and I met eyes. No Fetta. They had no other evidence at all to put on against Jovan.

"Very well," the judge said. "As to Mr. Mosley?"

Cathy, in a clear, loud voice said, "We would make a motion for a directed finding of not guilty at this time."

"Any argument with respect to your motion?"

"Very briefly, Your Honor. The state's witnesses, other than the assistant state's attorney, Allen Murphy, were all occurrence witnesses. *None* of them said or testified that Mr. Mosley did anything other than simply being there. He was merely present . . . We would ask Your Honor to direct the verdict of not guilty at this time."

"State?" the judge said.

Andy Varga stepped forward. "Mr. Williams," he said, referring to Anton, "puts the defendant at the scene at the time of the beating. In his statement to Mr. Murphy, the defendant acknowledges knowing what was going on, acknowledges the sharing in some of the proceeds, even if that is albeit just a soft drink." Andy mentioned some other testimony, ending with the summary, "He admits to getting a couple of punches in. I would submit that we have sustained our burden."

The judge looked from Andy Varga to Cathy and back. "The motion for directed finding is respectfully denied."

35

"You have a right to present evidence on your behalf."

Jovan leaned in, huddling with the lawyers. His lawyers. Sometimes he still couldn't believe it.

He listened as they talked. They were confused that the state hadn't called Fetta and surprised they hadn't called other police officers or detectives—there had been so many of them involved in his arrest and the time he spent in that little room. Jovan had been steeling himself to see Fetta and challenge him (at least with his eyes) to say that Jovan had anything to do with that fight when he knew damn well he hadn't.

Plus, he was looking forward to Cathy ripping Fetta's testimony apart. Yesterday, trying to make him laugh, Cathy had told him that since Fetta was a rapper, she was thinking about rapping her cross.

"Yo, Fetta, East to the West," Cathy had said, joking, throwing up a gang sign with her hands. "Yo, where were you on August sixth?"

He had surprised himself by laughing. He had thought sometimes that he might never laugh again, certainly not about his case. But Cathy was one of the funniest people he'd ever met.

Cathy looked at him now. "I subpoenaed the detectives just in case," she said. "And two of them are here. We're going to have to call them. We need to show how long you were in that room and how many times you denied hitting Thomas."

"Mr. Mosley." Judge Brown's voice boomed through the courtroom, startling him.

Jovan and his lawyers turned to the judge.

"You have a right to present evidence on your behalf," the judge said. "Or you have a right to remain silent. Have you made the decision on whether or not you're going to testify?"

He looked at Cathy and Laura. They had talked about this—Cathy had been thinking he shouldn't take the stand, while Laura seemed more conflicted about it. He was conflicted too. He wanted *so badly* to get on that stand and tell the jury exactly what had happened. And yet, he could see that the state's attorneys were good lawyers. Although he had prepared himself to square off against them for the last five years and nine months, he couldn't help but think about the mock cross-examination he'd undergone with Eddie and Laura. It had been harder than he'd thought. Either way, both his lawyers had told him many times that this was his decision, one that only he could make.

He looked back at the judge. "No." His voice cracked. It was the first time he'd spoken aloud to the courtroom since the trial began. He cleared his throat. "No, I haven't, Judge."

Judge Brown dipped his head and peered at him. Jovan felt a flutter of nerves. "Have you discussed the matter with your attorneys?" the judge asked.

"Yes."

"And as of yet, you have not decided whether or not you're going to testify?"

Jovan crossed his hands on the table in front of him. It was his decision. He had to make it, and if he ever wanted to practice law later, he would have to make all kinds of hard decisions. And so, just like a lawyer would, he squeezed his hands tighter, sat up straighter, and said, "No, sir."

36

"Let it roll, he's killing himself."

The camaraderie I'd noticed the first day between Cathy and the state's attorneys had continued throughout the trial. As we waited for the judge to return from lunch that day, I was touched by the state's attorneys. They sauntered over to our table and asked how we were doing. Then they dropped the concern and launched into jokes about parts of their case, about Dr. Jones's testimony and certain ghastly aspects of the autopsy. Such comments would usually be offensive, but I'd learned that the absurdity of gallows humor was the only way these guys coped with both the stress of their jobs and the evil they so often encountered. I looked the state's attorneys, clearly kind and intelligent men who had an enormous amount of work to do and a mammoth weight of responsibility on their shoulders. I understood then that it would probably have been easier for everyone involved—the PDs, the state's attorneys—to continue Jovan's case rather than to spend time they didn't have to see if he might be innocent.

The camaraderie even extended between Cathy and the detectives. As we were talking, Detective Howard, one of the officers who'd arrested Jovan and had been key in his interrogation, came into the courtroom, wanting to see if he had to testify. He was a cheerful African-American man with a big presence. He and Cathy, who'd met before, chatted like they were at a church social.

"Hey, how are you?" Cathy said. "Good to see you."

"You too. I saw you when? On that one?"

They both burst out laughing and talked about some average, run-of-the-mill stabbing case they'd both been involved with.

"So what are we doing here?" Detective Howard waved a hand at the witness stand, where he would soon be sitting.

"Ah, you know, the usual," Cathy said. "I'll take you through your investigation, your records."

They both paused at mention of the records. Since there were essentially none. But they both recovered and went back to talking about the stabbing. One of the state's attorneys made one more joke about the trial. And then everyone dropped the topic and skidded over to the prospects of the Bears, avoiding the fact that a man's life hung in the balance because, six years ago, another life had been cut short.

At the end of the lunch break, it was our turn

The jury returned to the courtroom. "On behalf of Mr. Mosley," Judge Brown said, his voice booming, "do you wish to present any evidence?"

I stood from the table. "Yes, Jovan Mosley would like to call Anita Owens."

At the back of the room, someone opened the courtroom door and Anita Owens, a medium-sized black woman, her long hair braided into cornrows, stepped inside. Wearing a blazer and pants, she walked down the aisle, while the courtroom, now even more crowded, watched her in silence.

We had decided that Anita Owens would be the sole character witness on behalf of Jovan because we thought Delores was too emotional to be cross-examined—it would be painful for her and ineffective for the case. Plus, character witnesses can only testify to very limited things. They can't go on about what a great guy the defendant is, how he's really nice and likes puppies. A character witness can only testify to those traits that show a character unlikely to commit the crime the defendant has been charged with. Since Jovan was accused of hitting a man and contributing to his murder, Anita could essentially only testify to his reputation for peacefulness.

I had been talking with Anita every night on the phone, prepping her for her testimony, listening to her rave about Jovan. She had worked with him at the law firm while he was in high school, and their boss had been difficult, she said, but Jovan always kept his cool. Anita had been writing Jovan regularly while he was in jail, and she missed him and worried about him. During our conversations, which would often last an hour or more, I frequently had to stop Anita to remind her that her testimony had to be very specific or it would draw objections.

On the stand now, Anita testified that she was a nurse tech for Jackson Park Hospital. Before that, she'd worked as the office service clerk for a law firm in the Loop that handled medical and accident cases. There were about twenty people at the firm, she said, and she managed the file room, as well as the copying and the mail and supplies.

"Did you ever have occasion to work with Jovan Mosley?" I asked.

"Yes," Anita answered. "Our office had a part-time position open, and I asked my immediate supervisor if it was okay if I would hire, since it was part-time, a high school student."

She went to Dunbar Vocational Career Academy, Jovan's high school, and interviewed students, she testified, and after the interviews she hired Jovan. "There was something about his personality as I talked to him and described his duties that [told me] he would be the right person for the job."

I asked what Jovan's duties were at the firm.

"Mainly filing, sometimes copying, whatever had to be done. But mainly his duties also included doing bank runs or messenger deliveries. . . . In our kitchen, we had a pop machine that had cash in it, coins in it, and [Jovan] would have to empty those coins out and take them over to the bank and bring back cash."

She worked with Jovan for about a year and a half. But even after he'd worked only a couple of weeks, "everybody would pull me over and say, 'Where did you get this guy from? We really like him.'"

Jovan was a peaceful person, she continued, smiling at the memory of Jovan and then shooting Jovan an adoring glance. "Whatever job or whatever task he was given, he did it just so, and he got praised for that, you know. There was never 'No, I'm not going to do this' or 'I'm not going to do that.' Jovan did just so."

"Did you ever hear anyone say anything against Jovan with respect to his reputation for peacefulness?"

"No, I never did."

I asked her how long Jovan had worked for the firm.

"About a year and a half."

"Why did his employment end?"

"Jovan told me that he wanted to go to college and further his education and so he told me that . . . he was thinking about leaving."

That was all I could get from Anita without pushing the limits of the law. "Thank you, ma'am."

"You're welcome."

I looked at my watch. Two fifteen. I had to teach at Loyola Law School at three, and I couldn't miss class because I'd taken off the previous week to prepare for the trial. But I would be able to leave soon, I figured. The state probably wouldn't cross Anita, since her testimony had been relatively inconsequential.

"Cross-examination?" the judge said.

"Yes, sir," came a voice from behind me.

I turned and saw Ethan Holland getting to his feet. He smoothed his auburn hair with his hand and buttoned his well-tailored suit. I sat next to Cathy, who looked as surprised as I did. Jovan narrowed his eyes and glared at Holland, as if trying to warn him off with his eyes.

And then Holland began what was undoubtedly the most intense cross-examination of the trial.

Jovan watched as the youngest state's attorney looked at Anita. He was so grateful to her for coming here today, and what she'd said about him had lifted his heart. But now he was wary.

"Ma'am," Ethan Holland said, still across the room from Anita, "you said that you worked with the defendant for approximately a year and a half, is that correct?"

"Yes." Anita had a great smile, and she sent one to Holland now.

"And specifically the only thing that we're concerned with," Holland said, "is your testimony regarding the defendant's peacefulness, is that correct?"

Anita glanced at Jovan. Jovan knew she probably didn't understand the legal reasons why she couldn't speak at length about things other than this 'peacefulness.' It had taken him awhile to understand.

He kept his face blank, though. Cathy and Laura had told him that, unlike a coach on a sideline, neither he nor they could give a witness any kind of sign or even encouragement.

Anita looked back at Holland. "Right."

"And specifically, counsel asked you about the defendant's reputation in your law firm for peacefulness, correct?"

"Right."

"And that reputation you said was born out of tasks that you gave him that he performed peacefully?"

"Well . . . the person who owned the law firm . . . he could be a very hard person. He is a very hard taskmaster, and Jovan would have to be peaceful you know and a humble person in order to work under a person like that."

Holland took a few steps toward her, making Jovan more nervous. "Let me ask you this. The law firm is downtown, correct?"

"Yes, it is."

"Is it in a big building?"

"Yes, it is."

"It is a work environment, correct?"

"Right."

"People wearing suits."

"Right."

"Lawyers are there, correct?"

"Right."

"Support staff is there?"

"Right."

Holland continued his questions like that. Jovan saw what he was doing—pointing out the professional nature of the office.

"Are you aware of people at the firm who did not carry out their tasks peacefully?" Holland asked.

"Most everybody there—who worked there—did, you know."

There was a pause. Laura glanced at Jovan and nodded, like, *She did a good job.* It seemed like it was over, but Jovan still had that wary feeling.

"What you're really saying," Holland continued, moving closer to her, "is that nothing that the defendant did when he was working down at a law firm was violent, correct?"

Now he seemed to be making fun of her.

"Right," she said, her voice lower.

"You also said that you had conversations with people in the firm *spe-*

cifically regarding the defendant's reputation as being peaceful, correct?" His tone made it clear he didn't believe her.

"Right."

"Who are these people that you had these conversations with?"

"The attorneys who worked in the office, the receptionists, the secretaries, the paralegals."

"Let me ask you about the attorneys," Holland said, his voice getting louder, again moving closer to the witness stand. "*When* did you have a conversation with attorneys in that office *specifically* regarding Jovan Mosley's reputation for being peaceful?"

It seemed he was calling her a liar now. *Leave her alone,* Jovan wanted to yell.

Anita shot him a distressed glance. This wasn't what she had signed up for.

Laura stood. "Objection."

Jovan felt a little relief.

"Basis?" the judge said.

"No specific instances raised on direct." Jovan knew what that meant too. The law stated that on cross-examination of a character witness, the attorney could inquire into specific instances where the witness saw certain character traits but only if "specific instances" of those traits were raised during the direct examination. Since Laura hadn't raised any specific times at the firm, she didn't think Holland should either.

But the judge didn't agree. "Objection overruled. This is cross-examination."

Ethan Holland repeated his question. "Regarding only the attorneys that worked at the law firm, how was it that you had a *specific* conversation about the defendant's reputation for peacefulness while at that law firm?" He made it sound like she was stupid.

"Well, sir," Anita said, like she was trying very patiently to explain, "when Jovan would be given tasks to do, sometimes he would go on deliveries, sometimes you know like somebody would be . . ." Her voice died off for a second, as if realizing her testimony was wandering.

"You know, if it's raining outside, you may not want to go outside in the rain, if it's snowing, below zero, and Jovan would do those tasks. He would not argue back with anyone, you know? So he was a peaceful person."

She looked at Jovan with a pained expression. She knew her explanation sounded weak, and she wanted so badly to do a good job for him. Without moving any of his facial muscles, he tried to send her a signal with his eyes: *You're fine. Thank you.*

There was a pause in the courtroom. Everyone began to shift gratefully in their seats.

But it wasn't over.

Shocked, Jovan, Cathy, and I watched as Ethan Holland turned back, again, to Anita Owens. She looked miserable.

"Really what you're saying," Holland continued, "is that the defendant, when taking on tasks at your law firm, did not complain, correct?"

"Yes, sir." Anita's voice was small. She was done arguing.

"That's *not* the same thing as having a reputation for being a peaceful person, isn't that right?"

"I would assume not, sir."

Holland started prowling in front of the jury box. "Let me ask you this." He gave a slight scoff. "Your opinion of the defendant was gained through your own personal interaction with the defendant at the law firm, correct?"

"Yes, and watching him handle his tasks."

"And really, the reputation that you're talking about here today in court was something that you learned on your own, correct?"

"Well, no, sir. . . ." Anita sat up straighter and spoke louder, as if willing to try and explain her point again. She talked about how different people in the firm said wonderful things about Jovan.

Holland asked her for specific conversations with the lawyers, the paralegals.

"Sometimes my boss would yell at Jovan," she said, "and sometimes it would be overheard by others in the office you know because that's the way my boss was, and Jovan would not . . ." She stopped and caught her breath. "You know, like if somebody is . . ." Anita dropped her voice as if imitating a man. "If somebody is, 'I want you to get over there and do this and I want it done right now.' Jovan did not get angry. . . . He wasn't a violent person. That is what I'm saying. He didn't get angry."

Holland stopped prowling and faced the witness stand, and his voice rang out with scorn. "So I guess what you're saying is that the defendant didn't *attack* anybody at work? Is that your testimony?"

"Right."

Holland scoffed again. "Did anybody else attack other people at work?"

"No."

"So, really, the defendant would be in the same boat as everybody else at the law firm in terms of his reputation for not attacking supervisors." He looked at Anita with contempt. "Is *that* correct?"

Anita had a confused look on her face. "Right, or anyone else." After another, similar question from Holland, Anita tried again, gamely, to explain. "If Jovan missed, wasn't at work a day, they might say, 'Anita, where is Jovan? We really miss him.' They really and truly liked him."

"I understand that ma'am," Holland said in a condescending voice. "We have established that the defendant was well-liked at the law firm. . . . My question—*again*—in the absence of any reason to talk about his specific reputation for peacefulness, give me one concrete example, a conversation that you had with somebody at your law firm specifically about his peaceful character."

"Well, the incident like I said when my boss yelled at him. Again they asked me—he did not have to be a peaceful person. If he was—he was— the person that asked me, he said, 'Anita, I noticed that Jovan didn't even get angry when—he just went and did what he was told,' so to me that is being peaceful, you know."

Anita Owens was faltering, her words starting and stopping and then tripping over each other. She sent a beseeching glance my way. So did Jovan. His eyes said, *Make it stop.*

Holland moved close to the bench so that he and Anita were only a foot or so apart. He leaned in with his body. "Your *answer* . . ."—his voice was loud and angry, and he said the word *answer* as if it had air quotes around it, implying it had been pathetic—"And correct me if I'm wrong, is that you can't think of a *single* conversation where you discussed—"

I stood. "Objection."

"Just a moment, please," the judge said. "Continue your question."

"Thank you, Your Honor." Holland looked at Anita Owens and crossed his arms. "I think your answer is that you *can't* give me *one* conversation that you had with other people in the law firm regarding the defendant's reputation at that law firm for peacefulness, correct?"

"Objection," I said loudly.

"Basis?" the judge said.

"Asked and answered."

"Overruled."

I sat down, feeling sick for the way Anita was getting beat up.

But she seemed to have some fight left in her. "Well, can I ask you a question, sir? Would you give me a definition of peacefulness then since it seems like I'm looking at peacefulness in one aspect and you're saying it's different?"

A couple of the jurors nodded, looking at Holland.

"Could you answer my question, ma'am?" he said with disdain.

She looked up at the judge for help and got none. Turning back to Holland, she said, "I would say, like I said before, the peacefulness that they talked of is how he performed and did not get angry at my boss."

"You don't remember where this conversation took place, do you?" Holland accused.

I knew what he was doing. Technically, Holland was following the law school formula for cross-examination—always get an answer to your question. Anita Owens hadn't specifically answered his question about when she'd had a conversation about Jovan's peacefulness and with whom. But the other thing they teach you in law school about cross-exams is, *Know when to sit down and shut up.*

Anita Owens paused and thought for a moment. "It was in the paralegal's office . . . the paralegal at the time was Deb Finki . . . and in her office, and like I said, she had overheard [the boss] yelling at Jovan—"

"Let me ask you this," Holland said, interrupting her. "Did [the boss] yell at other people in your office?"

"Yes. He did."

He asked if anyone else attacked the boss for having him yell at them.

"No."

From behind me I heard fierce whispering. I turned to see Eddie, Cathy's husband, and his friend Steve Shobat, a respected criminal lawyer who'd been giving Cathy advice during the trial and its prep.

Eddie gave me an intent stare with his dark eyes. "*Objection,*" he said.

He whispered fast a couple of other objections I might try. So did Steve.

I turned back to Cathy. She glanced at me, shaking her head—*Don't object*—then she turned back to watch Ethan Holland and Anita Owens.

"Did you have other conversations about other people in your office and *their* 'peaceful reputation'?" Now Holland's tone was contemptuous, making no effort to hide the fact that he was mocking her.

"Yes," Anita said defiantly.

"Who?"

She mentioned a name, then explained, "one of the attorneys that worked there."

"And he had a reputation in your law firm as being a peaceful person too?"

"Yes, he did," Anita said firmly.

"How did that 'conversation' come up?" There was no ambiguity in his tone—he was clearly deriding her.

"Well . . . I mean . . . it's just . . ." Anita had begun to lose her fire for this verbal joust. "You don't walk around and say is this person—" She looked at Jovan, as if to say, *I'm sorry. I don't know what else to do.* "We were having a conversation."

"That is *exactly* my point," Holland said, his voice thundering through the courtroom. "You don't walk around saying 'I like this person. They've got a really good reputation for peacefulness,' do you?"

The jury looked alarmed.

"No, sir," Anita answered, beginning to get teary.

Jovan shot me a look that said, *Help her!*

I leaned over to Cathy. "Jesus, what should I do?" I whispered. The cross-examination had grown painful to watch, and there was no reason to beat up this poor woman, one of the least important people in the trial.

Cathy chewed the gloss off her lower lip as we watched Holland decimate our witness. "Let it roll," she whispered back, looking at Holland. "He's killing himself."

"That's not really how it happens, is it?" Holland was saying, nearly yelling at Anita now.

"No, sir," she said, crying now, but trying to stop her tears.

At the state's attorneys' table, Andy Varga and Jim Lynch had their heads down, facing their notes.

Holland stalked even closer to her. "You don't sit around by the water cooler and say, 'That clerk we have. I'm not worried about him attacking the boss at all,' do you?" The scorn was so thick, and, to my mind, so misguided. The jury looked mortified.

"No, sir." Anita's voice was small, defeated. She wiped at her streaming tears with the sleeve of her blazer.

"Now, ma'am, the Jovan Mosley that *you* knew was the Jovan Mosley at the downtown law firm, correct?"

"Yes, sir." Anita Owens's voice was almost undetectable. She sniffled and shot a look of apology to Jovan, who looked close to tears himself.

"Surrounded by lawyers, correct?" Holland asked.

"Yes, sir."

"Surrounded by other office workers, correct?"

He'd made his point already, about fifteen times, that Anita only knew Jovan from a nice, clean, shiny downtown law office, not in the "hood."

I looked at Cathy. "Asked and answered," I whispered quick, like, *Please let me make the objection.*

She shook her head no and continued to watch Ethan Holland with fascination.

"He dressed appropriately, correct?" Holland asked.

"Yes, sir."

"*That* is the Jovan Mosley you knew, correct?"

"Yes, sir."

"Nothing further, Your Honor," Ethan Holland said with pride. Technically, he'd done a good job of beating up the witness, getting her to finally admit to the point he was making, but it had been devastating to watch.

As he took his seat, the courtroom sat in shocked silence. On the stand, Anita Owens dropped her head in her hands.

I turned to Cathy and said in a low tone, "I want to redirect."

"I think we should leave it alone."

"But he massacred her." I glanced at the defeated figure of Anita Owens. "I can clean up a few things. Even if I'm doing it just to make her feel better."

"Redirect?" the judge asked.

"Let me," I whispered to Cathy.

Cathy looked around the crowded courtroom. All eyes—from those of the jury, the state's attorneys, the judge, and what were now approximately one hundred spectators—were on us. Except for Anita Owens's. She looked at the floor of the witness stand, hunching forward as she swiped tears from her face.

The quiet grew and filled with intensity as everyone watched, waited for our decision. Cathy let the moment drag on. And on. Until it felt like several minutes had passed.

Finally, she smiled, looked me in the eye, and whispered, "I *love* this shit."

I gave a surprised laugh.

Cathy glanced at Anita, then back at me, and shook her head.

Reluctantly, I stood. "Nothing further, Your Honor."

37

"No matter what happens,
I'm so glad I took your case."

Even Cathy had to admit that Detective Howard was very likable on the stand. He testified that he treated Jovan well and fed him numerous times. Cathy wanted to laugh. To hear him tell it, it was like Thanksgiving, with all the feeding sessions.

Specifically, Detective Howard testified that on the second day Jovan was in custody, he returned to work at eight a.m. (Jovan was in custody long enough for detectives to work entire shifts, go home, sleep, and return to work another shift.) But before he got to the station, Detective Howard said, he went to McDonald's and got Jovan "a sandwich, hash browns, and a juice."

"Did you write that down anywhere?" Cathy asked him.

"No."

"This has been six years?"

"Yes, ma'am."

"But you remember that on March seventh you got him hash browns and a juice?" Cathy let the incredulity roll off her tongue and into the courtroom.

The heads of the jurors snapped back to Detective Howard.

"For the three years that I was a detective, anytime I had a defendant in custody overnight, that was my standard operating procedure."

Another practice that was standard, Detective Howard testified, was that the police officers interviewed Jovan in sets of two so that "one person will do the speaking and the other person will do the writing."[137] Detective Easter was his cohort, and was the officer writing most of the notes when they were in the room.

Detective Howard explained that such notes, or GPRs, are written by the detectives during an investigation to record witness interviews and "just about anything that happens during an investigation." Generally, he testified, GPRs were preserved with the entire police report.

"Are they done by civilians?" Cathy asked him, remembering Fetta's handwritten GPR.

"No."

"Where are the GPRs for Jovan Mosley?" Cathy asked.

A pause. Then, "I have no idea."

Cathy let that hang in silence for a second, then moved on. Detective Howard testified that he hadn't personally read Jovan his Miranda rights when he was arrested, but someone had, he was sure. He admitted that the arrest record, drafted shortly after the arrest, did not mention the giving of any Miranda rights.

Detective Howard testified that over the course of the days Jovan was interrogated, he "denied everything."[138] Jovan admitted he had been at the scene but denied having hit anyone, stating a minimum of five times that he had never touched Howard Thomas.

Cathy asked about supplemental reports, generally written by the police at the end of an investigation.

Detective Howard testified that the one supplemental report in Jovan's case was written by Detective Hill, but that he had collaborated on it. "I told Detective Hill what I did, parts of the case."

"Do you know when you had those conversations with Detective Hill?"

"After the investigation was over with."

"Well, the report didn't get drafted for three and a half months, did it?"

"That is true," Detective Howard said.

She asked him about the lineup report. "Are you aware if it was drafted *fifteen months* after the actual lineup?"

"Yesterday it was printed out, but I am not sure when it was written."

"There is a note in there that it was drafted because a review of the file showed no reports about the lineup, is that right?"

"Yes."

"And the lineup occurred on the sixth of March at eleven thirty in the evening, correct?"

"Yes."

"Mr. Mosley was identified in the lineup. Is that correct?"

"Yes."

Cathy stopped. Anton Williams had said he told the detectives Jovan had been there but he hadn't done anything. But often what the cops "remember" is very, very different from other witnesses. Cathy debated whether to ask the question. She looked at Jovan. She knew she would do anything for the kid.

She turned back to Detective Howard. "He was identified as simply having been there but not taking part, isn't that correct?"

Detective Howard's face remained impassive. "Yes."

Cathy stopped herself from looking triumphant. "And the identifier was Mr. Anton Williams."

"Yes."

Detective Howard denied cuffing Jovan to the wall during the interrogation.

Cathy asked whether any of his "brother detectives" had done that. She didn't know why, but she got a kick out of asking ASAs about their "brother and sister attorneys" or cops about their "brother and sister police officers."

Detective Howard denied that any other officer had cuffed Jovan.

"When you went to interrogate Mr. Mosley," Cathy said, "those kinds of visits with Mr. Mosley, they were confrontational, is that fair?"

"Yes."

"Did you ever present Mr. Mosley with a pen and ask him to write a statement of facts for you?" Again, she was referring, obliquely, to Fetta's bullshit freestyle rap of a GPR.

"No, ma'am," Detective Howard said with sarcasm. "This is not TV."

She had been starting to gather her notes, but now she froze. "I'm sorry?"

"No, ma'am. This is not TV."

Cathy blinked at the detective and cocked her head. "I agree. Thank you *very* much. I have nothing further."

Under questioning by the state's attorney, Detective Howard denied that he told Jovan he could go home when he admitted he was a participant in the fight. He denied telling Jovan that if he admitted hitting Howard Thomas he would be just a witness in the case. As for the Miranda rights, he didn't recall reading them himself, but Miranda rights were read to the defendant at some time.

Cathy stood up again. She wanted another go at him. "You have no idea where the GPRs [are] that contained his five denials?"

"I did not handle them. I do not know where they're at, ma'am."

After a few clarifying questions, she asked, "When is the last time that you saw the GPRs that contained Mr. Mosley's five denials?"

"Since the time that Detective Easter was writing them up."

"And they're gone now, correct?" She let her voice ring through the courtroom.

Detective Howard's was much quieter. "I do not know where they're at, ma'am."

"But Mr. Mosley's admissions seem to survive, correct?" Her sarcasm was palpable.

Jim Lynch's stood quickly, his tall frame leaning over the table. "Objection."

The judge sustained it.

Cathy showed the witness a report. "Do you recognize that report?"

"It is a supplementary report."

"Is that Detective Hill's report?"

"Yes. It was created by Detective Hill."

"Can you tell us when he created that report? Does June of 2000 sound about right?"

"Yes."

"About three and a half months after Mr. Mosley's arrest?"

"Yes."

Cathy paused to let that information settle in again.

Then she called Detective Clarence Hill.

Detective Hill, who was the lead detective on the case along with Detective Williams, was a reserved man. Whether he was nervous or not a good speaker, Cathy didn't know. He testified with several pregnant pauses, especially when asked about the lineup reports. As had Detective Howard, Detective Hill denied that they had cuffed Jovan to the wall inside the interrogation room.

"Let me ask you this," Cathy said. She picked up the lineup report and held it aloft. She crossed the courtroom and showed it to the witness. "Did you generate that document months and months after the lineup?"

"It could have been. . . ." Detective Hill scrutinized the document. The crowd in the courtroom, Cathy noticed, was entirely silent, as if everyone understood the importance of this testimony. "Without knowing . . ." He stopped and looked at the document some more. "Without being able to find the created date on here—" Once again he stopped.

Cathy took a few steps closer to him. "Did you generate that document," she said, in a don't-mess-with-me kind of voice, "because you had reviewed the file and noticed that there was absolutely no lineup report?"

"If there was no lineup report, there needed to be one for the case." He paused.

Cathy did too.

"That is correct," Detective Hill said. Then, seeming uncomfortable with this admission, he added, "It would be correct that I needed one for the case."

"Is that why you drafted the one that you're reviewing now?"

"Yes. I drafted . . ." Again, a heavy pause. Finally, Detective Hill looked up from the document. "I would have drafted the lineup report because there was no lineup report."

They wrangled for a bit about the date the lineup report was created.

"You were the only one who drafted any kind of reports with respect to Mr. Mosley's arrest and statement, am I correct?" Cathy asked.

"The only report I know in this case as it relates to Mr. Mosley, that I am aware of right now, is the report that I typed, yes."

"That is because all of the other GPRs with respect to his statements are gone, isn't that correct?"

Detective Hill waited a moment, then, "I later learned that those GPRs were gone. Yes."

"Where are they?" Cathy said, her voice demanding.

"I don't know if they ever existed. I just heard that the GPRs were gone. Someone said the GPRs were gone."

"Who told you that they were gone?"

"One of the detectives, but I don't know if they had . . ." Another pause.

"We were looking for GPRs," the detective said, as if starting his explanation over. "We were asked to look for any GPRs as it relates to Mosley, and no one could find any."

Cathy asked a few other questions, then crossed her arms and looked at her witness. "GPRs are not something that you shred, correct?"

"No."

"In fact, you, during the course of this investigation, created several GPRs, isn't that correct?"

"Yes."

"You created about twelve, is that right?" Cathy asked, referring to the total number of GPRs created for the other defendants.

"I don't remember the number, counsel," Detective Hill said with a grim voice that bordered on irritated.

"You and your GPRs made a thing called a timeline, didn't you?"

"I believe so. Yes."

"And in your timeline, on nineteen occasions you refer to the times that the different people were interviewed, correct?"

"I believe so, yes."

"That means that time is very important in investigations, would you agree?"

"Time is an important factor in investigations, yes."

They went around and around about when the supplementary report on Jovan's case had been created—both agreed it was months after the interrogation, but Detective Hill continued to assert that he couldn't tell exactly when, based on the document itself.

Cathy let it drop. She asked him what he used to create that report.

"That report was done based upon me talking to the other detectives who were involved in the case . . . ," Detective Hill said, "and what they did, me typing what they did into the computer. And if there were GPRs, I would have used the GPRs to populate that report."

"Did you use Mr. Mosley's handwritten statement that was taken by the assistant state's attorney in drafting your report?"

"Yes, any previous documentation that we had prior to that point, I would have used—I would have referred to all that in order to draft my report."

She stopped and took a wide stance, staring at Detective Howard, tired of all the grappling about his authoring of reports. "Now, this midnight lineup that took place . . . were you there or not there for the lineup?"

"For Mr. Mosley's lineup? I was there for the lineup."

"And you, in your lineup report, didn't indicate that Mr. Mosley had been identified as doing anything—simply that he was identified, isn't that correct?"

Detective Hill paused, blinking at Cathy.

Everyone waited for his answer. He hadn't been allowed in the courtroom during Detective Howard's testimony. Would he testify the same?

"That's correct," he said finally.

Cathy hid her relief, then shifted the questioning around to address Detective Maverick Porter's interrogation, in which he got Jovan to confess. "Did you see him go in that room?" she asked.

"Yes, I did."

Detective Hill testified that he was sitting at a typewriter, writing a report, when Detective Maverick Porter went into the interrogation room by himself.

They haggled over what report he was writing at the time.

"I know that I was typing at the typewriter and Detective Porter said . . ." A pause. "Came to me and said . . ." Another pause. "And said that he's . . . he's admitting to being involved or he's got something to say, something to that effect."

"He came out and told you that *he's giving it up!*" Cathy held a rolled-up stack of papers like a baton, her voice growing loud as she repeated the words of the detective.

Detective Hill looked fed up with the questioning. "I believe that might have been his words. Yeah."

Hill testified that after Porter came out, he went in the room. At this point, Jovan had been in custody for well over a day. Hill testified that Jovan was crying, although he couldn't remember if it was exactly after Porter came out or sometime later.

It killed Cathy to think of Jovan in that little room, by himself, crying. She looked at Jovan now and they held each other's eyes for a second.

She turned back to Detective Hill and began verbally wrestling with him, attempting to show how his police report, authored months after the event, was in many places verbatim of the confession written by the state's attorney. Detective Hill admitted that he had "paraphrased" parts of the confession in his report, but she couldn't get a good, complete answer, because the state's attorneys kept objecting and the judge kept sustaining.

She looked once more at Jovan, who gave a little nod like, *It's okay.*

She decided to pack it up and sat down.

Jovan looked at Cathy through the bars of the bullpen. He had been thinking about this and thinking about this. "I want to testify," he told her.

"It's your decision, but I don't think you should. The burden was on the state to prove you threw two punches. It is *their* burden." She pointed down the hall toward the courtroom. "And I don't think they did that beyond a reasonable doubt."

Jovan struggled to focus hard on what she was saying, but his mind was exhausted, twisted.

"Think about what they did to Anita on the stand," Cathy said, her voice rising. "Think about that! She was just a *character* witness, Jovan. She was the *least* important witness at this trial, and look what they did to her! Remember what they did to her!"

Tears sprang from Jovan's eyes. That someone had come into that courtroom to help him and had been destroyed like that was killing him. It had been a nightmare, almost worse than jail. Because in jail, he still believed that the legal system would give him justice; that the legal system was *good*. But that—what they'd done to Anita?—there wasn't a shred of good in that.

And then he remembered that his shot with the legal system was almost over. The trial was drawing to a close. And he could be spending the rest of his life in jail for something he didn't do. More tears began to fall.

"Jovan," Cathy said insistently. She grasped the bars with both of her hands and leaned her face in. "I can't, in good conscience, subject you to the torture they'll put you through on the stand when their case was crap. Absolute crap! And . . ." Her voice faltered. And when you've already been through so much."

Jovan put his hands on the bars below hers and bent slightly at the waist, as if holding himself up. When he looked up at Cathy, his face was nearly even with hers, her blond hair framed by steel rods.

"I promised the jury you would testify," she said. "And I always keep my promises. I've never told a jury I'd do something, present some evidence or whatever, and not done it. And trust me, I really don't want to start now, on *your* case."

Her voice was full of emotion, and Cathy stopped to take a breath. She and Jovan looked at each other through the old steel bars, and both felt they didn't have to talk anymore.

His eyes said, *I want to trust you. But I promised myself I wouldn't let anyone tell me what to do again.*

She gave the briefest of nods. *I know. And this is your decision. Yours.*

A door closed down the hallway—maybe the judge leaving for the day? But otherwise there were no sounds down at the bullpen, no one around. Jovan was the only inmate left. Tears splashed his cheeks. Suddenly he could not stop crying, could not imagine a time when he would not be crying.

"I really didn't do anything," he said to Cathy, gulping back his tears. "I really didn't."

Cathy reached forward and grabbed Jovan's arms. She began crying too. "I know, I know." They both continued to cry. "We're going to have our answer tomorrow." She tried to take a breath. "Listen," she said, "I'm glad I know you. I think you're a good kid. I think you're telling the truth. No matter what happens, I'm so glad I took your case."

They looked at each other, both crying, holding tight to each other's arms.

38

"Do it because it's right, it's fair, and it is time."

Cathy drove her French-blue Mercedes down Highway 55, heading south. Her mother, Rosanne O'Daniel, was Cathy's "rock," although most other people, Cathy knew, would describe her as a sweet little thing. She'd been giving her mom an update on the trial every day. She called her mom now and told her about the day's testimony, about her conversation with Jovan in the bullpen. And with that, she let the tears come again. "Mom, if they don't acquit him, he's going to disappear back into that broken system."

"It's in God's hands," her mom said over and over. "It's good you did this. You've done your best."

Cathy didn't think anything could make her feel better, could drive away that image of Jovan crying behind those bars, but her mother's voice and her calming words did the trick.

Back at SuperMax, Jovan spoke to no one. He marched to the three phones that hung on the far wall of the day room—those that could only be used for outgoing collect calls. He acted like he had important things to discuss. He picked up the receiver and hunched forward, so his face would be covered. He acted like he was talking low. But really, he was crying again, letting the tears stream down his neck and soak the collar of his DOC shirt.

None of the other inmates bothered him. They all knew his trial was on, that it was about to come to a close.

I could be found guilty, Jovan thought over and over. It seemed impossible when he had done nothing wrong. But he couldn't get away from the fact that he might be going to prison for the rest of his life.

He hunched his back, hung his head lower, and cried some more.

Cathy and I spent much of the night on the phone, planning the closing argument. We looked up famous closings from people like Clarence Darrow. We called our friend Beth Kaveny, who was in Hawaii, a master trial lawyer herself, and consulted with her. We struggled again over whether to let Jovan take the stand in his own defense.

I tried Jason a few times, but didn't reach him.

I called Cathy back and told her I was missing my husband.

She listened intently, as Cathy always does, refusing to sugarcoat things. "That's a bitch," she said. "He'll be home soon." But Jason wasn't due back for at least four days, and the sound of that—*four days*—seemed as long as a decade.

The next morning, I went back to the bullpen and yelled, "Mosley!"

Jovan made his way through the mass of prisoners to the bars. He looked like hell. He had barely eaten or slept in over a week, and his suit and shirt were limp from sweat and hung awkwardly on his wasted frame. He told me that he'd managed to sleep a few hours this morning. He'd also gotten some cologne sample cards from a guard's magazine and rubbed them on his suit.

Cathy arrived and strode back to the bullpen, a grim expression on her face. We huddled with Jovan, him in a corner of the bullpen, us just outside the bars, our three faces only inches apart.

"I don't think you should testify," Cathy said. Her voice was definitive now. "It's still your decision, always has been. But here's what I'm thinking. They'll never get you to admit guilt, right? But they'll pick apart your memories of that night. They'll do their damnedest to make you look guilty of *something*.

"It's your decision," she said again.

Jovan took a deep breath and closed his eyes.

Five minutes later, we advised the judge that Jovan would not testify. We were ready for closing arguments.

Ten days before, the trial of Jovan Mosley had started with a tiny group of people witnessing the jury selection and opening arguments. But word about Jovan's case had spread. People had heard that a guy had been in county for a long, long time, a guy whose lawyers said he'd been forced into a confession.

So by the time Jim Lynch stood to his full height, ready to deliver the state's closing argument, the courtroom was packed. Every row in the gallery was jammed, people sitting shoulder to shoulder. Along the sides, the overflowing crowd leaned against the walls. At the back of the courtroom, people stood three feet deep, trying to see over those in front of them.

Jim Lynch gave a fervent closing about the power of a group, explaining that the law said if Jovan hit Howard Thomas even once, he was responsible for every single blow. Outside the courtroom, Lynch is a playwright and author, and his argument was delivered with powerful oratory skills. The jury was rapt.

I wrote on my notepad and shoved it at Cathy. *NO ONE TRIED TO STOP THIS FIGHT. Not Jovan, but also not Anton, not Fetta, not the Barnes brothers, not Jori, not Joseph Saunders.*

Cathy read the note but was too focused on Jim Lynch to respond.

Mr. Thomas and his family had suffered, Lynch said, and they did so because of the actions of a group.

Lynch stalked across the courtroom, unveiled a photo of a badly beaten Howard Thomas. "A group can accomplish *this.*"

He explained the accountability instruction again. That instruction meant, he said, that Jovan Mosley was "accountable for *every* blow."

Right then, one of the jurors, Andrea Schultz, began to cry. She held a Kleenex to her face. Soon, two other jurors joined her, while others wiped at tears that seemed ready to fall.

Lynch ended his argument quoting the famous phrase, "United we stand, divided we fall." Referring to the accountability instruction, he went on to say, "But in the law of the state of Illinois, united they stand and united they will fall because they are guilty of first-degree murder and armed robbery."

I wrote on Cathy's pad, *Match his passion.*

She did more than that.

In a red suit with black piping, her feet encased in high patent-leather pumps, Cathy walked slowly from the counsels' table until she stood in front of the jurors, at the very center of the jury box. She held a few sheets of paper with notes, but those notes were rolled in one hand, and that hand hung at her side. She looked at the jury, sweeping them all into her gaze. No one in the courtroom spoke.

I stood and moved into Cathy's chair to be closer to Jovan, whose eyes were locked on Cathy's back. "You okay?" I whispered.

He looked at me, terrified, mute, then back at Cathy.

In typical Cathy style, her closing was no-holds-barred. "Good morning, ladies and gentlemen. You just heard a fifteen-minute speech.[139] About two seconds of that speech were devoted to Jovan Mosley and what they say Jovan Mosley did. Well, I don't know about you, but did you feel like you were in the wrong courtroom on Monday and Tuesday when over and over and over again witness after witness, *their* witnesses, got on that stand and told you he was there, but he did not hit him, [was] not part of the group? The group is made up of people who beat this poor man to death. That group was Marvin, Frad, and Larry Wideman.

"We know who did it. It's not a whodunit. Mr. Mosley was not in that group. And how do we know? Ask Anton Williams, their witness. Ask *their* witness. We have seen a modern courtroom miracle. We have seen the miracle on 26th Street, the miracle of the state proving Mr. Mosley didn't do it with their own witnesses. *Eyewitnesses. . . .*"

At the state's attorneys' table, Varga, Lynch, and Holland shifted in their seats and gazed at the table in front of them.

"They don't want you to look at what Jovan Mosley did do if anything," Cathy said. "Ignore Anton Williams. Ignore their own witness. That's what they're asking you to do. Folks, we can't ignore Anton Williams, their witness, and we can't ignore Jori Garth. Jori and Anton and the Barnes brothers . . . they all heard arguing, not a robbery, not 'Let's get his money,' and certainly not 'Let's get his bottle of pop. . . .'

"Those were the people on the street. Those were the people who saw it, not the detectives, not the trained prosecutors who come on the scene later. Their own witnesses.

"All these days later, it comes down to two punches and a sip of pop. Two punches and a sip of pop. Unless you believe Jovan Mosley threw two punches, you cannot convict him of murder. Unless you believe Jovan Mosley drank a sip of pop, you can't convict him of armed robbery.

"They came right out in opening statement and said, 'Let's front this. Nobody's ever going to put that bat in Jovan Mosley's hands.' Well, that's an understatement. Not only does [no one] ever say he had the bat in his hands, everyone said he didn't hit Mr. Thomas.

"You're not part of the group unless you do something to help the group, and Jovan Mosley was not part of that group. He was not on that team. Their witness, Anton Williams, told you that over and over again."

I glanced at Jovan. He was looking at the ceiling, swallowing hard. I hadn't known Jovan Mosley very well ten days ago. I knew him now. I knew he was trying, desperately, not to cry as Cathy and I had told him not to. Tears could be read as guilt, we'd said. Jovan swallowed again. With his head level, his eyebrows up, he gazed heavenward. I reached under the table and took his hand in mine.

Cathy kept rolling, reviewing in detail first Anton Williams's testimony, then Jori Garth's.

Next, Cathy turned to the issue of the missing police records. The police, she said, "told us [of] the need for notes, accurate notes, in a murder investigation. This is an extremely, as every murder is, an extremely important thing to get right. Someone's died. Someone's *died*. The notes ought to be right. They ought to be accurate." She paused and let her gaze scroll up and down the rows of jurors. "They ought to exist."

I looked at Jovan again. His eyebrows were scrunched together, his mouth pursed, but he was taking his eyes off the ceiling more and more to look at Cathy.

"As jurors," Cathy said, "you've all been given notes, notepads, notebooks. You're allowed to take notes. That is our justice system's way of recognizing that memories can be fragile. Memories can fade even if it's only within the space of one week. It's our justice system's recognition of how important it is to get the details right."

That, she said, is why so many notes did exist on the case—notes about

Frad's case, Marvin's, Red's, notes about interviewing the Barnes brothers. So why were there no notes or GPRs in Jovan's file? The file of one of the alleged murderers?

Cathy next moved to the detectives themselves and Allen Murphy, the assistant state's attorney who took Jovan's statement. "The detective and the state's attorney . . . they weren't there. They're not eyewitnesses. They are professional witnesses who came along after the fact. Nineteen-year-old Jovan Mosley, from the minute he was arrested, was outnumbered, and he was outmatched."

She spoke of how long he'd been in that interrogation room. "Do you think one time anybody ever came to tell him that he hadn't been identified in a lineup? Do you think anybody ever came to tell him Anton Williams says you're entirely innocent? Of course they didn't.

"Ladies and gentlemen," Cathy said, "their philosophy was don't bother me with the facts and don't pester me with the truth. I'm going to talk to him and talk to him and talk to him and talk to him again and again and again and again and again. . . . They knew Anton said he was there and didn't do anything. They knew that. And they worked on him, and they worked on him, and they worked on him.

"Over the course of twenty-seven hours, the detectives came to him, and then they went home. And two other detectives came, and then *they* went home. Three different shifts, five different 'I was there but I didn't hit that man. I didn't rob that man. I did not rob that man.' Does that sound familiar? Of course. It's the same thing we heard from the people that were there—Anton and Jori.

"Twenty-seven hours later, Detective Porter enters the room. Detective Hill says that after Detective Porter entered the room and spent some time with Mr. Mosley, Detective Porter came out and told Detective Hill, 'He's giving it up!'

Cathy mentioned that Detective Hill had never asked Porter how he'd gotten him to 'give it up.' He only knew that when he went in that room again, Jovan was crying. "We just know that Maverick Porter, 'the closer,' does not want you to hear about the labor pains. He just wants you to see the baby. He isn't here. We didn't hear from him."

Cathy pointed at the state's attorneys. "The burden of proof is on them. . . . We don't have to call anybody. Jovan Mosley doesn't have to testify when the state's own eyewitness gets up there on that stand and says he didn't do it, he can't add a single thing."

Cathy paused to let that sink in. I was still grasping Jovan's hand under the table. We were both sweating.

"You heard from Anita Owens," Cathy said. "She . . . talked to you about what it was like to work with Jovan Mosley in the law firm. She liked him. That was clear. She thought he was a good kid. She met him when he was in high school, and she hired him to do an important job to represent that law firm. She trusted him with money, and she told you about his character and reputation."

Cathy turned and faced the state's attorneys' table. "And what did they do?" she said with loud incredulity. "They got in her face. They screamed at her. They tore her to shreds, and they broke her into tears! And she left this courtroom in tears."

"Objection!" Andy Varga said, standing from his seat.

"Congratulations!" Cathy said over him.

"Just a moment, please," Judge Brown said, asking for the basis of the objection.

Andy Varga tossed off a vague objection: "Arguing facts not in evidence."

The judge looked at the jury. "You heard the evidence. You saw the evidence." Then he looked at Cathy. "Continue."

Cathy jumped in almost before the judge had finished speaking. "Anita Owens has no bone to pick. She has no ax to grind. She wasn't there on the street either. She's not an eyewitness. But she told you about the year that she spent with Jovan working, and they got in her face and screamed at her."

Cathy turned and looked at Jovan. Their eyes met for a long moment. Then she turned back to the jury. "I wasn't going to put my client through that again, not after the six years he's already been through. To have them get up in his face and scream at him when their own witnesses got on the stand over and over again and told us he was there, but he didn't hit anybody."

I felt Jovan shaking. When I looked at him, I saw his tears had begun to stream. I took my hand from his and placed it on his arm, giving him what I hoped was a reassuring squeeze.

When I looked at the jury I saw that Andrea Schultz was crying again. So was another juror, a thin Polish woman. I peered at them, trying to discern why they were crying: Because they felt bad for Jovan? For Anita Owens? Or, as we all should, were they thinking of Howard Thomas and his family?

"[Jovan] has no burden in this case," Cathy said, "but he called Detective Howard, and he called Detective Hill. We made the police our witnesses in this case." She crossed her arms and paused, looking at the jury intently. "That's not a usual occurrence," Cathy explained. "The detectives have to be called by the defendant to say he didn't do it? What's going on? . . . I called them because they won't.

"And the detectives tell us about feeding him. . . ." Cathy's tone had grown weighty with sarcasm." About giving him drinks, and all that stuff. He got McDonald's. It's a wonder they had time to question him, they were so busy feeding him.

"Ladies and gentlemen, you heard from the state's attorney how important it is that a statement be voluntary. . . . It's so important that the state's attorney spent a page and a half of a seven-page document talking about the good treatment of Jovan. That's how important it is. And the detectives know darned well how [important] it is. And they didn't bother to make one note anywhere about any of the things they did, let alone even noting the advice of his rights, his *Miranda* rights. The most basic thing that happens when you're arrested. It's not in the arrest report."

Cathy paused, taking in the jury with her gaze. Andrea Schultz dabbed at her eyes with a Kleenex. A few jurors were stoic. Many had seemed aggrieved.

From the counsels' table, Jovan and I studied those faces too, looking closer at Andrea Schultz. It was impossible to tell what they were thinking, which way they were leaning.

"Every witness, including the coroner, who was an excellent witness, a very credible person, every witness that testified talked about the importance of notes." Cathy paused, then repeated, "The importance of notes. . . . This is a murder case. It does not get any more serious than this. . . .

"Detective Howard told us time is real important to him. He drafted twelve general progress reports. . . . He noted the time things happened. But he didn't have one report about Jovan Mosley."

I looked at Jovan. He'd folded his top lip inside his mouth, trying to stifle his tears.

"Those [reports] have vanished. The same thing for Detective Hill, for Detective Porter. Everybody who came into contact with Jovan Mosley and wrote those reports." Another pause, then, enunciating with jabs at the air with her notes, Cathy said, "They have all vanished.

"Think about that, ladies and gentlemen. Those are the reports where Jovan was asked what happened. And he said, 'I was there, but I did not hit that man.'" She crossed her arms now, stopping, letting the air hang heavy. "Those. Are. All. Gone."

Cathy glanced over her shoulder at the state's attorneys. "When they get back up here—because they get the last word because it's their burden and it should be—don't let them tell you . . . missing reports are just details. Maybe they're just details to them. They're definitely just details to the police. They're not just details to Jovan Mosley. This is the most important day of his life. Those are not just details."

She took a breath and let it out audibly. "Missing reports. Is it reasonable, or is it reasonable doubt? Of course it is. Reasonable doubt is not something you're going to find an instruction on. You don't need one. You know it when you see it. You know it when you hear it, and you have seen it and you have heard it over and over and over again this week."

Cathy talked about Allen Murphy, about how he was not an independent witness, he was the lawyer for the police. "Assistant State's Attorney Murphy never told Mr. Mosley if you admit to two punches and a sip of pop, I'm going to charge you with first-degree murder, and I'm going to charge you with armed robbery. Of course he didn't tell him that. . . . Do you really believe that Jovan Mosley is so sophisticated that he said just enough for the approval of charges on first-degree murder and armed robbery? Do you really think Jovan said, 'Let's go rob a guy, let's go beat him. Oh, you got money? Well, I don't want the money, but I want a sip of that pop.' . . . I like Jovan but he's not sophisticated and smart enough to pull that off—two punches and a sip of pop—just enough to get the charges to stick."

Cathy put her notes on the podium, her hands behind her back, and looked at the jury. "They talk about group, group, group, group. Folks, the most important group is right here." She pointed at them. "This is the group that matters. I will go on to other cases soon. The state will go on to other cases soon. The judge will go on to other cases soon." She turned, looked at Jovan, then back at the jury. "But this is Jovan Mosley's day in court, and you are the group that matters the most to him. He wasn't part of any group, and you heard it over and over again.

"Now is the time for you to do what you think is fair. You have all of the evidence. You have inherited the power to do what is fair from a system that has been alive and well for two hundred and twenty-nine years in this country. Why? Because it works. The system works, and it's something that we all should be thankful for. . . . You are quality control. You are the great equalizers. You have heard the evidence this week.

"Do what you think is fair. Do what the evidence merits. Find Mr. Mosley not guilty. Because Mr. Mosley is *not* guilty." She paused, looking down. Finally she raised her face. "And do it because it's right, it's fair, and it . . . is . . . time." I heard a catch in her throat.

When she sat down, she wrote a note on my yellow pad: *I almost lost it.*

After she had taken a few breaths, Cathy wrote me another note: *Did the crier cry for us?* She meant the juror Andrea Schulz.

I wrote her back, *Yes, but not as much. She makes me nervous.* I sat up, about to push the notepad toward Cathy. Then I added one more line: *If crier is foreperson, we're in trouble.*

39

"The jury has a question."

Delores Mosley listened as Cathy spoke to her. "Make *sure* you eat something," Cathy said. "We have no idea how long we'll be waiting for the verdict."

Delores swallowed hard, nodded.

Delores left the courtroom and went to the first floor of 26th and Cal and found the snack bar—the Gangbangers' Café, she'd heard it called. The rectangular room was filled with silent, grim-faced defendants. Few lawyers in the snack bar, Delores noted, except a couple leaning over the formica countertops, handing out business cards, hustling for work.

Delores looked up at the list of food choices—chips, sandwiches, hot dogs, fries.

She ordered a hot dog and took a spot at a counter. She looked at the hot dog and thought, *I can't eat. I can't eat until I know the verdict.*

But she heard Cathy saying she should eat something. She knew she was right.

She picked up the hot dog and took a small bite. It tasted warm, comforting. She took another bite, then another, this one larger. She kept eating, and she couldn't believe it but she noticed that she felt okay. Strangely. She was still scared, but somehow not as scared as she had thought, not as scared as she had been for almost six years.

She kept chewing and she thought, *No, I'm not that scared at all.*

While the jury deliberated and the judge went back to his chambers, Cathy and I and the state's attorneys lingered in the courtroom chatting, packing up our notes and exhibits.

The sheriff came into the courtroom. "The jury has a question."

The air got tense. Jury questions are like snippets of their deliberations. You get to know what they're thinking and debating, and therefore what verdict they might be leaning toward. We'd already had two minor questions—about what had happened to Marvin and Red, and where Jovan had been since he was arrested. The judge hadn't given them any additional information, just told the jury to deliberate.

Now the sheriff went and got Jovan from the bullpen, and the judge returned to the bench, zipping up his black robe. He took the question, read it to himself without a flicker of a reaction, and then read it aloud. "Can we convict him of something less than first-degree murder?"

No one responded. Cathy and I locked eyes. The question was ominous. Jovan searched our faces, wearing a panicked expression.

"They can only consider the crimes he's been charged with," the judge said. "I'm inclined to tell them that, and tell them to keep deliberating. Any objections?"

Cathy swallowed hard, but shook her head no.

The sheriff gestured for Jovan to stand and led him back to the bullpen, as he shot terrified glances over his shoulder at us.

Cathy was white. She looked as if she were struggling to keep her composure.

"You want me to talk to him?" I asked.

She gave me a silent nod.

Alone in the bullpen, Jovan sat on the bench with a blank stare. He stood when he saw me and grasped the bars. I put my hands over his.

"What do *you* think about the question?" he asked me.

It was one of the hardest things I would ever do, but I told him the truth. I told him it sounded as if they were thinking of convicting him of something.

Jovan's despair was palpable, and I couldn't stop thinking about what would happen to him if he was convicted. I tried to console him, but we both knew I couldn't do anything. No one could except the jury. And who knew how long it would take them to decide Jovan's future? They could return with a verdict in three minutes or three days. In the meantime, we all had to keep our strength up. It was the only thing we could control right now.

"Eat something," I told Jovan, nodding at the white paper plate on the bench.

When I returned to the courtroom, I found that Cathy had gotten her mojo back. She stood with the state's attorneys, trying to butter them up.

"C'mon," she said. "If he gets hit, you have to recommend a lenient sentence. You have to. You've already got the guys you want for this."

Cathy never stopped working.

40

"How can someone say they didn't do it, after signing a paper that says he did?"

In the jury room behind Courtroom 600, the walls were a dirty, dingy yellow. The room was stark. Old oak chairs sat in front of a long, scarred wood table. A few tall windows let in the anemic gray November light, yet they were set so high up in the wall that jurors couldn't see outside.

But Andrea Schultz wasn't thinking about what was outside those windows. She cared only about her duty as a juror, and now as the foreperson of that jury. She knew she had to do the right thing, that they had no room for even the tiniest error. And that scared the hell out of her.

During the trial, it struck Andrea as profound that Jovan was so attentive and worried, while his codefendant, Frad, appeared nonchalant, although admittedly she'd only seen portions of Frad's trial, since he had his own jury. She also noticed that when the lawyers had to address the judge, and the judge gave the defendants the option either to stay or to leave, it was always Jovan, only him, who stayed in the courtroom.

She looked around the jury room now, taking in the eleven other people who would decide Jovan Mosley's fate, and she was gripped with a sense of what an awesome, overpowering, *overwhelming* responsibility they were faced with. She had known, absolutely known, as the trial came to a close, that she would be the foreperson, that her fellow jurors would select her, and that she would accept. She couldn't explain it; it was just a sense she had. And she was right.

She cleared her throat now and addressed the group. "We haven't been able to talk about this for days," she said, "so everybody needs to get it out—any emotions, any thoughts. Just spew."

She started the spewing process. And found herself sobbing. She couldn't help it. She knew, as she told the other jurors, that a young man's life was in their hands.

After everyone else had their say, Andrea, a former project manager in marketing, let the jury know that they were going to work on this case with a process. Using her managerial skills, she led the jurors in a discussion about the witnesses and the evidence, using their notes and their memories.

When they had concluded, Andrea told the group that the big hang-up for her was that Jovan had *signed* the confession. And he wasn't denying he signed it. If he admitted to throwing a few punches, and a few punches made him responsible for what the group had done, then how were they supposed to get from a signed confession to a not-guilty verdict?

The fact was Andrea Schultz wanted to give Jovan a not-guilty. She had felt from the start that he was innocent, and she was even more convinced now. And even if he wasn't innocent, even if every word in that confession was true, she suspected that Jovan Mosley had been in jail ever since his arrest, and personally, Andrea felt he'd suffered enough for two punches.

But ultimately, she told the jury, none of her feelings mattered. The jury instructions had been clear, and they had to evaluate the evidence through the lens of those instructions.

The jurors discussed the case some more and came up with two questions, which they asked the sheriff to send to the judge: *Where has Jovan been since the fight? Where are Marvin and Red now?*

The thought behind the questions was that if the other guys had been convicted, then someone was paying for Howard Thomas's death. And the jury felt certain that *someone* had to pay.

The judge sent back an answer: *You have all the information you need, keep deliberating.*

They batted around some ideas and thoughts in the jury room, discussing how even if Jovan had thrown a few punches, a first-degree murder conviction didn't seem right. Out of curiosity more than anything, they sent out another question: *Can we convict him of something less than first-degree murder?* The answer was the same.

Feeling frustrated, Andrea got the jurors talking again. They discussed the fact that the only people who knew the truth about what had happened were the victim, the defendants, and the witnesses. In terms of witnesses, all the jury had were those the state had called, and neither had seen Jovan throw a punch.

Andrea noticed that Alfonzo Lewis, a young black juror who sat halfway down the table, was strangely quiet. He'd been a little late every day, which Andrea knew because she'd always been the first one in the jury room. Alfonzo admitted that he had wanted to be on the jury because he was upset with his supervisor at work and needed a break.

Andrea turned her attention back to the other members of the jury. "How can someone say they didn't do it," she said to them, "after signing a paper that says he did?"

Suddenly Alfonzo spoke up. "How many times has someone put a piece of paper in front of you and said, 'Just sign here, and you can read it later'?"

Looking at him, something clicked in Andrea's mind. She thought of all the real estate closing documents she'd signed in her life, all the doctors' office forms.

"Think about it," Alfonzo continued, "it happens all the time, so how hard is it to believe that he signed that thing after being in a room for that long, not eating or sleeping?"

Andrea Schultz found herself nodding. She leaned forward and told Alfonzo Lewis to keep talking.

41

"Weird seeing you.
We're waiting on the Mosley verdict."

Cathy and I left the courthouse in search of food. "Where do attorneys eat and wait for verdicts around here?" I asked. I thought of Petterino's, the place across the street from the civil courthouse where most lawyers awaited the fates of their cases. I could see the polished red leather booths and the sparkling glasses behind the bar.

"There isn't any one place." She stopped outside on the steps, shivering, looking up and down the block.

At the end of that block was the white monolith—SuperMax. Cathy and I stared at it for a second and I know we were both thinking, *Please, God, don't make him have to go back there, or someplace like it, for the rest of his life.*

Cathy pointed to the left. "There's a Mexican joint that way."

We found the restaurant—a place with plastic booths and fake tile floors. We ordered enchiladas and margaritas, then left the food largely untouched, cheese congealing, while we sucked down the cocktails. Our mood wobbled between despondency at the mere thought of a guilty verdict and relief that the trial was over.

Cathy's husband, Eddie, joined us for a bit, as did Steve Gallagher, a student of mine who'd performed some research. As all trial partners do, Cathy and I relived for the guys, ad nauseam, the big moments of the trial and the small. Like fishing stories, trial anecdotes grow with each sip: *Did you see his mouth fall open when you impeached him? It was THIS big.*

We told Eddie and Steve about Anton's definitive testimony that Jovan hadn't done anything. We told them of Cathy's questioning of the cops and Ethan Holland's destruction of Anita Owens, and finally the decision not to put Jovan on the stand. We told them the little stuff too—Cathy calling Jovan "Vizzle" whenever she wanted to cheer him up or kidding him about rapping her cross to Fetta, our thought that as the only women in the courtroom we should use a table runner and colored, scented paper.

At some point, Steve left and Eddie went outside to take a phone call.

Briefly, we tore ourselves away from the trial and talked about other things—our families, Cathy's kids, the looming deadline for my next book. When it was just us, Cathy and I talked in shorthand now. We were no longer two attorneys who vaguely knew each other from the legal world. We were friends. Exceptional friends.

Cathy shot me a concerned look. "Did you get to talk to Jason last night?"

I shook my head.

"You guys all right?"

"Ah, sure. We've never had problems." It was true.

A lawyer walked up to our table. It was easy to spot the lawyers around 26th and Cal. No one else in the neighborhood wore a suit.

"Jim." Cathy's eyebrows rose. "Weird seeing you. We're waiting on the Mosley verdict."

She introduced me, and I shook hands with the guy. He and Cathy talked about a judge they knew, someone who Cathy said "didn't know his ass from a motion to quash." Then it hit me—*Jim* was Jim Fryman, one of Jovan's public defenders.

"Why did it take so long?" I said, interrupting their conversation. The margarita had made me bold. And blunt.

"Excuse me?" he said.

"Why was Jovan waiting for a trial for almost six years while you were his lawyer?"

He blinked a few times. He said he wasn't Jovan's public defender for the first year and a half.

"What about the other four years?"

He mentioned something about the judge on the case being transferred and a state's attorney becoming ill.

Cathy beamed me a look: *Shut up.*

I wanted to ask, *Why didn't you defend that kid? Why didn't you help someone who says he was forced into a murder confession after being cuffed to a wall for days with no food or water or sleep or even a bathroom break?* But I closed my mouth. He probably had helped as best he could. And after being at 26th and Cal that week, I had a sense of how impossibly hard it was to work in the criminal justice system. Often, there simply wasn't enough time to care.

When Fryman was gone, Cathy and I returned to our discussion of all things trial.

"Oh, my God," Cathy said, her face growing animated, happy. "Do you remember when I was crossing Murphy?" She meant Allen Murphy, the assistant state's attorney.

"Of course. You did a great job, but he's a pro, so it's hard to get points from—"

"No, no," she interrupted me, holding up a hand. "Please tell me that you remember the *beginning* of the cross. When I asked him about the 'B team'?"

I burst out laughing. In the tension of the rest of the trial, I'd almost forgotten. "Oh, my God, you asked him if being on the B team of Felony Review had anything to do with talent. It was hysterical! Did you see his face?"

Cathy coughed up a swallow of margarita and started laughing too. "He was so pissed!"

"*So* pissed."

"He wanted to kill me!"

"And Jim Lynch and I just looked at each other, and we were trying not to crack up."

"Are you serious?" She put her hand over her mouth and kept laughing. "The state's attorneys caught it?"

"Of course they caught it! They objected. And then they wanted to crack up."

Cathy laughed harder, pounding on the table. "I did that for you!"

"What do you mean?" I said.

"I did that for you. I just wanted to give you a little gift."

"What?" Now it was my turn to choke up some of my drink.

"Absolutely." Her laughter grew louder. "Just a little something from me to you to lift you spirits."

"You're whacked." I cracked up even more. "You're fucking whacked."

"B team . . ." Cathy choked out between fits.

"B team!" I said. "You asked him if the B team was a reference to talent!"

"Jesus, that was *pants*-pissing funny."

The laughter was a relief. I felt like I hadn't laughed in years somehow. Cathy must have felt the same, because her laughter grew and grew along with mine until we were shrieking.

"Please, misses," the owner of the restaurant said, coming over to us. "Please you stop."

We looked around the restaurant and realized that the ten or so patrons were all staring openly at the crazy women, which only made us shriek more, sending delicious whooping laughs throughout the place.

"Please, misses," the owner said again.

"Okay, we have to stop," I said.

"That's not a reference to talent, is it?" she said, quoting herself

"C'mon," I said, trying to gulp back the laughter that wanted to boom out of me. I tugged Cathy out of the booth and led her, both of us still dissolving into laughter, toward the small, one-toilet bathroom in the back.

When we got there, I closed the door and Cathy and I fell on each other in hysterics.

"We have to stop," Cathy said.

"I know, I know." But I couldn't. She couldn't either. It was as if a pressure relief valve had blown and we couldn't turn it off. "B team!" we kept saying. "Reference to talent!"

Finally, wiping tears and clutching stomachs, we managed to tamp it down.

"Thank you so much for doing this with me," Cathy said.

"Thanks for letting me."

"Here's to Jovan," Cathy said, holding up an imaginary glass.

I did the same. "To Jovan."

Afraid to speak of what could happen, we hugged then in the cramped confines of the bathroom in that Mexican restaurant. We clutched each other in a different way than we had outside, like soldiers who have gone to battle together, and still don't know if they're going to win the war.

42

"You're there for the moment that this person's life is about to change forever."

How to describe hearing a verdict being read?

Maurice Possley, an award-winning Chicago criminal justice reporter, said that the reason he was so drawn to the courtroom beat was the verdict. "You're there for the moment that this person's life is about to change forever."

Back in Courtroom 600, I knew exactly what he meant.

"They're back," I told Jovan when I went to retrieve him from the bull-pen for the last time.

Sweat beaded on his upper lip. His expression was one of horror.

The deputy opened the cage, keys jangling.

Back in the courtroom, it was deadly silent. The three male state's attorneys stood at their counsel table, hands clasped behind their backs.

The deputy walked us to our table, and after he unlocked the hand-cuffs, Cathy and I arranged Jovan so he stood between us. I felt him trembling.

"Breathe," I told him. "Breathe."

He shook his head and swallowed.

"Breathe," I said again.

In utter silence, the jury filed into the jury box.

Alfonzo Lewis gave Jovan a look—a barely perceptible jut of his head, entirely unreadable. He sat and looked down.

Cathy and I shot each other a question with our eyes: *What did that mean?*

Jovan had been adamant that he wanted Alfonzo on the jury. We trusted his intuition.

Jovan's trembling increased.

"Uh-oh," Cathy said under her breath when she saw Andrea Schultz was the foreperson.

He's sunk, I thought. I couldn't look at Jovan, but I grabbed his arm with both of mine. Cathy did the same from the other side.

Jovan Mosley felt the air in that courtroom. It was alive. More alive than anything he'd ever felt. He was shaking. He couldn't help it. It was like all that energy was somehow inside him, and it was impossible to control.

The judge opened the verdict forms and read them to himself. What did they say? What did they say?

He had been waiting for this for so long. So long.

He kept shaking. He couldn't help it. Cathy was on his left side, holding tight to his arm. Laura was on his right, doing the same. They were squeezing so tight, like they were holding him up and wouldn't let him fall.

But he knew it wasn't up to them anymore.

"In the matter of *The State of Illinois v. Jovan Mosley,*" the judge read, "the people find Jovan Mosley . . ."

Jovan tried to breathe. He knew his mouth was open. But no air would get in there.

". . . not guilty of armed robbery."

A happy shout rang out in courtroom. Was that his mom?

He smiled—smiled really, really big. But then it hit him: *That's only one verdict, that's the easier one.*

His happiness was replaced by the feeling of drowning.

The judge studied the next verdict form. He looked at the jury, then back at the form, then up at Jovan. *What?* Jovan thought. *What?*

Cathy and Laura were squeezing him so hard now his arms were pinned tight to his side. He looked up at the ceiling, said one more prayer. Tears began streaming down his face, but he couldn't push them away because his lawyers wouldn't let him go. So he kept his eyes on the ceiling, trying to stop crying. They'd told him not to cry, but he would never be able to stop these tears. No matter what happened.

"In the matter of *The People of the State of Illinois v. Jovan Mosley*," the judge read, "the people find Jovan Mosley . . ."—a pause—"not guilty of first-degree murder."

Thank you, God! Thank you, God!

Another happy shout, this one followed by some sobs. Definitely his mom.

Finally his lawyers let him go. He turned to Cathy, hugging her, his angel. They grabbed Laura then, all of them wracked with sobs of relief.

43

"Remember, you have to look both ways."

Following a trial, jurors are often quick to leave, but our jury stayed. In fact, they all sat in the jury room, when they could have gone home immediately, and asked Judge Brown if they could speak with Cathy and me.

When we went in the jury room, some were weeping. They said they all felt very connected to the case and were emotionally drained by it.

The state's attorneys popped their heads in the room, and the jury erupted with questions for them.

I was surprised at the candor of the state's attorneys. They leaned against the wall and good-naturedly answered all the questions they could. They didn't seem upset that Jovan received a not-guilty, and I wondered if that was because of Jovan's particular case or if they had to adopt such an attitude in order to do their job properly. Also, like any trial lawyer, the state's attorneys knew that there is much to be learned from twelve people who have scrutinized your every movement and utterance for so many days.

"Do you guys hate me for that cross of Anita Owens?" Ethan Holland asked.

"Yes!" they answered. They berated Holland for his cross, and Holland's co-counsels ribbed him. Ethan Holland took the abuse in stride.

They wanted to know why Jovan hadn't taken the stand, and Cathy explained her reasoning.

"Why didn't you call Fetta?" one of the jurors asked, causing the others to ask things like, "Yeah, where was Fetta?" and "Why wasn't he arrested in this case?"

The state's attorneys gave vague responses. (We would later find out from a *Chicago* magazine story that the state's attorneys spoke to Fetta weeks before trial and learned he had been drunk the night of the beating, and the things he'd written in his statement were based solely on things he'd heard others say.)

The jury then told us what had really made them say "not guilty."

"It was Alfonzo," Andrea Schultz said, nodding to the young black juror Jovan had insisted on keeping on the panel. (It was only later that Jovan told Cathy and me why—he thought Alfonzo looked like Kanye West. This is not necessarily a great reason to choose a juror.)

When we left the jury room, the jurors hugged us.

Andrea Schultz said, "You make sure you take care of that kid."

I promised her I would.

Jovan had to be locked up again after his verdict.

"Why?" Delores Mosley asked Cathy. "I want to hug my baby."

Cathy explained that he had to be processed—records had to be changed to show he'd been found not guilty, he had to be removed from the roster of the county jail for the first time in nearly six years. Apparently processing usually took many hours, so Cathy, Eddie, and I drove to their town for dinner. Along the drive, I called my husband in Mexico, but I didn't reach him. We had spent lots of time apart before, but something about us felt wrong. I spent most of the drive crying, whether from the relief of the verdict or something else, I didn't know. I called different family members and told them about the verdict, crying with each retelling.

At an Italian restaurant in Burr Ridge, Cathy, Eddie, and I drank bottles of wine and toasted again and again: *Here's to Jovan!* Eddie did the duty that anyone who is friends with a trial attorney must—listening to the war stories. Again.

Meanwhile, Jovan was okay about going back to SuperMax. He had people to say good-bye to, guards to thank, and there was one more thing he needed to do at SuperMax. The truth was, he *really* wanted to do it.

It was tradition in SuperMax that if an inmate won his case and got a not-guilty, he would be tossed in the shower and a bucket of ice would be dumped on him, the prison version of dumping Gatorade on a winning coach. When Jovan had left the deck that morning, he'd told the other inmates that if he got a not-guilty, he'd throw *himself* in the shower.

After his verdict, Jovan waited three hours in the bullpen before they transported him back to SuperMax. The Christian Deck went silent when he entered, everyone wanting to ask but fearing the answer. Jovan walked slowly through the day room for his last time, everyone's eyes on him. He went to the shower. Calmly, he pulled off his shoes, his tie, his suit—clothes that he had worn every day for over a week now. Then he took off his DOC shirt and tossed it in the garbage. Standing in nothing but his underwear, he could feel everyone waiting. Then he turned on the shower and stepped under the fall of water.

Cries of celebration went up from the deck. Soon he felt ice pouring over him, then he was swarmed by inmates thumping his back and hugging him.

By the time Jovan was released from SuperMax, it was nearly two in the morning.

He'd been told the county had lost the clothes and money he'd been arrested with. He left jail with a Bible and the suit on his back. The jail system provided him with a bus card, but when he stepped out onto California Avenue, nothing but the wind was barreling down the deserted street.

Over the past years, when he had been transported back and forth from the jail to the courthouse, he'd felt fresh air for the briefest moments. But he had been in handcuffs then. Now he was standing on his own, no one around him. He could go anywhere, do anything he wanted, *be* anything he wanted. He was elated and scared. His knew his cousins had come to his grandmother's house and taken his stuff while he was in jail. He had nothing now—not a wallet or a coat or a home.

He was like a brand-new human being, turned loose into a cold Chicago night.

He took a step toward the street. *Where am I going to go?* he thought. *What am I going to do?* But he made himself take another step and another, until he reached the deserted street. He hadn't crossed a street by himself for nearly six years.

Remember, he told himself, *you have to look both ways.*

He swiveled his head back and forth. To the right, he could make out the courthouse, the place that, until this moment, had ruled his fate. He looked to the left. The city looked more spread out that way, more open. He looked down from his perch on the curb; he looked at the street, the one he'd been fantasizing about, the one that would take him away from this place. Despite the fact that there were no cars, he looked both ways, and then again and again.

And then he took that step.

Epilogue

A day after Jovan's verdict, Frad Muhammad was found guilty of first-degree murder and armed robbery. When I heard the news, I felt a pang of sympathy for Frad's public defenders. They'd been given a hard case, they put up a good fight, and they lost. But they had done the right thing by giving Frad a vigorous defense.

I understood now that it's not the responsibility of a criminal lawyer to decide innocence or guilt. That's the job of a judge or a jury. The role of attorneys is to represent their clients to the absolute best of their abilities. Those who assume criminal defense lawyers aren't doing their job (or aren't doing it well) by representing people who might be guilty are incorrect. The entire point of a lawyer is to give *everyone* a chance to lay out their case; to provide checks and balances to the hunches of cops and the faith of prosecutors; to make sure the defendant was arrested fairly, interrogated fairly, and tried fairly.

In preparation for Frad's sentencing, Victim Impact Statements were submitted from the family and friends of Howard "Bug" Thomas, along with condolence cards and notes. (Victim Impact Statements give the victim, or the victim's family, an opportunity to address the court before sentencing.)

Howard Thomas's family had received a multitude of sympathy cards after he died. Even the employees of Howard's local post office had written to say how much he would be missed. James Cashman, a Union League Club member, wrote, *Howard was a good, honest and spiritual man who I was privileged to know in his professional capacity as an attendant at the Union League Club.*

The statement written by Bug's daughter was the most moving. *The death of my father has brought me to understand my own mortality,* she wrote. *I am almost consumed by death; it is constantly on my mind. . . . I would love to know what gave them the right to think that it was okay to take his life? I would love to know if they truly feel any remorse for intruding into and ruining our lives like they did? . . . What I lost was a friend, as well as a father. I never got the chance to say good-bye. I never got to tell him I LOVE HIM! So in closing, I would love to see them deprived of life for as long as the law allows and then some. . . . Please let justice prevail in this case.*

For the death of Howard Thomas, Marvin Treadwell received a sentence of thirty-two years; Red was given forty-three. Frad Muhammad was given the heaviest sentence of fifty-five years. If he serves his entire sentence, he will be eighty years old when released.

A Clean Slate was the second book I published, and it was about a Chicago woman who loses five months of her memory and has to start over.

But after Jovan's verdict, I realized that I had no idea what a clean slate was. I couldn't even imagine one until I watched Jovan after his release.

Saundra Westervelt, a criminologist who studied innocent men freed from prison (called exonerees) wrote, along with her coauthor Kimberly Cook, "The enduring images of exonerees are of vindicated individuals reunited with family and friends in a moment of happiness and relief, tearful men embraced by supporters who have long fought for their release. We think of these moments as conclusions, but really they're the start of a new story, one that social science is beginning to tell about how exonerees are greeted by their communities, their homes, and their families, and how they cope with the injustice of their confinement and rebuild their lives on the outside."[140]

Westervelt and Cook's work discussed how exonerees often suffer from feelings of worthlessness, fear, and rejection. "Many exonerees simply feel helpless. Depending on their length of incarceration, they return to a world dramatically different from the one they left. Technology such as ATM machines or cell phones is confounding and many struggle just to relearn the basics of walking (for sustained periods or by negotiating space), eating with utensils, and sleeping."[141]

"It's not easy being gone," Jovan said to me one day after he'd gotten out of SuperMax. "It's amazing how much the world can change in six years. And it changed *a lot.*"

Jovan had been in jail during 9/11. He missed the proliferation of computers, of the Internet, and of cell phones. The programs, software, and innovations that had arisen since his incarceration were overwhelming. He didn't have a computer, much less an e-mail account. He didn't know what Google was. The present was a foreign country.

There was also the gap in his emotional development. "I was a teenager when I went in. When I got out, I was a grown man, although I still felt nineteen a lot of the time."

Marsha Adger, the woman whom Jovan met while she was preaching in SuperMax, stepped up to the plate, big time, and offered to let Jovan stay with her and her son. She and Lisa Taylor (the guard who had formed the Christian Deck and cried when Jovan read his poem) had begun their own "after-care" ministry, where they helped people once they got out of jail. When Jovan was released, Lisa told Marsha that Jovan's mom didn't have room for him or money to move to a bigger place. Marsha had never had another inmate live with her, but she knew Jovan was a gentleman, a good kid, and she wanted him to be able to get a job and eventually go to school. She opened her heart. And her home.

Cathy and I let Jovan get settled over the weekend, but the Tuesday after the verdict, Cathy picked up Jovan at Marsha's and the three of us met for a celebratory luncheon. We drank champagne in a sunny restaurant west of the Loop. Jovan was wide-eyed at everything—the kindness of the waiter, the glittering cutlery, the bustle outside the windows. When he looked at the menu, he became overwhelmed.

"I feel like I've been in a time capsule," he said. "I don't know what to do." He looked at the menu again. "I don't even know what some of these things are." He looked up at Cathy and me. "Tell me what to order." He was not used to choices.

"Do you want a steak?"

"I don't know." He shook his head in slow, ponderous swings, as if an answer to this dilemma might never present itself.

As we debated the massive menu, Jovan flinched at loud noises, constantly looked over his shoulder when he saw something out of the corner of his eye. Cathy and I were buzzing with a strange energy ourselves. It was surreal to see this man, whom we'd encountered only as a prisoner, sitting across from us, debating the merits of a baked potato versus those of the asparagus.

Eventually, after twenty minutes and much discussion, Jovan ordered the steak. He beamed with pleasure as he ate it, savoring it.

The next day I signed up Jovan for a Hotmail account. I sent an old computer to his house along with a tech guy, and over the phone I taught him how to use the Internet.

The day after that, I got an e-mail from Jovan that said only two words in capital letters. *THANK YOU.*

But for both Jovan and me, the journey was far from over.

About ten days after Jovan's verdict, after a celebratory Thanksgiving dinner, during which my family repeatedly toasted to Jovan, I went with my husband to Manhattan. It was there that things between us fell apart. Or at least when the fault lines became evident.

I've tried to place a distinct story behind what happened to my marriage, but I have no simple explanation for the rupture. Even now I can't summarize it, not because it's a mystery but because it's a multilayered story with no good or bad, no right or wrong.

All I know is I returned from that trip to New York, and despite all my friends' reassurances to the contrary, I had a persistent thought: *I am getting a divorce.* And I was right. Jason and I went from being the perfect couple to being in a world of hurt. Since I couldn't seem to keep my life together, I focused on helping Jovan with his. All of his belongings had indeed disappeared from his grandmother's house while he was in jail. He had no clothes, no books, nothing. I called friends and family around the country, asking them to donate clothing, new or used, for Jovan. Stacks of it poured in from my friends, from Jason's buddies, and from my sisters and their husbands in Phoenix

I filled my car with their donations and drove to find Jovan at Marsha's, where we turned her living room into a boutique. We went through the clothes, setting aside the ones that were too small for Jovan's expansive shoulders, which were many. He'd gained weight since getting out of SuperMax. The first week he ate nothing but steaks. Then he'd gone on to visit all the other foods he loved but hadn't eaten in nearly six years. After eating bologna every day for lunch, after the slop they were fed for dinner at county, he craved every kind of food, would try anything. When he went to a restaurant, even if it was a McDonald's, he studied the menu at length, wanting to find something he hadn't tried before. As long as it wasn't shellfish (he was allergic), if he hadn't tasted it, he would order it.

But there was more at work than just rejoicing at the return of regular food.

Since Jovan's release, he had noticed a difference in the way he felt about himself. He had a vague sense of being insignificant and useless, along with a clear realization that he was very, very behind in life. He was twenty-five years old and felt he had nothing to show for it. He tried to ignore the feelings, to just steer clear of them. But sometimes they overtook him and he was surrounded by melancholy.

It was then that he turned to the thing that had always soothed him—food. Lean when he was released, Jovan quickly strode past 230 pounds, making many of the donated shirts simply too small. But people had been generous, so we had more than enough to choose from, even a watch we found at the bottom of a bag from my sister, Katie, and her husband, T.J. Jovan had not owned a watch since he'd been arrested almost six years before.

Later, he would jokingly tell me, "It was like I had been in W.A.— Watches Anonymous—for all that time. And then Katie and T.J. gave me the watch. It was like walking an alcoholic into a liquor store. In terms of watches, I was back on the path to destruction."

As Jovan put the watch on, I looked around Marsha's house and pointed to the room where he'd been trying on clothes. "Is that your bedroom?"

He shook his head. "I'm staying downstairs." He gestured for me to follow him.

Jovan led me to an unfinished basement. Before Jovan's arrival, it had apparently been used for laundry and storage. But in a corner, bare wooden struts formed the bones of what could be made into a room. And inside that room was a roll-away bed and a chair on which sat his T-shirts. An old desk on the left held the computer I'd given him.

Looking around the place, I wanted to cry. Jovan was beyond lucky to have a roof over his head. He was unbelievably fortunate to have a friend in Marsha who had allowed him stay in that basement room. But the dark basement, to me, looked a lot like a prison cell.

Jovan met my eyes.

"It's great," I said.

Jovan nodded and looked around. "Yeah," he said. "Yeah."

In a way, friendships are determined by who in your world has time for friendship. When a girlfriend becomes pregnant and has her first kid? She has no time. And so your friendship simply isn't as strong. And when that friend's kid goes off to school, when manageable amounts of time open in her schedule? Often you're the one who's crazed then, maybe just starting a new job or moving to a new city.

When my husband and I crashed, I found myself with all sorts of time. Although I was incredibly lonely, always feeling adrift and apart, I rarely returned the multitudes of phone calls I received from friends and family. The only people I wanted to talk to were people who didn't know me well, who didn't know Jason and me, who didn't look at me with gut-wrenching God-I-feel-so-sorry-for-you looks, because while I intensely appreciated how much they cared, I already felt sorry enough for myself.

What I realized was Jovan had time for friendship, and so did I, and neither of us knew what the old Jovan and the old Laura were like. Neither of us had any preconceived notions about our personalities, our relationships, what we found funny, what we found interesting.

We e-mailed back and forth, and once I mentioned to him that I was blue. He called me almost right away. "What's wrong, Laura?"

"Nothing, I'm okay."

"There's something about your voice. And your e-mails. You're not a hundred percent."

I got teary. It was Jason, I told him. We were having problems. We were trying to figure out those problems, but it felt like it was all unraveling. And fast. Meanwhile, I had to write a book, and I was teaching again, and—

Jovan interrupted me with a soft voice. "You can only do so much, Laura. That's one of life's lessons. You can't be the answer for everything."

He told me about the demons he'd fought since getting out of jail, the worthlessness, the melancholy.

Later, he would say, "It was like being nothing, nobody, no man, deadbeat man, not accomplishing anything," he said. "I was behind in the world, just stuck, just behind everyone."[142]

Unfortunately, many things Jovan faced solidified that feeling. To the state, for example, Jovan was persona non grata when he got out of Super-Max. Jovan had an ID when arrested, but during his jail time the county lost it, and so one of the largest hurdles he faced was obtaining some form of identification. For most of us, getting a license if you've lost one or had it stolen is a pain. You have to find your Social Security card or passport, maybe dig up a bill with your current address. But what would you do if you had none of that, not even one thing?

Jovan had never had a passport. His Social Security card and birth certificate had been misplaced by his family while he was imprisoned. None of these forms of identification could be recovered when he got out, and he certainly didn't have a utility bill to show where he'd been living the last few years.

He and Marsha Adger went from one state building to next, from one federal authority to another, asking for help. When they hit another wall, they went back to square one and started all over again, trying to find someone to say that Jovan existed.

But the remarkable thing about Jovan was that he never forgot to recognize how remarkable life was. "Bitterness is a choice I make every day," he said. "And I choose not to do it."

In January 2006, a couple of months after the trial, we had a reunion.

Andrea Schultz, the foreperson, and I were the first to arrive at the tea café off Michigan Avenue. Andrea's brown hair was still short, and she was bright-eyed behind her glasses. "Laura!" she said, hugging me tight.

We sat at a table in a pool of sunshine, although the door kept opening, blasting freezing air inside.

"I've been so touched by Jovan and this case," Andrea told me. "It's changed the way I look at everything in life. But I worry about Jovan every day." She had already seen Jovan—when she'd taken him shopping after learning he had enrolled in community college but had no supplies.

I was worried about him too. I looked at my watch. What worried me most at that instant was his finding the tea shop. The act of getting around the city stymied Jovan. Before he'd gone to jail he hadn't needed to wander far from whatever neighborhood he was living in. But now he had enrolled in community college, and he had to maneuver around the city for school, job interviews, and church. When he was first out of SuperMax, Cathy and I tried to pick him up and take him places where he needed to go, or his mother would rent a car and drive him somewhere. But that couldn't last forever. As he began to navigate the city himself, meticulous directions would have to be given, and even then something always went amiss. If he took a bus, inevitably he was on the wrong one. When he finally had access to a car, he would get completely turned around. Once, when I'd set up an interview for him for a law clerk job, he became so confused by the streets in the Loop that he was nearly an hour late.

But at the café, a minute later Jovan walked in. Alfonzo Lewis arrived next. He still looked like Kanye West. He and Jovan hugged like brothers.

Cathy was the next to show. "Yo, Jovizzle!" she yelled, coming through the door. They embraced, and she took a seat to my right. She squeezed my arm. "Hi, girl," she said.

I asked how she was, and she told me she was as crazed as ever. She'd just been hired to represent Mickey Marcello, one of the defendants in the highly profiled "Family Secrets" trial. Many of the defendants, such as Mickey's brother, James, and Joey "the Clown" Lombardo, were accused of plotting the murder of the Spilotro brothers (the slayings that formed the basis for the 1995 movie *Casino*).

"Any more pro bono cases like Jovan's?" I asked.

"No way. No more pro bono work. It was too hard."

I knew she didn't mean the money she'd lost working on Jovan's case (hundreds of thousands of dollars, which she could have made on other cases). She didn't mean the physical toll, although Jovan's case had exacted that from her too. What she meant was the emotional strain.

"Honest to God . . ." I could hear tears making her throat tight as she looked at Jovan across the table. "Honest to God, if we had lost him, *I* would have lost it. I don't know if I could've dealt with it."

A minute later, Eddie Shishem, Cathy's husband, arrived and we all sort of beamed at each other. It's practically unheard-of for a criminal defendant to reunite with his lawyers and jurors.

"What are you doing these days?" Eddie asked.

Jovan told him he had started school in the mornings at Daley College.

He wanted to get a degree in criminal justice. "It's hard," he said. "*Hard*. I don't know how to keep up."

We all glanced around. The world was difficult enough for us, people who'd been actively living in it. And then here was Jovan, dumped unceremoniously back into the world, like an American dropped into Bangkok with nothing but a pat on the back and a *Good luck to you*. Would he be able to survive?

Someone mentioned school again, and we all tossed in study suggestions. Jovan explained how studying had been tough, not just because he wasn't used to it, but because he'd also landed a job working nights at a construction site. Although we'd been looking for law clerk jobs for him, so far nothing had materialized.

"But he had to quit the construction job," I said.

Jovan nodded, his eyes dipping toward the table.

"Why?" Eddie asked.

"The boss didn't have a building permit," Jovan said, "and the cops kept showing up."

Everyone winced. That was all Jovan needed—another run-in with the cops.

He saw our glances and shook his head. "It's okay," he said. "Laura still has me looking for law jobs."

"You can work a few hours a week at my firm," Eddie said. "Just to get you going."

"For real?"

"For real."

"Thank you," Jovan said, nodding his acceptance. "*Thank* you."

Alfonzo turned to Jovan. "So many blessings, kid. You do not know what goes on in a jury room or what kind of people have your life in their hands. It was the toss of a coin."

Cathy and I looked at each other. I could tell what she was thinking. The coin was still in the air.

Jovan filed a civil rights lawsuit against the city and the detectives who were involved in his case. At their depositions, none of the detectives could explain the missing GPRs. And as to why the lineup report was authored a year and a half after the fact? No one had an explanation for that either. They all admitted that although the postdated lineup report stated Jovan had been "identified," it didn't say what, if anything, he'd been identified as doing. Maverick Porter, "the closer" (who had not been involved in the lineup), also admitted that it was standard practice at Area 2 to not just include if the suspect had been identified and also whether he was a striker or a shooter or whatever the witness said he'd done.[143]

None of the detectives recalled taking Jovan to the bathroom. None recalled giving Jovan food, with the exception of the detective, who, as he'd testified at trial, said that he'd purchased McDonald's for him.[144]

Marvin, Frad, and Red were subpoenaed by the city to testify. At Marvin's deposition, he told the attorneys he hadn't received a visitor, or even a letter, since he'd been sentenced to jail. When Marvin was asked about his confession in which he said "my guy" (Jovan) threw a couple of punches, he said, "I lied in my statement." The attorneys asked why, and Marvin said because the cops were scaring him. They were "all over" him, he said, which led him to say stuff he shouldn't have.

Lawrence "Red" Wideman refused to testify, saying he didn't have to do anything he didn't want to do. That wasn't exactly true, since he was in a state pen, but he was right that he didn't have to give a civil deposition. And so he didn't.

At Frad Muhammad's deposition, Frad was asked, "Did Jovan have anything to do with the murder of Howard Thomas?"

Frad answered with a simple, "No." Later, he said, "Jovan didn't do anything."[145]

When Frad was asked whether he knew the subject matter of Jovan's civil case, he responded, "He was incarcerated for five and a half years for something he didn't do. I'd sue their ass too."[146]

Shortly after, the city revised their witness list, adding one short name—*Gregory Reed*. When I saw that name, a moment passed before I recognized it. But then I remembered. Apparently, Fettuccini Corleone had agreed to testify at last.

As the date of Fetta's deposition neared, Jovan was still taking it one day at a time.

He awoke every day between three and three thirty a.m., just like he had at SuperMax. His body clock had been permanently altered.

Often at that time, his breath would only come in shallow gasps as he wondered what would become of him. When he was younger, the future was nothing he worried about. And in jail, you could focus on only one thing—survival. But now time seemed to spread out in front of him, and he feared whether he could do enough, whether he could do the right thing, with that time.

His heart would pound. He would flip onto his back and raise his face a little, trying to suck in air, trying to suck in some ease, some feeling that things would be okay.

He felt better when he was working at Eddie's law office. He did a little of everything there—filed court documents, faxed and sent correspondence, answered the phones, and did just about anything else anyone needed. Jovan was happiest when a few minutes of downtime allowed him to read a motion for summary judgment or pore over a deposition transcript that had just come in the mail. He tried to figure out what was going on in the cases. He considered how he would have written something differently if he were a lawyer, how he would have asked a different question.

He liked getting alternative views of the law from the various attorneys who shared Eddie's office space—one did defense work, another plaintiffs' personal injury, another divorce.

He liked it most when Cathy called the office, always yelling, "Vizzle!"

There was another thing that was picking up his spirits. After dating different women once out of jail, he had found someone special. Her name was Andrea Anderson, the niece of Marsha Adger.

Meanwhile, some people were wary of the friendship Jovan and I had developed. At a writers' conference, I had drinks with another author and told him about Jovan and how I was thinking of writing a book about the whole thing.

"You know how that book ends?" he said. "He kills you—two punches."

Other friends expressed similar skepticism. A friend who was overserved one night told me, "He's going to steal from you."

They worried that I was giving too much, taking too much responsibility, but to the contrary, it was Jovan who was giving so much to me. Jovan didn't know he was handing me advice when he told me how he dealt with potential bitterness—making it a choice every day. Hell, *I* didn't realize he was giving advice. But as it became clear that my marriage was ending, I started carrying his words in my head. I pulled them out when I opened a closet in my house and saw half of it empty; when I sat across a restaurant table from my husband and tried to fix a dollar amount to our life together so that we could split it fifty/fifty; when I packed away framed photos of us because to look at them felt like a swift knife blade to my gut.

I modeled myself after Jovan and chose not to be bitter. In the space left behind where bitterness may have resided, I realized something, namely that certain relationships burn brighter than others. That's obvious to everyone from the start—obvious to the couple, to the people around them. But sometimes those couples flame so bright they burn faster, they turn to ash sooner. What the world doesn't realize is that the beauty of the flame is so much better than the beauty of counted years.

The odd thing was that just as Jovan had found happiness with his girl-friend, Andrea, I was starting to date for the first time in well over a decade.

Once, as I drove him to work following a meeting for his civil case, he listened to me talk about my impending divorce.

"So you're dating again?" he said when I'd finished.

"Yeah, I am." I told him how I adored my husband, always would, but our time together had ended.

We stopped for traffic, and I took a peek at Jovan. He had that look he got—eyebrows knitted together, nose scrunched up—that meant he was thinking hard.

"I'm going to let you in on some inside information," Jovan said.

"Okay." I couldn't imagine where the conversation was going.

"Men aren't emotional."

"What are you talking about? I've seen you cry at least fifteen times."

He glared at me. "I'm talking about *dating*. When men date, we act like we're emotional, and we say things to make you *think* we're emotional. But we're not."

I told him I doubted this theory. I didn't say that I wasn't looking for dating advice from a guy who had been in a jail for almost six years.

He shook his head like he knew better. "Look, just listen to me. I'm going to give you some rules, all right?" He breathed out heavily, as if he were about to impart the secrets of the Sphinx, then launched into a list of dating must-do's: *Withhold sex as long as you can to see if the guy sticks around. If he does stick around, he really likes you. Beware of gifts that seem heartfelt, because men know they can buy a teddy bear in a lobby gift shop and you'll swoon and think, Oh, he thought of me!*

The rules weren't that bad. I nodded. Jovan went on and on. There seemed no end to the rules.

Traffic picked up, and I hit the gas pedal. Soon we were speeding along, to the tune of Jovan's advice: *Don't call too many times in a day. You'll look needy, and needy freaks us out. Be careful of guys who've never been in a long relationship. Something could be really wrong there.* . . . I pulled off at the Congress exit and stopped in front of the building where Jovan worked.

He was still talking. "Don't let them tell you they just want to be friends . . . That's crap because—"

I put my hand on his arm, stopping him.

"What?" He looked at my hand, like he was surprised at the interruption.

"How did we get here?" I asked.

"Where?" He glanced outside the window. People rushed by on Jackson Street, gabbing into cell phones, darting between cars.

"Here." I gestured with my hand between the two of us. "How did we get *here*?"

Jovan looked around one more time. He shrugged. We laughed. "Wait," he said. "I've got more."

As the time drew near for Fetta's deposition, I dug out his handwritten police statement. *Jason gets in and gives him [Howard Thomas] two or three punches. . . . Jason, you really didn't do anything but pass a couple licks maybe God will forgive you.*

I felt a tickle of fear when I read that. I believed in Jovan. I believed he had never touched Howard Thomas, but it still nagged me that there could be someone who thought he did.

At the time, I was working on the second and third novels of a mystery trilogy, which involved a Chicago attorney moonlighting as a private investigator. I had already interviewed a California PI, but I needed to talk to someone in Illinois about what it was like to work in the state, in Chicago. Someone directed me to an investigator named Paul Ciolino, and I called him.

I started out asking Ciolino research questions for my novel, but I quickly veered toward Jovan's case and in particular to Fetta, hoping Ciolino could help find his phone number. I wanted to chat with Fetta before his deposition. I *had* to know what he was going to say. I told Ciolino I had an address for Fetta from the subpoena. But I had already called Directory Assistance and tried to get a phone number, and there had been no listing for a Gregory Reed at that address. How could I get his cell phone number?

"These guys don't have cell phones," Ciolino said. "Or if they do, they get prepaid ones and throw 'em away. You'll have to go find him. What's the address?"

I gave it to him. It was deep on the Southeast Side.

"What do you look like?" Ciolino said.

"Excuse me?"

"What do you look like?" he repeated, sounding irritated.

I mentioned my Web site, said there were photos of me there.

I heard the clicking of fingers on a keyboard. "Shit," he said once he'd found my site. "Be at my office tomorrow morning at nine." He rattled off an address on West Jackson and hung up.

I decided to do an Internet search on Paul Ciolino and found that he was a widely respected investigator who'd been featured on CNN, *20/20*, *48 Hours*, and *The Early Show*. He'd developed something of a specialty for investigating cases on behalf of death row inmates and helping to exonerate them. Many of the cases even involved forced confessions like Jovan's. I had unintentionally hit the PI jackpot.

The next morning, I drove to the Loop to meet with Ciolino. When I reached Jackson Street it was a zoo of construction and commuters. I'd just about found Ciolino's address when I heard a loud, "Caldwell?"

I turned to see a massive white truck, the kind you'd envision on a cattle ranch in Texas, hogging the curb and most of the left lane. A big guy, maybe fifty, with steel-gray hair hung out of the open window. "You're late," he barked. "Get in."

I hurried around the truck and used all my strength to pull myself up into the cab and the passenger seat.

He asked me for Fetta's address, then he floored the truck, getting on the Dan Ryan and heading for the South Side. "So what did this guy say to the cops again?"

Twenty minutes later, we got off the highway and drove past some sketchy neighborhoods. It was a weekday, in the middle of the morning, and yet in front of convenience stores, packs of people (including a number of kids) hung out on the curb as if it were Saturday night. A few blocks later, the neighborhood grew desolate but for one guy on a street corner here, another one there.

Ciolino started pointing to them, ticking off the names of the different gangs they belonged to. "That guy's a Black Disciple. That one's a Gangster Disciple. That one's El Rukn."

"How can you tell?"

"They control certain blocks. Those kids are lookouts in case someone from another gang comes into their block."

"What happens then?"

"We get the fuck out of here."

We pulled up in front of a brick building with six units. The blinds on every unit were closed tight.

Ciolino leaned over me in the passenger seat to see out the window. He grunted. "Pretty nice. Probably some housing authority money." He sat up. "Let's go."

He was out of the truck in a second, his large frame sauntering up the front sidewalk, and I followed.

At the front door, Ciolino buzzed the apartment listed for Fetta's address. No answer. No name on the buzzer. Still, he buzzed again, then tried the others. Nothing.

Ciolino and I walked up and down the street, asking about Fetta, but no one knew anything. We got back in the truck and talked about what it was like to be a PI in Chicago. After a while, we got out and buzzed the apartment again. Then we got back in the truck and talked. Then we buzzed again. This seesaw went on for hours.

At some point, I told Ciolino I was grateful for his efforts in finding Fetta, and I appreciated the information he'd shared on the life of a private investigator, but clearly Fetta wasn't home. Maybe it was time to go.

"Give it a little more time," Ciolino said.

And so time passed. Finally, Ciolino looked at his watch. "C'mon," he said, once again getting out of the truck.

Dutifully, I followed him down the walk, but this time he veered to the right, walked around the side of the building, and, stepping over refuse and abandoned foldable patio chairs, made his way to the back of the building.

When we got there, Ciolino pointed at the windows of one apartment, then he raised his arms like two leather-clad batons. *BOOM, BOOM, BOOM, BOOM, BOOM!* Ciolino banged on the back window so loud, it sounded like gunfire.

BOOM, BOOM, BOOM, BOOM, BOOM! He kept at it, producing a constant, deafening sound that seemed as if it could cause an earthquake. I saw window blinds being pulled back from apartments on the block. A couple of people opened their windows and stuck their heads out to see what was happening.

Suddenly the back door of the apartment popped open, and there stood a sleepy-looking black man in green boxer shorts and a yellow T-shirt. I recognized him from the lineup photos. Fetta.

"Guess you're not going to leave," he said in a slurry voice, gesturing with a glass full of clear liquid. "You might as well come in."

I shot a look at Ciolino, who gave me an innocent shrug. "These guys sleep till at least eleven," he said. "Ya gotta smoke 'em out."

The apartment inside was tidy and decently furnished.

"You got a great place here," Ciolino said.

"My mother's," Fetta slurred over his shoulder as he led us in a slight stagger through the kitchen and to a front room. The place was nice, much nicer than anyplace I had expected to find Fetta, but it was also dark. No lights were on. All the windows were closed tight, the shades drawn.

Fetta took a seat on a squat chair and pointed across a coffee table at a couch. As I sat, my eyes darted around the place, and my heart rate skipped faster and faster. I was, I realized, in a blacked-out apartment on the Southeast Side with two men I didn't know, one of whom was the infamous Fetta.

Fetta took a slug from his glass. I peered at it, and he caught my look.

"I started today like I start every morning," he proclaimed. "Bacon. Eggs." He held up his glass. "Vodka!"

"A great way to kick off the day," Ciolino said amiably, lowering himself onto the couch. "Is it all right if we call you Fetta?"

"That's what they call me," he said, his eyelids at half-mast.

"So, I hear you're a rapper."

"Yeah. Freestyle. I'm about to shoot a video. I live in L.A. mostly."

Ciolino asked a few more polite questions about Fetta's music career, then nodded at me as if to say, *I got you in here, now it's your show, sister.*

"So, Fetta," I said. "I know you're giving a deposition tomorrow."

"Yeah, they just kept after me and kept after me," he said. "But I got nothing to say. I never had anything to say! I didn't see Jovan do nothing."

"You were there the night that fight happened, right?"

"Yeah, and I was drunk." He lifted up his glass as if to emphasize the point. "This is what I do. I rap and I drink. You get that?"

I nodded. I made what I hoped was a simpatico expression.

"And I was so drunk that night," Fetta continued, "that I don't even remember it. I don't know who did what. I got hit by the bat, and I didn't even know that until the cops told me."

"Did you tell the cops you didn't remember anything?"

"Yeah, I told them that!"

"Did you see Jovan hit that man?"

"No."

"Did you see him get involved in the fight in any way?"

"Hell, no."

I pulled out the handwritten statement he'd written. "So why did you write in here that Jovan, or Jason, as you wrote, had thrown a couple of punches?"

He cupped his glass with his hands and leaned on his knees, sighing. "I think I was drunk when I wrote that too. And the cops told me to say that."

"They told you that Jovan had thrown a few punches?"

"Yeah, and I'd heard that around the hood."

"Who from the neighborhood told you that?"

"Red, I think. Maybe Marvin."

"Did Anton Williams or Jori Garth ever tell you that?"

"No."

"Did you tell the cops that Jovan being involved was only what you'd heard but you hadn't seen anything yourself?"

"Hell, yeah, I told them that."

"Did they know you were drunk when you wrote the statement?"

He gave an exaggerated shrug and gestured with his glass. "You tell me."

Ciolino threw me a look: *Anything else?*

I shook my head.

Ciolino grunted and hoisted himself off the couch. "Thanks, Fetta. We'll let you get back to your day now."

Fetta and I stood too.

"I gotta go to the hospital," Fetta said. "I'm supposed to be having a baby today. I got this girl, ya know, and they called me last night from the hospital, talking about inducing or some shit."

I blinked. "If they induced her last night, she's probably had the baby already."

"Yeah?" Fetta took another slug of his vodka.

"Congrats," Ciolino said, holding out his hand. "I'm sure you'll make a great father."

Chicago magazine ran a story on Jovan called "Long Time Coming," which gave an in-depth report of Jovan's case and the length of time he'd been incarcerated.[147] Jovan, Cathy, and I were interviewed at length, and a photo of the three of us adorned the article. It concluded:

> *No single culprit is to blame . . . it is in a defendant's interest to put off going to trial; sometimes the state wants a delay. A clubby collegiality gives prosecutors and public defenders a shared interest in processing defendants through a system that was designed to be adversarial, and local judges typically do little to speed things along. The result is inertia, and the cost of maintaining it is borne by the accused, who may languish behind bars for years before answering the charges against them in court. The cost to taxpayers to support a prisoner in jail: about $23,000 per year.*

After the article appeared, many of the state's attorneys and public defenders on Jovan's case began to give Cathy some good ribbing at 26th and Cal. ASA Allen Murphy stopped saying hello. It was as if they all knew the system sucked, and they all knew people like Jovan got lost, but no one was supposed to discuss it. Certainly not to the press.

"It's like being children of abusive parents," Cathy said. "We all know the bad things that go on, but we don't talk about it. Not to each other, much less to anyone on the outside."

But as always, Cathy kept her sense of humor. The day I turned forty, she sent me a text message: *Happy BDay 2 U; I just want to scream; You're fabulous and 40; And NOT on the B-team!*

Meanwhile, things were moving fast for Cathy's "Family Secrets" case, which would turn out to be the fourth-largest mob trial ever in the United States. Eventually, although some of the defendants received life sentences, Mickey Marcello, Cathy's client, was sentenced to only eight years.

One night, Cathy and I went to a party for a mutual friend. I was thrilled to see her, because neither of us had much free time lately. My novel *The Good Liar* had been released, and I was promoting the book, as well as working on the mystery trilogy. The effect of writing a trilogy was that for years I was always on a deadline, in addition to teaching law school and trying to date again.

As we sat at the party, wineglasses in hand, I asked Cathy what was going on with work. There had been a mountain of issues in the post-trial phase of Mickey's case, so when I posed that question to Cathy, I expected another good episode of the Mickey Marcello story.

Instead, she raised her free arm with a massive shrug. "I'm swamped with pro bono cases."

"What?" I asked, incredulous. "You swore you would never do another pro bono case after Jovan."

"I know. And I'm not going to after this. Trust me. But you wouldn't believe it. There's this one guy—it's a post-Katrina fraud case—and he was getting screwed so bad." She rolled her eyes and shook her blond hair back and forth. "It was just so ridiculous, I *had* to take the case for free. Then there was another guy. Oh, you wouldn't believe what has happened to him. The cops were terrible. And then there was this other guy . . ."

———

A few years after the verdict, I was given an alumni award from Loyola University Chicago School of Law, in part because of my work on Jovan's case. I brought Jovan, along with my father and uncle, to the black-tie gala, though Cathy couldn't attend. The gala was held at the John B. Murphy Memorial Building on East Erie. The place, with its domed ceiling and stained-glass walls, had been built in the 1920s and had only recently been open to the public for events. Tuxedoed law professors and well-known attorneys from around the city filled the palatial room.

As we ate a scrumptious meal and sipped wine, I looked at Jovan, clad in a black suit and chatting with a judge. I remembered the time I invited Jovan and his mom to my cabin on Lake Michigan. The sand there is fine and white, the beach rarely populated. Sometimes the lake is cobalt and wavy, sometimes it's teal and flat as a pond. That day, the wind blew and waves splashed against a couple of kids in pink bathing suits.

"It looks like the ocean," Jovan had said. "Or at least what I think the ocean would look like." He glanced at me. "I've never seen the ocean."

I remembered how we went to an outlet mall later, and we had to pull Jovan away from the display cases of men's watches because he wanted them all.

Now he was wearing a watch. Now he was leaning across the table to chat with a law professor. He hadn't seen the ocean yet, but I knew he'd get there.

That night, I was the first of three alumni to receive the award and the only woman recipient. Therefore, I was the only one with the potential for a massive wipe-out if my skirt caught on my stiletto heels. When my name was called, I crossed the ballroom and lifted my skirt, climbing the stairs as delicately as I could. I made my way to Dean David Yellen, who stood smiling, holding the award—a heavy block of glass carved into a flame.

As I took it from him, I glanced at the podium and realized that the top was slanted and that there was no place to put the award. Nervous, I shoved it back at the dean. I turned to the crowd. "This is what happens when you start giving people awards. They make the dean do their work. He's going to carry my purse to the bathroom after this."

The crowd laughed. I saw my father raise his wineglass and give me a thumbs-up.

The room settled into silence again. I hadn't known what to say before. All though the dinner, I'd been anxiously going over, and then dismissing, potential remarks in my head. But suddenly I found my words.

I talked about Jovan. I quickly told the story of his arrest and trial. When I mentioned how long he'd been in county jail, I heard a few gasps from the usually unflappable lawyer crowd. I talked about how he had been released.

"He stepped out into that street," I said, "into a freezing cold Chicago night, and he had nothing."

I talked about how he was now on the dean's list at Daley College, how he wanted to finish his undergrad degree at Loyola, and how, ultimately, he wanted to be a lawyer.

I talked about how lucky I was to have followed my father, uncle, and grandfather into the legal profession; how the law could be stubborn but that it could also be an amazing tool. I spoke of how Jovan and his trial had given me a newfound respect for the law and, more important, the human spirit. The legal system had its problems and Jovan was, in many ways, a victim of it. And yet Jovan had believed in that system, and in the end it had worked in his favor. The law had taken way too long. It had stolen much from him. Ultimately, however, it had restored us both.

I looked at Jovan. I could barely see him with the bright lights in my eyes. "Jovan," I said, swallowing a lump in my throat, "if you want to join me in this profession, I would welcome you. I would welcome you with open arms."

In the back, one of the professors leapt to his feet and started clapping. A second later, others at his table did the same thing. More attorneys followed, quickly standing and hammering their hands together. I saw my dad tugging on Jovan's sleeve, pulling him to his feet.

A ballroom full of lawyers gave Jovan a standing ovation. Just a few weeks later Jovan was accepted as a student at Loyola University Chicago.

Note

Summary judgment was granted on behalf of the city and the detectives in Jovan's civil rights case (meaning it was dismissed). As of the writing of this book, the case had been appealed to the Seventh Circuit Court of Appeals, but no ruling had been made.

Acknowledgments

Thank you so very much to my agent, Amy Moore-Benson, the champion of this book, and to Hilary Redmon, my stellar editor, for making it shine. Thanks also to everyone at Free Press and Simon & Schuster, especially Sydney Tanigawa, Carisa Hays, Andrew Dodds, Carol de Onís, Dave Cole, and Ellen Sasahara.

Thanks also to everyone who read the book, helped with research, or offered advice, especially Sean Mulroney, Rob Kovell, Rob Warden, John Conroy, Kevin Davis, Dick Devine, Maurice Possley, Paul Ciolino, Jason Billups, Steve Cochran, Les Klinger, Liza Jaine, MK Meador, Marcus Sakey, Katie Caldwell Kuhn, Margaret Caldwell, Christi Smith, William Caldwell, Eric Rayman, Matthew Caldwell, Meredith Caldwell, and all of my students at the Life After Innocence Project at Loyola University Chicago School of Law (a project which was inspired by Jovan), especially Erica Greene, Emily DeYoe, Megan Tomlinson, and Eric Shah.

Most of all, thanks to Jovan and Cathy.

Author's Note on Sources

Long Way Home is the story of Jovan Mosley and his harrowing journey through the criminal justice system. It's also the account of his lead attorney and my co-counsel, Catharine O'Daniel, and the trial that changed all of us. And finally, the epilogue of *Long Way Home* is about the aftermath of that trial.

In part, *Long Way Home* is a memoir. It reflects what I remember from being Jovan's attorney and his friend. When I wasn't present for certain events, it also reflects what I learned about those events through participant interviews, trial and deposition transcripts, police records, television reports, and newspaper and magazine articles (especially Katherine Millett's *Chicago* magazine article titled "Long Time Coming"). Cathy and Jovan have contributed their accounts, and I have presented them to the best of my ability. In order to allow us to discuss the case, Jovan specifically waived the attorney-client privilege. Any mistake in the telling of the accounts is inadvertent.

I am indebted to the many police officers, detectives, state's attorneys, public defenders, criminal defense lawyers, judges, defendants, and former prisoners who spoke with me and answered my endless questions. I am also indebted to many excellent works, including *Defending the Damned* by Kevin Davis (Atria Books), *Unspeakable Acts, Ordinary People* by John Conroy (University of California Press), *Courtroom 302* by Steve Bogira (Alfred A. Knopf), *Interrogations, Confessions, and Entrapment* by G. Daniel Lassiter (Springer), *Innocent: Inside Wrongful Conviction Cases*, by Scott Christianson (New York University Press), and *Wrongly Convicted: Perspectives on Failed Justice* edited by Saundra D. Westervelt and John A. Humphrey (Rutgers University Press).

Endnotes

1. At her request, this is a pseudonym.
2. Dream Town Realty, www.dreamtown.com, April 4, 2009.
3. Chicago Police Department Area 2 Supplementary Report, August 25, 1999, p. 3.
4. Chicago Police Department Area 2 Supplementary Report, August 25, 1999, p. 1.
5. Trial transcript, *The People of the State of Illinois v. Frad Muhammad,* testimony of Detective Charles Williams, November 15, 2005.
6. John Conroy, "Detective Laverty Did the Right Thing—and Paid for It for Years," *Chicago Reader,* January 5, 2007.
7. Tom McNamee, "Daley Likes Easy Fights the Chicago Way: He's Quick to Slam Lakefront Dwellers on Museum, but Where Is He When It Comes to Burge?" *Chicago Sun-Times,* September 24, 2007.
8. John Conroy, "Town Without Pity," *Chicago Reader,* January 11, 1996.
9. Ibid.
10. Hernan Reyes, "The Worst Scars Are in the Mind: Psychological Torture," *International Review of the Red Cross,* Volume 89, September 2007.
11. Ibid.
12. Deposition transcript of Charles Williams, *Jovan Mosley v. City of Chicago et al.,* May 29, 2008; deposition transcript of Clarence Hill, *Jovan Mosley v. City of Chicago et al.,* June 6, 2008, p. 10.
13. Deposition transcript of Charles Williams, *Jovan Mosley v. City of Chicago et al.,* May 29, 2008.
14. Trial testimony of Anton Williams, *The People of the State of Illinois v. Jovan Mosley,* November 15, 2005.
15. Ibid.
16. Ibid.
17. Ibid.
18. Ibid.
19. Ibid.
20. Kevin Davis, *Defending the Damned* (New York: Atria Books, 2007).
21. Ibid.

22. Deposition transcript of Gregory Reed, *Jovan Mosley v. City of Chicago et al.*, April 4, 2008.
23. Ibid.
24. Chicago Police Department Case Supplementary Report, dated at bottom August 20, 2000.
25. Deposition transcript of Derail Easter, *Jovan Mosley v. City of Chicago et al.*, June 4, 2008.
26. Chicago Police Department Case Supplementary Report concerning lineup of February 17, 2000.
27. Deposition transcript of Gregory Reed, *Jovan Mosley v. City of Chicago et al.*, April 4, 2008.
28. Ibid.
29. Ibid.
30. Ibid.
31. Ibid.
32. Ibid.
33. Deposition transcript of Derail Easter, *Jovan Mosley v. City of Chicago et al.*, June 4, 2008.
34. Ibid.
35. Trial transcript, *The People of the State of Illinois v. Frad Muhammad*, testimony of Victoria Ciszek, November 14, 2005.
36. Ibid.
37. Deposition transcript of Gregory Reed, *Jovan Mosley v. City of Chicago et al.*, April 4, 2008.
38. Ibid.
39. Ibid.
40. Ibid.
41. Ibid.
42. Chicago Police Department Case Supplementary Report, dated at bottom August 4, 2000, p. 14.
43. Chicago Police Department Case Supplementary Report concerning lineup of February 19, 2000.
44. Trial transcript, *The People of the State of Illinois v. Frad Muhammad*, testimony of Detective Robert Bartik, November 15, 2005.
45. Chicago Police Department Case Supplementary Report, dated at bottom August 4, 2000.
46. Ibid.
47. Ibid.
48. Ibid.
49. Deposition transcript of Charles Williams, *Jovan Mosley v. City of Chicago et al.*, May 29, 2008.
50. Chicago Police Department Case Supplementary Report, March 5, 2000.

51. Deposition transcript of Edward Howard, *Jovan Mosley v. City of Chicago et al.*, June 6, 2008.
52. Chicago Police Department Case Supplementary Report, regarding Jovan Mosley and concerning lineup of March 5, 2000.
53. Deposition transcript of Gregory Reed, *Jovan Mosley v. City of Chicago et al.*, April 4, 2008.
54. Ibid.
55. Ibid.
56. Ibid.
57. Ibid.
58. Deposition transcript of Derail Easter, *Jovan Mosley v. City of Chicago et al.*, June 4, 2008.
59. Ibid.
60. Trial transcript, *The People of the State of Illinois v. Jovan Mosley*, testimony of Detective Edward Howard, November 16, 2005.
61. Trial transcript, *The People of the State of Illinois v. Jovan Mosley*, testimony of Anton Williams, November 2005.
62. Richard Leo, "False Confessions: Causes, Consequences and Solutions," in *Wrongfully Convicted: Perspectives on Failed Justice*, edited by Saundra D. Westervelt and John A. Humphrey (Piscataway, NJ: Rutgers University Press, 2008).
63. Melanie Eversley, *USA Today*, Dec. 16, 2009 (citing *Chicago Tribune*).
64. John Conroy, *Unspeakable Acts, Ordinary People* (Berkeley: University of California Press, 2000).
65. Ibid.
66. Ibid.
67. *Perspectives* magazine (online), Ohio University, http://news.research.ohiou.edu/perspectives/index.php?item=116.
68. Scott Christianson, *Innocent: Inside Wrongful Conviction Cases* (New York: New York University Press, 2004).
69. Ibid.
70. Ibid.
71. Ibid.
72. *In re Marvin M.*, 383 Ill.App.3d 693 (2008).
73. *People v. Smith*, 108 Ill.App.2d 172 (1969).
74. Ibid.
75. *Frazier v. Cupp*, 394 U.S. 731 (1969).
76. Deposition transcript of John Laskey, *Jovan Mosley v. City of Chicago et al.*, May 18, 2009.
77. Deposition transcript of Maverick Porter, *Jovan Mosley v. City of Chicago et al.*, May 29, 2008.
78. Deposition transcript of Catharine O'Daniel, *Jovan Mosley v. City of Chicago et al.*, July 22, 2008.

79. Deposition transcript of Maverick Porter, *Jovan Mosley v. City of Chicago et al.*, July 22, 2008.
80. Trial transcript, *The People of the State of Illinois v. Jovan Mosley*, testimony of Allen Murphy, November 16, 2005.
81. Innocenceproject.org/understanding/false-confessions, May 1, 2009.
82. Ibid.
83. Ibid.
84. Ibid.
85. Ibid.
86. Ibid.
87. Transcript of testimony of Jori Garth before the Grand Jury of Cook County, March 8, 2000.
88. Transcript of testimony of Anton Williams before the Grand Jury of Cook County, March 8, 2000.
89. Kevin Davis, *Defending the Damned* (New York: Atria Books, 2007).
90. Katherine Millett, "Long Time Coming," *Chicago* magazine, September 2006.
91. Deposition transcript of Edwin Korb, *Jovan Mosley v. City of Chicago et al.*, May 19, 2008.
92. Ibid.
93. Scott Christianson, *Innocent: Inside Wrongful Conviction Cases* (New York: New York University Press, 2004).
94. Ibid.
95. Ibid.
96. Katherine Millet, "Long Time Coming," *Chicago* magazine, September 2006.
97. Steve Bogira, *Courtroom 302* (New York: Vintage Books 2005).
98. Katherine Millet, "Long Time Coming," *Chicago* magazine, September 2006.
99. Steve Bogira, *Courtroom 302* (New York: Vintage Books 2005).
100. Kevin Davis, *Defending the Damned* (New York: Atria Books, 2007).
101. Ibid.
102. Deposition transcript of Edwin Korb, *Jovan Mosley v. City of Chicago et al.*, May 19, 2008.
103. Ibid.
104. Deposition transcript of Jovan Mosley, *Jovan Mosley v. City of Chicago et al.*, May 30, 2008.
105. Steve Bogira, *Courtroom 302* (New York: Vintage Books, 2005).
106. Ibid.
107. Steve Mills and Maurice Possley, "Will Taping Interrogations Fix the System?" *Chicago Tribune*, June 21, 2005.
108. Steve Bogira, *Courtroom 302* (New York: Vintage Books, 2005).
109. Ibid.

110. Deposition transcript of Roy Kwilos, *Jovan Mosley v. City of Chicago et al.*, July 16, 2008.
111. Ibid.
112. Deposition transcript of Derail Easter, *Jovan Mosley v. City of Chicago et al.*, June 4, 2008.
113. Deposition transcript of Charles Williams, *Jovan Mosley v. City of Chicago et al.*, May 29, 2008.
114. Deposition transcript of Roy Kwilos, *Jovan Mosley v. City of Chicago et al.*, July 16, 2008.
115. Ibid.
116. Deposition transcript of Edward Howard, *Jovan Mosley v. City of Chicago et al.*, June 6, 2008.
117. Deposition transcript of Roy Kwilos, *Jovan Mosley v. City of Chicago et al.*, July 16, 2008.
118. Ibid.
119. Ibid.
120. Ibid.
121. Transcript of hearing for Motion to Suppress Statement, *The People of the State of Illinois v. Wideman,* April 16, 2003.
122. Ibid.
123. Myron Orfield, "Deterrence, Perjury, and the Heater Factor: An Exclusionary Rule in the Chicago Criminal Courts," *University of Colorado Law Review,* 1992.
124. Ibid.
125. Ibid.
126. Trial transcript, *The People of the State of Illinois v. Jovan Mosley,* November 14, 2005.
127. Trial transcript, *The People of the State of Illinois v. Jovan Mosley,* testimony of Derek Barnes, November 14, 2005.
128. Trial transcript, *The People of the State of Illinois v. Jovan Mosley,* testimony of Ronald Barnes, November 14, 2005.
129. Trial transcript, *The People of the State of Illinois v. Jovan Mosley,* testimony of Jori Garth, November 14, 2005.
130. Trial transcript, *The People of the State of Illinois v. Jovan Mosley,* testimony of Anton Williams, November 15, 2005.
131. Trial transcript, *The People of the State of Illinois v. Jovan Mosley,* November 15, 2005.
132. Ibid.
133. Trial transcript, *The People of the State of Illinois v. Jovan Mosley,* November 16, 2005.
134. Trial transcript, *The People of the State of Illinois v. Jovan Mosley,* testimony of Allen Murphy, November 16, 2005.
135. Ibid.

136. Trial transcript, *The People of the State of Illinois v. Jovan Mosley,* November 16, 2005.

137. Trial transcript, *The People of the State of Illinois v. Jovan Mosley,*, testimony of Detective Edward Howard, November 16, 2005.

138. Ibid.

139. Trial transcript, *The People of the State of Illinois v. Jovan Mosley,* November 17, 2005.

140. Saundra D. Westervelt and Kimberly J. Cook. "Coping with Innocence after Death Row," *Contexts* 7(4): 32–37.

141. Ibid.

142. Deposition transcript of Jovan Mosley, *Jovan Mosley v. City of Chicago et al.,* June 5, 2008.

143. Deposition transcript of Maverick Porter, *Jovan Mosley v. City of Chicago et al.,* July 22, 2008.

144. Deposition transcript of Edward Howard, *Jovan Mosley v. City of Chicago et al.,* June 6, 2008.

145. Deposition transcript of Frad Muhammad, *Jovan Mosley v. City of Chicago et al.,* March 5, 2008.

146. Ibid.

147. Katherine Millett, "Long Time Coming," *Chicago* magazine, September 2006.

About the Author

Formerly a civil trial lawyer, Laura Caldwell is now a Distinguished Scholar in Residence at Loyola University Chicago School of Law. She has taught international criminal law and advanced legal writing and is the director and founder of Loyola's Life After Innocence Project. The project, inspired by Jovan Mosley, works with wrongfully convicted individuals or other innocent persons affected by the criminal justice system in order to help them reenter society and reclaim their lives. Caldwell is the author of ten novels, including the Izzy McNeil novels. Her work has been translated into thirteen languages and published in over twenty countries.